The Art of
What Works

The Art of What Works

How Success Really Happens

William Duggan

McGraw-Hill
New York   Chicago   San Francisco
Lisbon   London   Madrid   Mexico City
Milan   New Delhi   San Juan   Seoul
Singapore   Sydney   Toronto

The McGraw·Hill Companies

1 2 3 4 5 6 7 8 9 0 DOC/DOC 0 9 8 7 6 5 4 3

ISBN 0-07-141206-9

McGraw-Hill books are available at special quantity discounts to use as premiums and sales promotions, or for use in corporate training programs. For more information, please write to the Director of Special Sales, Professional Publishing, McGraw-Hill, Two Penn Plaza, New York, NY 10121-2298. Or contact your local bookstore.

This book is printed on recycled, acid-free paper containing a minimum of 50% recycled, de-inked fiber.

Library of Congress Cataloging-in-Publication Data

Duggan, William.
    The art of what works : how success really happens / by William Duggan.
        p.   cm.
    ISBN 0-07-141206-9 (hardcover : alk. paper)
    1. Business planning. 2. Leadership. I. Title.

HD30.28.D834   2003
658.4'012—dc21   2002153056

Contents

Preface		vii
Part I	**The Art of Expert Intuition**	I
Chapter I	Introduction	3
Chapter 2	An Eye for What Works	13
	The Problem of Intuition	13
	Goal Setting versus Coup d'Oeil	16
	Four Keys to Success	22
	Coup d'Oeil Today	26
	Coup d'Oeil in Science	30
	East Meets West	35
	An Eye for Business	41
Chapter 3	The Art of Success	43
	Adaptive versus Creative Response	43
	Creative Imitation	48
	Build on What Works	51
	Johnson & Johnson	53
	Marriott	53
	American Express	54
	Creative Structure	58
	DuPont	60

General Motors 61
Standard Oil 64
Sears 66
The Art of Japanese Business 68
The GE Way 72
The Erratic Goddess 76
Creative Success 80

Part II **The Advantage of Expert Intuition** **83**

Chapter 4 Plan-to versus Can-do 85
The Triumph of Planning 85
Strategic Flexibility 90
Honda Takes Off 94
What's a Good Plan? 97
Coastline Pool Consortium 98
Strategic Intent 101
Core Competence 104
Creative Planning 106

Chapter 5 Change versus Charge 109
The Fifth Discipline 109
Great Groups 113
Knowledge Management 119
The Achievement Network 121
Organizational Change 125

Chapter 6 Forces versus Sources 129
Five Forces and Three Strategies 129
Does It Work? 134
Competitive Intuition 138
Grounded Research 140
Five Sources 144
Competitive Insight 145
Expert Analysis 147

Part III **The Application of Expert Intuition** **149**

Chapter 7 Arrows in the Quiver 151
Brainstorming 152
Is It SMART? 155

	SWOT	156
	Creative Stimulation	157
	Bootstrapping	161
	Normal Science	165
	What-Works Scan	167
	Wei Wu Wei	171
	Quality	173
	Dialogue	176
	Reengineering	178
	Game Theory	181
	Trotter Matrix	183
	S-Curve	185
	After-Action Review	187
Chapter 8	The Art of Synthesis	193
	Whose Strategy Is It?	194
	The McKinsey Way	196
	Strategic Synthesis	206
Chapter 9	The Way of What Works	211
	In Search of Success	215
	Let Go	220
	The Hero's Journey	224
	Creative Strategy	229
Appendix	Right versus Might	233
	Schools of Social Strategy	234
	In Search of What Works	236
	GRAD	238
	Globe-Trotter	242
Notes		351
Index		271

Preface

LEONARDO DA VINCI, the original "Renaissance man," stands out in history for his achievements in both science and art. He made scientific advances, especially in anatomy and mechanical invention, and he painted two of the most famous pictures of all time: the *Mona Lisa* and the *Last Supper*.

How did he do it?

A famous quote by Leonardo himself reveals the secret:

> As you cannot do what you want,
> want what you can do.[1]

Leonardo da Vinci was an artist of what works.

He tells us that his creative method starts by giving up "what you want." This contradicts conventional wisdom: Doesn't everything start with a vision, a goal, a desire? According to Leonardo, no. You have to give those up. Instead, you "want what you can do." That is, first you see what you can do, then you know what goal to set. You don't know what problem you can solve, what painting to paint, what desire to fulfill, until you see how to do it. You do what you can, not what you want.

But still we ask: What can you do?

That depends on how much you know, how much you've learned, and what skills you master. You can only do what you or someone else has done in the past, but in new combinations to suit the present. The more you study the experience of others, and the more you practice yourself, the more you can do. What works in the future is some combination of what worked before in the past. Great scientists, great artists, great business leaders—they don't "reach for the stars," they grasp what works.

Four centuries later, we hear an echo of Leonardo's secret in the words of a modern Renaissance man:

> The operative assumption today is that someone, somewhere, has a better idea; and the operative compulsion is to find out who has that better idea, learn it, and put it into action—fast.[2]

This quote comes from Jack Welch, who rivaled Leonardo in the range of his achievements. Welch ran General Electric, the world's largest conglomerate, for 20 years of stunning success, from 1981 to 2001. At a time when other companies sought greater focus on one or two major businesses, Welch succeeded in a dozen different sectors, from aircraft engines to mortgage insurance to a major television network.

For Welch, a good idea was something that worked before somewhere else. You search for what works, and that tells you what you can do. Then you go ahead and do it. As Welch saw it, his main job was to spread this method through General Electric's many different companies. Contrast that with the dot.com craze of the same era, where pie-in-the-sky business plans brought the stock market to its knees. Like Leonardo da Vinci, Welch was an artist of what works.

This book tells how Leonardo and Jack Welch did it. And not just them: We find dozens of others throughout the ages. Napoleon Bonaparte, Bill Gates of Microsoft, Ray Kroc of McDonald's, and top companies like Nokia, Marriott, Johnson & Johnson—the list goes on and on. The art of what works is the secret of strategy, a timeless truth for success in business or any other field.

This book presents principles, tools, and examples to help you apply the art of what works yourself. We study success, to see how it happened. Our trail leads mostly through business strategy, but it leads also to science, art, war, government, the nonprofit sector, psychology, and Eastern and Western philosophy. We hunt for success from many angles. Time and again, in case after case, the answer turns out to be the same: the art of what works.

But how can success be the same? Every sector is different. Every business is different. Every year something changes. Don't we miss key factors by looking at what is the same?

Yes, every situation is unique. But every situation is made up of elements that are similar to something in the past. The combination is new, but the elements are not. In the art of what works, the answer is always different, but the question is always the same: What past successes can I draw from and combine in this new situation? The more you learn and the more you study past achievements, the more likely it is that a new situation will look familiar, and the greater your chance of success.

Certainly there are differences among successful strategies, but much is gained from studying what is the same. The structure of every success looks alike, although the content changes from case to case. Such is the art of what works.

We can see a close parallel in yet another field: mythology. In his landmark study *The Hero with a Thousand Faces*, Joseph Campbell describes a common "hero's journey" in myths across the globe:

> A hero ventures forth from the world of common day into a world of supernatural wonder: fabulous forces are there encountered and a decisive victory is won: the hero comes back from this mysterious adventure with the power to bestow boons on his fellow man.[3]

There are countless myths in the world, but only one hero's journey. So too with success: Amid great variety, you find the same story again and again. Furthermore, we will find that our strategists see what to do not in bits and pieces but all at once, in a flash of insight that starts them off on a hero's journey of the sort that Campbell describes.

There are many, many artists of what works—or perhaps, as Campbell might claim, there is only one, with a thousand faces depending on the situation and times.

Maybe one of these faces is you.

The Art of
What Works

PART

I

The Art
of Expert
Intuition

Introduction
The Problem of Strategy

I N 2001, the Nobel Prize in economics went to Joseph Stiglitz, George Akerlof, and Michael Spence for showing how and why markets again and again fall prey to imperfect information. Stiglitz explains their main idea:

> In the field of economics, perhaps the most important break with the past—one that leaves open huge areas for future work—lies in the economics of information. It is now recognized that information is imperfect, obtaining information can be costly, there are important asymmetries of information, and the extent of information asymmetries is affected by actions of firms and individuals.[1]

What this means for business strategy is that you can never predict the future, no matter how hard you try. You can gather more and more data and analyze them night and day, but you still can't know which strategy will work and which will not. Whatever you do, your information remains imperfect. It will not yield an answer to what your strategy should be.

Does this mean that we just give up? Is strategy a problem we just can't solve?

Not quite. There is an answer. It's just very different from what we expect. And it's been around for a very long time, since the first full scholarly study of strategy more than a century and a half ago.

That study is *On War* by Carl von Clausewitz, published in 1832.[2] Strategy began as a military science, and over the years it spread to other fields, especially business. Although military strategy goes back in time as long as war has existed, the scholarly study of strategy starts with von Clausewitz. The word *strategy* entered the English language only in 1810, at the height of Napoleon Bonaparte's military success.[3] Napoleon won more battles than any other general in history, before or since. *On War* explains how he did it.

Von Clausewitz uses a vivid term for imperfect information: the "fog" of war.

> The great uncertainty of all data in War is a peculiar difficulty, because all action must, to a certain extent, be planned in a mere twilight, which in addition not unfrequently—like the effect of fog or moonshine—gives to things exaggerated dimensions and an unnatural appearance.

According to von Clausewitz, four key elements of strategy will help you make it through this fog of uncertainty.

First, you enter the fog with "presence of mind"—you expect the unexpected. Don't go in thinking that you already know what to do. Be ready for surprise.

Second, you cut through the fog in a flash of insight. That flash is a *coup d'oeil*,* which is French for "glance." To von Clausewitz, a coup d'oeil is "the rapid discovery of a truth which in the ordinary mind is either not visible at all or only becomes so after long examination and reflection."

Third, a strategist follows through on the coup d'oeil with "resolution." To von Clausewitz, resolution is "removing the torments of doubt . . . when there are no sufficient motives for guidance." There is no way to prove that your coup d'oeil is right, to

*Pronounced "koo-DOY."

convince every doubter with facts and figures. Despite the doubts, you follow through.

Fourth, the doubts are much reduced when "strategy . . . turns to experience, and directs its attention on those combinations which military history can furnish." These combinations are the very content of the actual coup d'oeil. You see in a flash a new combination based on what worked in the past.

Presence of mind, coup d'oeil, resolution, and combinations from history—these four elements were the secrets of Napoleon's success. To von Clausewitz, they formed the essence of strategy that others could also use.

Today, more than a century after von Clausewitz, modern research has given these four elements a growing body of scientific support, plus a modern name: *expert intuition*.[4] Psychologists describe expert intuition as "recognition-based decision making," where you see something similar from the past in the current situation. The greater your expertise, the more situations you see as familiar. A novice, in contrast, sees each situation as new and unique.

Key scholars of expert intuition include Herbert Simon, who won the 1978 Nobel Prize in economics, and the psychologist Gary Klein, who studied firefighters, emergency room nurses, and soldiers in battle. We also find expert intuition in the "science of science," the study of how scientists make their discoveries, as told by the great historian of science, Thomas Kuhn.

Expert intuition shows up in philosophy, too, especially in the Pragmatism of William James and other leading scholars of his time. In *The Metaphysical Club*, Louis Menand tells how Pragmatism became America's core philosophy at the start of the twentieth century, when the country teemed with competing religions, cultures, and traditions from around the world. In the face of so many theories to choose from, Pragmatism tells you to pick whichever one works the best for you in your current situation.

We find a similar strain in Eastern philosophy: Taoism in China and Zen in Japan. Expert intuition runs through two ancient Tao classics from the fifth century B.C., the *Tao Te Ching* by Lao Tzu and *The Art of War* by Sun Tzu. Centuries later, Tao merged with Buddhism to become Zen. Japanese masters of crafts and martial arts today study expert intuition through Zen classics like *The Book of Five Rings* by Miyamoto Musashi, a great samurai of the Middle Ages.[5]

In war, in science, and in Eastern and Western philosophy, expert intuition is the art of what works. You do what you can, not what you want to, based on what worked in the past. And the past includes what happened to you 5 minutes ago as well as ancient truths. Your expertise comes from outside, not inside. You learn it from others. The more you learn, the deeper and faster your intuition will be, and the shorter your path to success.

We see this in von Clausewitz. He equates experience with military history. Thus, experience is not just your experience, but all of human experience. A prime example is Napoleon himself. He was only 26 years old when he won his first campaign. It took place in northern Italy against a superior Italian and Austrian army. Napoleon had never fought before in open-field warfare, yet he won a dozen battles without losing one.

How did Napoleon do it? Through study. He tells us himself:

> The principles of warfare are those that guided the great captains whose high deeds history has transmitted to us—Alexander, Hannibal, Caesar, Gustavus Adolphus, Turenne, Eugene of Savoy, Frederick the Great. . . . The history of their eighty-three campaigns would constitute a complete treatise on the art of war.[6]

Eighty-three campaigns involve hundreds of battles. Napoleon studied these battles at military school. Then, when he went into battle himself, he drew ideas from those battles like arrows from a quiver. In his first campaign, he especially drew from Frederick the Great of Prussia. Each battle that Napoleon fought added more to his expertise. But its original source was books.

And so we answer an age-old question: Can you teach intuition? The answer is yes, through study, practice, and example. This is the timeless truth of success. As we turn to business, our principal subject, we see that the same truth applies there, too. Business is just another arena of human achievement, like war or science or Japanese crafts, where the coup d'oeil of an expert ignites the spark of the art of what works.

In business strategy, our study of the art of what works begins with Joseph Schumpeter, an Austrian economist in the early twentieth century. Schumpeter said that entrepreneurs create economic growth—not the other way around. That is, entrepreneurs do not just take advantage of what economic growth produces. They see opportunities that no one else sees and turn them into economic growth. In a key essay, "The Creative Response in Economic History," Schumpeter cites "personal intuition and force"—otherwise known as coup d'oeil and resolution—as the key to successful entrepreneurship.[7]

In *The Mind of the Strategist,* by Kenichi Ohmae, coup d'oeil and resolution show up again as "insight and a consequent drive for achievement."[8] In *The Growth of Firms in Japan*, Ryuei Shimizu calls them a "sixth sense" and "spiritual courage."[9] Ohmae and Shimizu cite these elements as the key to Japan's tremendous business success in the decades after World War II. And in *The Origin and Evolution of New Businesses*, Amar Bhidé shows that successful entrepreneurs don't dream up ideas on their own; they take them from other businesses, like Napoleon drawing on the actions of great generals before him.[10]

Another study of business success, *Built to Last*, by James Collins and Jerry Porras, also features the art of what works.[11] It shows us how the most profitable American companies through the twentieth century changed strategy time and again when a coup d'oeil showed them the path to success. The same thing can be seen in *Strategy and Structure*, a classic study by Alfred Chandler of four successful companies—Dupont, Sears, General Motors, and Standard Oil—that managed growth by changing their structure.[12] The art of what works showed them how.

In addition to these scholarly sources, we find accounts of the art of what works in the success stories of individual companies, including Microsoft, McDonald's, Apple, Nokia, and many others. And General Electric spread the art of what works throughout its many companies as the "GE Way." From business newspapers and magazines, you can pick out current examples every day.

Yet the art of what works remains a secret. It is there, but most people fail to see it. Why? Because other explanations get in the way.

To see how that happens, let's return to the problem of strategy—imperfect information, our fog of war.

In the art of what works, a coup d'oeil cuts through the fog. But other schools of strategy offer other solutions to the problem. Let's look at three of the leading schools: strategic planning, the learning organization, and competitive strategy.

In the first school, classic strategic planning, you set a goal and plan activities that will enable you to reach it. If you keep to your plan, you'll reach your goal. But in *The Rise and Fall of Strategic Planning*, Henry Mintzberg warns against rigid adherence to plans.[13] Instead, he favors "emergent" strategy, where you adjust your plans over time as new information emerges. Nowadays, most strategic planners agree with Mintzberg. James Quinn, for example, offers a similar view and calls it "logical incrementalism."[14] The message: In the face of imperfect information, keep your strategy flexible.

The second school of strategy, the learning organization, gives a different response to dealing with the fog of war: One person cannot possibly master enough information to develop a complex strategy, but a team can, so everyone in the system needs to work together. The best summary of this school remains *The Fifth Discipline*, by Peter Senge.[15] And in *Organizing Genius*, Warren Bennis supports the idea with several case histories.[16] The message: In the face of imperfect information, work as a team.

The third school, competitive strategy, cuts through the fog of business with economic analysis. The leader of this school, Michael Porter, uses economic research and analysis to give a firm a better understanding of its economic position in an industry, with special emphasis on the positions of competitors throughout the entire value chain.[17] The message: In the face of imperfect information, squeeze as much as you can from the information you have.

Flexible planning, teamwork, and thorough analysis—those are the answers given by the three leading schools of strategy. Thus, most businesses handle strategy in one of these ways, instead of using the art of what works. But there is really no contradiction. You can combine one or all of these schools with expert intuition. Von Clausewitz considered them all important. Napoleon mastered them, too. But in the end they cannot tell you what your strategy should be. Only expert intuition does that.

But how?

The four elements of the art of what works—presence of mind, coup d'oeil, resolution, and examples from history—translate into tools and techniques that you can apply in your own situation. The other schools of strategy offer their own tools and techniques, so the art of what works can do the same.

Some tools use expert intuition directly. For example, boot-strapping involves making a rigorous study of what a successful strategist actually does, rather than asking the strategist to explain it—something that strategists can never do very well. The Trotter matrix from General Electric attacks a strategic problem by engaging in a treasure hunt to find out whether anyone else in the world has made any progress in solving any part of the problem. A what-works scan applies grounded theory to basic strategy research. And last but not least, the normal science version of the scientific method is very much like the art of what works.[18]

We can also add elements of expert intuition to tools from other schools of strategy. For example, an exercise in strategic planning or a team dialogue session in the learning organization often begins with the question, "What is our vision?" That's fine. In the art of what works, however, we arrive at that vision by asking first, "What works?" The vision comes second, after you see what path can lead to success. That avoids developing a vision that you have no way to reach.

As another example, in competitive strategy, you analyze the "five forces" that determine your competitive position: direct competitors, suppliers, customers, potential entrants, and substitutes. In the art of what works, these five forces also become "five sources," where you look for things that others are doing right and that you might do as well. The result is creative imitation based on what you find. Competitive analysis gives you the lay of the land, but it does not tell you what path to take. Only a coup d'oeil, based on what worked in the past, does that.

Using the principles of expert intuition, examples from business history, and practical methods is how you learn the art of what works. In the chapters that follow, we study these principles, examples, and methods in greater detail. At all times, we look first for other observers who came before. This is the first book to apply recent advances in expert intuition to the art of strategy, but the basic idea is as old as mankind. It's the ancient secret of success.

This book itself follows the art of what works. We take what others have found before us and make a new combination. The book reveals for the first time in one volume what many people from many fields have always known. In some ways, then, it speaks the unspoken. Successful people are like magicians: They put on quite a show, but they seldom reveal their secrets. But magicians know each other's tricks.

This book lets everyone in on the secret: how success really happens. And by using prior sources, it speaks with authority, derived from the work of dozens who came before us. Yet our method is more a treasure hunt than statistical research. We look for gems and pass up more than we find. For example, we pick out just one quote from everything that Leonardo da Vinci said through the years. It takes a lot of sifting. But now and then, we strike gold.

Here you find the results of much searching. It saves you the time needed to do your own searching. You will find that these results apply to all kinds of business situations, and even to other parts of your life. Some of our sources straddle self-help and business; after all, Americans buy more books on self-improvement than on any other subject, and most Americans work in business. Strategy applies to both business and life to a strong and equal degree.

In this personal realm, the art of what works offers nothing new. It offers something old: from ancient China to postwar Japan, from Napoleon Bonaparte to Jack Welch, from Microsoft to Nokia, from General Motors to General Electric. We find there not new ideas, but timeless truths, for work, for life, and even for love.

That's right, the quest for personal happiness can also benefit from the art of success. When you see what you can do and then set off to do it, no pleasure on earth is greater. Think of what you like to do best, or would like to do, then think of its going wrong. Now think of its going right. Successful action fills your heart with joy.

And even when the fog is too thick, when you can't yet see what to do, the art of what works still applies. Here is the earliest written trace, from the *Tao Te Ching* in the fifth century B.C.:

> Do you have the patience to wait
> Til your mud settles and the water is clear
> Can you remain unmoving
> Til the right action arises by itself?

> Study.
> Learn.
> Practice.
> Have patience.
> Keep your eyes open.
> Your coup d'oeil will come.

CHAPTER 2

An Eye for What Works
Expert Intuition in Strategy

IN THIS CHAPTER, we study the four key elements of expert intuition in strategy and decision making: presence of mind, coup d'oeil, resolution, and examples from history. The four elements come from *On War* by Carl von Clausewitz, the first scholarly study of strategy,[1] but we find them in many other sources from other fields as well.

The Problem of Intuition

In his autobiography, *Grinding it Out*, Ray Kroc tells how he founded the great McDonald's empire:[2]

It was a restaurant stripped down to the minimum service and more, the prototype for legions of fast-food units that later would spread across the land. Hamburgers, fries, and beverages were prepared on an assembly line basis, and, to the amazement of everyone, Mac and Dick included, the thing worked! Of course, the simplicity of the procedure allowed the McDonalds to concentrate on quality in every step, and that was the trick. When I saw it working that day in 1954, I felt like some latter-day Newton who'd just had an Idaho potato caromed off his skull.

This passage from Kroc is one of the most explicit statements on record of the use of expert intuition in business strategy. When he first saw the original McDonald's restaurant in San Bernadino, California, Kroc had a classic coup d'oeil. His resolution after that brought forth the McDonald's we know today.

Kroc refers directly to another legendary coup d'oeil, this one from science: Isaac Newton's discovering gravity when an apple fell on his head. Kroc converts Newton's apple to a potato, which he also cites as part of his coup d'oeil in the form of French fries.

Kroc showed great presence of mind. He expected the unexpected. When he went to San Bernadino, he had a very different strategic goal from starting a restaurant chain. At the time, he was selling Multimixers to soda fountains and restaurants across the country. A Multimixer is a machine that mixes six milkshakes at a time instead of only one. Kroc's goal was clear: to sell as many Multimixers as possible.

Kroc had heard that the McDonald brothers kept eight Multimixers going at full capacity. How did they do this? He paid a visit to the McDonalds' restaurant in San Bernadino to learn their secret. Whatever they did, he wanted to recommend the same thing to his other clients, so that they too would buy eight Multimixers, and so increase Kroc's sales. But during his visit, he changed his goal.

In the art of what works, the means precede the ends. The goal comes second, not first. How that happens is very hard to explain. It seems as if the world turns upside down, or a potato falls on your head. Successful strategists are seldom aware of their expert intuition. They just have it, and they go on from there.

Kroc's statement is also unusual because successful strategists very rarely cite past achievements as the key to their success. Why? In part, because they suppress the notion. Steven Jobs, founder of Apple Computer, once explained in an interview,

Creativity is just connecting things. When you ask creative people how they did something, they feel a little guilty because they didn't really do it, they just saw something. It seemed obvious to them after a while. That's because they were able to connect experiences they've had and synthesize new things.[3]

Here Jobs reveals one of the secrets of creative success: combining successful ideas from others. He himself was a stellar example.

Jobs's partner, Steven Wozniak, had already developed a small, inexpensive computer, which Jobs combined with the features he saw at a meeting with Xerox in December 1979. In the interview that this quotation comes from, Jobs explains how guilty he feels about claiming credit. During the meeting with Xerox, Jobs had a classic coup d'oeil, as he explains in another interview:

> They showed me really three things. But I was so blinded by the first one I didn't even really see the other two. . . . I was so blinded by the first thing they showed me which was the graphical user interface. I thought it was the best thing I'd ever seen in my life. Now remember it was very flawed, what we saw was incomplete, they'd done a bunch of things wrong. But . . . still . . . the germ of the idea was there and . . . within you know ten minutes it was obvious to me that all computers would work like this some day.[4]

Like Kroc's, Jobs's coup d'oeil changed his goal. He set out to combine the Xerox features with Wozniak's latest computer model. The result was the Macintosh, the first user-friendly, affordable personal computer.

These quotes from Kroc and Jobs are rare examples of journalists catching the art of what works in action. More often, a journalist asks about innovation, not imitation—what's new, not what's old. A recent example is *New Ideas about New Ideas* by Shira White, who interviewed 100 artists, sculptors, architects, and business leaders.[5] When you ask what's new, that's what you get. When you ask what worked, you get something else entirely.

Academic researchers also usually miss the art of what works. That's because they carry into their inquiries other theories of strategy. When you read about McDonald's or Apple in business textbooks or in teaching cases, you find analysis and discussion of economic factors, team dynamics, personal drive, and a variety of cultural, political, and social forces inside and outside the firm. You seldom read about what worked in the past. It's hard to find expert intuition in studies of business strategy. Other factors are easier to identify and explain.[6]

The elusive nature of expert intuition makes von Clausewitz stand out for his great achievement in pinning down the essence of strategy. It also helps us see why his achievement is still so poorly understood today. Expert intuition is easy to misunderstand or to miss completely. And even when von Clausewitz understood it, he struggled to find the words to explain it. So you can read von Clausewitz and miss it too—unless you know what to look for.

Goal Setting versus Coup d'Oeil

On War by von Clausewitz was the first full scholarly study of strategy, but it was not the first best-seller on the topic. That distinction goes to Antoine Jomini's *Summary of the Art of War*.[7] Jomini's book came out in 1838, six years after *On War*. For the next 50 years, Jomini won out over von Clausewitz in the world's military academies.

There are four reasons for Jomini's success. First, he was a French-speaking Swiss who served on Napoleon's staff. That meant he was rightly able to claim inside knowledge of Napoleon's strategy. Von Clausewitz, a Prussian, fought on the other side.

Second, Jomini wrote in French, the language of most of the literature on Napoleon, including Napoleon's own sayings and writings. Von Clausewitz wrote in German.

Third, Jomini wrote in a simple, elegant style. Von Clausewitz wrote in the dense, ponderous style of German academics of the day, in the intellectual tradition of Immanuel Kant.

Fourth, Jomini told a simple story of Napoleon's success. It made sense to the reader. If you wanted to use Napoleon's strategy, Jomini's advice was easy to follow. Von Clausewitz made everything complicated. He gave no step-by-step method for following Napoleon's strategy yourself.

Jomini's book is worth some study, because it stands out as the first scholarly work in the strategic planning school of strategy.

Also, the contrast between Jomini and von Clausewitz continues to this day.

In his book, Jomini states that strategy is "the art of making war on the map, the art of taking in the whole theater of war." He lists what strategy "thus includes":

1. Selection of the theater of war and the different combinations it offers
2. Determination of decisive points that result from these combinations and the most favorable direction to give to the undertakings
3. Choice and establishment of the fixed base and the zone of operations
4. Determination of the objective point, either offensive or defensive
5. Fronts of operations, the strategic fronts and the line of defense
6. Choice of lines of operations that lead from the base to the objective point or to the strategic front occupied by the army
7. Best strategic line to take for a given operation; the different maneuvers for covering these lines in their different combinations
8. Eventual bases of operations and the strategic reserves
9. Marches of armies considered as maneuvers
10. Depots considered in their relation to the marches of the armies
11. Fortresses foreseen as strategic means, as refuges for an army or as an obstacle to its march; sieges to make and cover
12. Points for entrenched camps, bridgeheads, etc.
13. Diversions and the large detachments that become useful or necessary.

We can see how this list by Jomini signals the birth of formal strategic planning. He tells you to plan out the "decisive points" and the "objective point" on a map, and then to determine the "lines of operations," "maneuvers," and "marches of armies" needed to reach those points. When other disciplines adopted strategic planning from the military, the decisive points and objective points became "goals," and the operations, maneuvers, and marches became "activities."

Note the order. For Jomini, determining goals comes before choosing activities. The ends precede the means. First you decide on your goal, and then you decide how to reach it. That's the opposite of the art of what works.

Jomini wrote his book in Moscow, where he founded a war college for the Russian army. But he won his greatest following in the United States. American army officers studied his book at West Point, either in the original French or in translations by professors. The first published English version came in 1854, in time to educate the last few classes of officers before the U.S. army split in two for the Civil War. A noted military historian, Colonel J. D. Hittle, tells us that on both sides, "many a Civil War general went into battle with a sword in one hand and Jomini's *Summary of the Art of War* in the other."[8]

Sure enough, the North and South studied their maps and came up with the same decisive points. They sent their armies on the march. The armies met in great battles of mutual slaughter.

Then, by accident, General Ulysses S. Grant discovered a different method in November 1862 at the battle of Vicksburg. When he became Union commander in 1864, he applied this new method more widely, and he won the war. His winning strategy was more like that of von Clausewitz than like that of Jomini. A shorthand for Grant's discovery is "mobile war."[9]

For von Clausewitz, Napoleon's success came from his putting his army in motion with no clear goal. Then, when he saw a battle he could win, he chose to fight. If he saw no battle that he could win, he just kept moving, out of reach of the enemy but always looking for a better time and place to attack. Napoleon passed up more battles than he fought. But in so doing, he won more battles than any other general in history.

At Napoleon's tomb in Paris, you can see the names of his greatest battles etched in the floor: Wagram, Austerlitz, Marengo, and so on. Not Berlin, Milan, or Vienna. Napoleon fought at places with no inherent strategic value. They just happened to be places where he saw at the moment a chance to defeat the enemy army.

And he "saw" by coup d'oeil. Napoleon's expert intuition came in the first instance from his thorough studies of past battles. He made no military innovations himself.

Some of Napoleon's own writings and sayings hint at the essence of his strategy.[10] For example, he gave full credit to the past achievements of the generals who came before him:

> The principles of warfare are those that guided the great captains whose high deeds history has transmitted to us—Alexander, Hannibal, Caesar, Gustavus Adolphus, Turenne, Eugene of Savoy, Frederick the Great. . . . The history of their eighty-three campaigns would constitute a complete treatise on the art of war.

Napoleon even mentions intuition as the method for seeing which battle he had a chance to win:

> The art of war consists, with a numerically interior army, in always having larger forces than the enemy at the point which is to be attacked or defended. . . . It is an intuitive way of acting which properly constitutes the genius of war.

And he describes coup d'oeil as a mix of the eye and the mind, where you see the path to success:

> The issue of a battle is the result of a single instant, a single thought. . . . The decisive moment appears; a psychological spark makes the decision; and a few reserve troops are enough to carry it out.

As a product of military school, Napoleon had mastered the tools and techniques of his day, but the way he combined them came from past achievements:

> Tactics can be learned from treatises, somewhat like geometry, and so can the various evolutions of the science of the engineer and the gunner; but knowledge of the grand principles of warfare can be acquired only through the study of military history and of the battles of the great captains and through experience.

Napoleon amassed great power, but he used it strategically. He never set a goal unless circumstances allowed it and he saw a way to achieve it: "I never truly was my own master, but was always ruled by circumstances."

And he never went into a situation with a theory on how to handle it. The theory arose from the situation. And so he declared, "To every circumstance its own law."

Not having theories or goals, Napoleon constantly changed his plans, depending on where he was able to win. He noted: I had few really definite ideas, and the reason for this was that instead of obstinately seeking to control circumstances, I obeyed them . . . Thus it happened that most of the time . . . I had no definite plans, but only projects.

A *project* in French is a course of action, a strategy. Napoleon launched a strategy when he saw that it had a good chance of success, not because it conformed to a goal. So to others, it seemed like he was switching goals all the time:

> The fact was that I was not a master of my actions, because I was not so insane as to attempt to bend events to conform to my policies. On the contrary, I bent my policies to accord with the unforeseen shape of the events.

Above all, he knew that his power came from winning battles, not from taking territory or achieving other goals:

> A battle is my plan of campaign, and success is my whole policy.

These quotes from Napoleon support von Clausewitz more than they support Jomini, especially with regard to the order of goals and activities. Jomini put the goal first; he said that Napoleon identified a strategic point and then concentrated his forces in order to seize it. In contrast, von Clausewitz said that the goal arises after the means to achieve it. So Napoleon decided what battle to fight only when he saw a way to win it.

This contrast between goal setting and coup d'oeil applies to strategy of all kinds. Following Jomini, in classic strategic planning, you choose a problem to solve and then look for a way to solve it. Following von Clausewitz, in the art of what works, you don't know what problem you can solve until you see how to solve it. And the "how" comes from expert intuition, that is, from past achievements in similar situations. So in business, you choose a specific goal—such as profits, market share, diversification, value creation, or unique position—only when you see a way to reach it.

Expert intuition is counterintuitive. Everyone knows that first you set your goal, and then you design your activities to reach that goal. That is, the ends precede the means. The notion that the means precede the ends violates common sense. No wonder Jomini was easier to follow than von Clausewitz: Jomini explained what most generals already thought.

In breaking with conventional wisdom, von Clausewitz found it hard to explain what he meant. He struggled for 20 years, from 1810 to 1830, and died before he finished. After his death, his wife, Marie, edited his papers and published them as *On War*. Even in a clear English translation, the heavy German philosophical style makes the book hard to read.

Sometimes the abstract prose of *On War* serves as camouflage. For example, Napoleon promoted officers on the basis of merit rather than for their noble blood, something that von Clausewitz could not praise too directly, as the Prussian army remained mostly in the hands of nobles. In the same way, von Clausewitz made sure to cite examples from a Prussian, Frederick the Great, as well as from the Frenchman Napoleon.

But all in all, *On War* is hard to read because of the difficult subject. Here is one of many examples from the text:[11]

> War in the real world, as we have already seen, is not an extreme thing which expends itself at one single discharge, it is the operation of powers which do not develop themselves completely in the same manner and in the same measure, but which at one time expand sufficiently to overcome the resistance opposed by inertia or friction, while at another they are too weak to produce an effect, it is therefore, in a certain measure, a pulsation of violent force more or less vehement, consequently making its discharges and exhausting its powers more or less quickly—in other words, conducting more or less quickly to the aim, but always lasting long enough to admit being exerted on its course, so as to give it this or that direction, in short, to be subject to the will of a guiding intelligence.

And that is only one sentence.

What von Clausewitz seems to be saying here is a version of this statement by Napoleon: "Instead of obstinately seeking to control circumstances, I obeyed them." That is, you pass up battles you can't win rather than trying and failing, and so the length and intensity of the war are within your "guidance" but out of your control.

This is a very difficult point to get across, and even from Napoleon it seems quite odd. Here we have the most successful general in history, who conquered Europe faster than the ancient Romans or the Holy Roman Empire before him, claiming that he never sought to control circumstances. It seems to make no sense. No wonder von Clausewitz poured on the words, as if he were attacking his subject from every direction in a valiant struggle to pin it down.[12]

Four Keys to Success

On War reveals three other keys to successful strategy that complement coup d'oeil: examples from history, resolution, and presence of mind. They all result from the same imperfect information that our Nobel Prize winners in economics cited.

Von Clausewitz sees war as "the province of uncertainty" for three-fourths of all decisions. Thanks to the "continual interposition of chance," a general "constantly finds things different from his expectations." So what is a general to do? Von Clausewitz offers this answer:

> Now, if one is to get safely through this perpetual conflict with the unexpected, two qualities are indispensable. . . . The first is figuratively expressed by the French phrase coup d'oeil. The other is resolution.

Here we find our first two elements of expert intuition: coup d'oeil and resolution. They arise from the uncertainty of all intelligence—the fog of war.

Von Clausewitz goes on to note that in military history, coup d'oeil first applied only to moving soldiers to the right place at the right time. A modern equivalent is hand-eye coordination in sports. Frederick the Great himself wrote an essay on this kind of coup d'oeil.[13] Yet von Clausewitz reports that coup d'oeil took on a wider meaning over time, so that "all able decisions formed in the moment of action soon came to be understood by the expression."

For von Clausewitz, coup d'oeil "must not be wanting in strategy, inasmuch as in it rapid decisions are often necessary." He gives a definition for coup d'oeil that applies to strategy in general,

> The rapid discovery of a truth which to the ordinary mind is either not visible at all or only becomes so after long examination and reflection.

Note that von Clausewitz says that coup d'oeil discovers a truth. But if information is always imperfect, and the range of possible intermediate ends and means is always subject to change, where does this truth come from?

Von Clausewitz goes on to explain. You run through a list of "ends and means" to assess "their effects and their mutual relations." That is, you consider possible courses of action and what they might achieve, until you find the best one. But then, "How does strategy arrive at a complete list of these things?" In theory, there are an infinite number of possible courses of action in any situation. And war is so uncertain that you can't arrive at an "absolute result." So where does strategy turn?

Von Clausewitz answers: strategy . . . turns to experience, and directs its attention on those combinations which military history can furnish.

Here we have examples from history, our fourth element of expert intuition. You search through courses of action that others before you took in similar situations, where you know the results they achieved. You don't copy any one strategy exactly, but rather make a combination based on several of them.

Thus, you don't apply a theory of war, you draw from previous examples. Von Clausewitz admits that such a method is limited because it covers only "circumstances such as are presented in history." In theory, there are many more possibilities than that—or are there? Von Clausewitz notes that a good theory is based on examples from history. Therefore, good theory has the same incompleteness as the list of examples it is based on. A theory that is not based on past examples will "lose itself in abstruse disquisitions, subtleties, and chimeras," instead of remaining "practical."

So coup d'oeil sees a combination of elements from history that can be applied in a new situation. As a result, von Clausewitz tells us, an expert can see much more than a novice:

> As the human eye in a dark room dilates its pupil, draws in the little light that there is, partially distinguishes objects by degrees, and at last knows them quite well, so it is in War with the experienced soldier, whilst the novice is only met by pitch dark night.

So the more history you know, the more of the truth you see. Yet in the end, that truth is still limited because it is based only on what the expert knows from past achievements in the field rather than on all theoretical possibilities. But good theory is itself based on past achievement, so the expert's truth is not so limited after all. The advantages of this method are that any theory so used must come from real examples, not chimeras.

The limited truth of coup d'oeil leads straight to another element of expert intuition: resolution. Von Clausewitz defines resolution as "removing the torments of doubt . . . when there are no sufficient motives for guidance." Coup d'oeil shows you what course of action to take, but its limited truth comes with plenty of flaws and uncertainties. You need resolve in order to engage in a strategy and stick to it, despite the obstacles and arguments against it.

So far we have found three of the key elements of expert intuition in *On War*: coup d'oeil, past examples, and resolution. Here is the fourth, presence of mind:

> From the coup d'oeil and resolution we are naturally led to speak of its kindred quality, presence of mind, which in a region of the unexpected like War must act a great part, for it is indeed nothing but a great conquest over the unexpected. . . . The expression

"presence of mind" certainly denotes very fitly the readiness and rapidity of the help rendered by the mind.

In order for coup d'oeil to work, the mind must be ready for the unexpected, which of course is a paradox: How can you expect the unexpected? What von Clausewitz means is, don't expect anything. Good theory, based on past examples, arms you for battle but "does not necessarily require to be a direction for action." It does not tell you what to do. Good theory builds learning through the generations, so that "each person in succession may not have to go through the same labor of clearing the ground and toiling through his subject, but may find the thing in order, and light admitted on it."

But in action, you leave theory behind. Theory should guide "the future leader" in "self-instruction, but not accompany him to the field of battle; just as a sensible tutor forms and enlightens the opening mind of a youth without, therefore, keeping him in leading strings all through his life." Presence of mind means being ready for the unexpected by mastering theory and then clearing it from your mind as you enter the field of battle. Theory based on past examples offers a guide, not a "director for action." The specific action is always unexpected.

Coup d'oeil, examples from history, resolution, and presence of mind: These are the four elements of expert intuition as found in von Clausewitz. Yet among the four, coup d'oeil stands out above the others:

> This facile coup d'oeil of the General, this simple art of forming notions, this personification of the whole action of War, is so entirely and completely the soul of the right method of conducting War, that in no other but this broad way is it possible to conceive that freedom of the mind which is indispensable if it is to dominate events, not be overpowered by them.

We see that the other elements support coup d'oeil, like three legs beneath the seat of a stool. Presence of mind makes you ready for coup d'oeil, examples from history give coup d'oeil its content, and resolution puts coup d'oeil in action. But all four are essential. Without the other three elements, coup d'oeil is ordinary intuition. All four elements together make expert intuition. That makes all the difference for success.

Coup d'Oeil Today

More than a century after Napoleon, modern science began to unravel the mystery of expert intuition. Today we find a body of evidence far beyond what von Clausewitz was able to piece together.[14] Sure enough, modern research confirms the four elements found in *On War*.

The study of intuition began as a branch of psychology research in the middle of the twentieth century. In recent decades, medical research has chimed in, too, with studies of the biology of the brain. The result is a common notion that there are two types of decision making: rational versus intuitive, or analytical versus naturalistic, or "left brain" versus "right brain." There is much debate on the details, including terminology and where in the brain different functions actually take place. But there is much consensus on the basic dichotomy of logic and intuition as two different modes of thought.

Herbert Simon has been an important figure in this debate, through books and articles from the late 1940s through the 1970s. Among the many studies that won him the 1978 Nobel Prize in economics were Simon's examination of the difference between master and novice chess players. He tried to develop computer models that mimic expert decision making. For Simon, chess is "semantically rich," in that an expert chess player knows a lot about the game. Chess may seem like a logic puzzle to nonplayers, but there is a vast amount of past expertise that you need to master in order to compete. There are various combinations of moves to learn that others developed before you, like the Dutch Stonewall Attack, the Staunton Gambit, or the Budapest Defense.

Simon concludes that "experts ... behave very differently from novices in semantically rich domains." They see situations as similar, with similar solutions:

> In particular, recognition of familiar patterns is a major component of expert skill, and experts can consequently replace a great

deal of heuristic search with solutions, or partial solutions, that they discover by recognition. Moreover, problem solving by recognition has all the characteristics of what is usually called "intuitive," "judgmental," or even "creative" problem solving.[15]

Many other researchers, both contemporary with and after Simon, have contributed to the study of expert intuition. One of the most recent and important of these researchers is Gary Klein. Rather than watching chess players or conducting laboratory experiments in which subjects make decisions in situations that the researcher designs, Klein studied real decision makers in action: firefighters, emergency room nurses, and soldiers in battle. In all these fields, expertise can mean the difference between life and death.

Klein interviewed his subjects about successful cases of rapid decision making. For example, a fire captain pulled his men out of a smoky building just before the floor collapsed, or an emergency room nurse snatched up an infant for instant treatment just in time to save the child. Klein asked them how they knew what to do. At first, they answered as we might expect. "I don't know. It was just my intuition."

But Klein kept at it. He asked them detailed questions about exactly what happened before and during their rapid decision. In every case, Klein was able to reconstruct what his subjects thought and did, and why. The answer was not just intuition, but expert intuition, very much as Simon described it. Because of their expertise, Klein's subjects saw something familiar that no one else saw.

Klein concludes:[16]

Intuition depends on the use of experience to recognize key patterns. . . . Experts can perceive things that are invisible to novices. . . . In the recognition-primed decision-making model (RPD), proficient decision makers . . . are able to detect patterns and typicality. They can size up a situation in a glance and realize that they have seen it, or variants of it . . . before. Their experience buys them the ability to recognize that a situation is a typical case.

Klein's work stands out as the fullest study we have to date of coup d'oeil in action. Note that he calls expert intuition "recognition-primed decision-making," to emphasize that the decision depends on recognizing something from the past in the current situation.

Klein also portrays goal setting in terms similar to those used by von Clausewitz. You don't choose a goal first and then take action. On the contrary, Klein tells us that the goal arises when you see that an action can succeed:

> What triggers active problem-solving is the ability to recognize when a goal is reachable.

Klein notes that this sequence seems "paradoxical" in terms of "the standard view" of goal setting, which we now know came from Jomini. According to Klein, a strategist evaluates the chance of success of a course of action "to determine whether to pursue that goal in the first place." And you can make that judgment based on what worked in the past:

> There must be an experiential ability to judge the solvability of problems prior to working on them. . . . Experience lets us recognize the existence of opportunities. When the opportunity is recognized, the problem solver working out its implications is looking for a way to make good use of it, trying to shape it into a reasonable goal.

In expert intuition, then, the course of action precedes the goal. Klein notes that the decision maker sees an opportunity to succeed and turns that into a goal, in the same way that Napoleon fought a battle only when he saw a way to win it. If he did not see a way to win, he just kept moving. Although separated by more than a century and a half, Klein and von Clausewitz stand together as our leading scholars of coup d'oeil.

More and more researchers are coming to agree with Simon and Klein. For example, a recent review of research on intuition by Robin Hogarth supports all of Simon's and Klein's major conclusions and adds more evidence from other studies as well. As a result, "People can be trained to develop their intuitive skills." That's what makes expert intuition "expert." And so Hogarth titles his review *Educating Intuition*.[17]

Yet science seldom speaks with one voice. We can find other research, especially in psychology, that seems to contradict the conclusions of Simon, Klein, and Hogarth. Let's take a closer look, to see if we can resolve the differences.

We recall that Simon equated creative problem solving with expert intuition that combines familiar elements. Yet a large body of psychology research defines *creativity* as just the opposite: making something new. This body of research has little overlap with research on intuition, thanks to the different definition of creativity.

For creativity, we also have a recent review of research, *Handbook on Creativity,* by Robert Sternberg, that mirrors Hogarth's review of research on intuition. Sternberg defines creativity as the ability to produce work that is both novel and appropriate. Creative work is original, unexpected, and useful.

Of course, if you look for things that are novel and original, you won't find expert intuition. And yet, even in Sternberg's *Handbook* there is one dissenting view, by Robert Weisberg. In his own work, Weisberg studied specific creative achievements in the arts—for example, by Picasso—and found that in each case they combined elements from earlier artists. So for Weisberg,[18]

> The reason that one person produced some innovation, while another person did not, may be due to nothing more than the fact that the former knew something that the latter did not. Furthermore, this knowledge may not have been of an extraordinary sort.

Or, as Sternberg puts it,

> Weisberg attempts to show that the insights depend on subjects using conventional cognitive processes (such as analogical transfer) applied to knowledge already stored in memory.

But the rest of Sternberg's review takes another path, that of "creative imagination" producing something new. So we might ask, does Sternberg find the secret? Does the research he cites tell us how the creative imagination works?

Hardly. A concluding essay by Richard Mayer reads like a lament:[19]

> Although creativity researchers have managed to ask some deep questions, they have generally not succeeded in answering them. . . . This Handbook will have served an important historic role if it re-kindles interest in the great unanswered questions concerning how people produce creative solutions to real problems.

Perhaps creativity research has not succeeded because in looking for what is new rather than for what is the same, it is barking up the wrong tree. We will return to this distinction between creative imagination and creative intuition in later chapters on business strategy.

For now, let's see what von Clausewitz had to say about imagination. He mentions it only once, saying that a general might have "a talent for forming an ideal picture of a country quickly and distinctively." That's good; you imagine the lay of the land in your mind. But to him, that's all imagination is good for:

> If this talent is then to be ascribed to imagination, it is also almost the only service which military activity requires of that erratic goddess, whose influence is more hurtful than useful in other respects.

For von Clausewitz, then, imagination is an "erratic goddess" that a strategist tries to avoid. Look for what's similar, not for what's new, as Simon, Klein, and Hogarth describe.

Coup d'Oeil in Science

We also find expert intuition in research on the "science of science"—that is, how scientists make discoveries. For our purpose, a scientist might be closer to von Clausewitz's general on a campaign and our own business strategist than to Klein's firefighters, nurses, and soldiers in battle. Klein's subjects must make decisions in a matter of moments. In science, in military strategy, and in business, decisions usually take more time.

The study of the use of intuition in science began in the early part of the twentieth century. Some scholars argued that science depended more on intuition than on logic. They included Henri

Poincaré, a distinguished physicist and mathematician, and Henri Bergson, a philosopher who won the 1927 Nobel Prize in literature. These scholars saw intuition as something opposed to the intellect that you could not explain. In later decades, scientists came to see intuition as a form of reasoning rather than as an irrational force that was in conflict with reasoning.[20]

For example, in *Intuition and Science*, Mario Bunge notes that scientific intuition comes not from unknown inspiration but from "previous experience" and "stored information"—that is, from expertise. Bunge uses another vivid term for scientific intuition: a "nose" for "the choice of problems, lines of investigation, techniques, and hypotheses." These activities amount to the scientist's course of action that is, a strategy.

We find our most telling description of expert intuition in science in the leading study of how science actually works: *The Structure of Scientific Revolutions,* by Thomas Kuhn. As it turns out, Kuhn endorses the role of expert intuition in science, in terms that come close to those of von Clausewitz in many respects. We note especially three of Kuhn's key observations: achievement precedes theory; expertise rests on concrete achievements; and science advances through evidence, not proof. Let's look at the three in turn.

Here is how Kuhn presents the core question of his study:[21]

> Why is the concrete scientific achievement, as a locus of professional commitment, prior to the various concepts, laws, theories, and points of view that may be abstracted from it?

In other words, achievement precedes theory. Conventional wisdom tells us the opposite: First you come up with a theory, and then you apply it. Thus, Kuhn sides with von Clausewitz, who told us to leave theory behind as we enter the field of battle. And in business, Ray Kroc saw the achievement of the McDonald brothers first. The theory of fast-food chains came after.

So for *theory* we can also read *goal* or *problem*. In expert intuition, you don't know what theory you need until you see a way to use it, just as you don't know what goal you can reach until you see a way to reach it, or what problem you can solve until you see a way to solve it.

Kuhn shows how, in case after case, scientific discovery precedes the acceptance of a theory to explain that discovery. For example, once there were many competing theories of electricity. Then Benjamin Franklin successfully showed that electricity flowed between objects. Only then did other scientists accept the "fluid" theory of electricity over the other competing theories. It was Franklin's concrete achievements, not his ideas, that won them over. Today, scientists know that electricity is not really a fluid and that it doesn't really flow, but the fluid theory still works for most everyday uses of electricity, if not for further advances in electrical sciences.

As for Kuhn's second key observation, he tells us that "the unit of scientific achievement is the solved problem." Experts do not simply apply a mass of past information to the present situation; they carry the past forward in units of achievement. Thus, Napoleon looked to the campaigns of the "great captains"—that is, to their achievements. He applied those achievements in different combinations to his own battles. Von Clausewitz called those achievements "examples from history." And Kroc saw the original McDonald's as a single achievement, not as a mass of information or as an application of a theory. Other scientists did not just take up the mass of Franklin's ideas; they repeated and modified his successful experiments, using and adapting the same equipment.

Kuhn makes a direct link between intuition and expertise based on past achievements:

> Intuitions are not individual . . . they are the tested and shared possessions of the members of a successful group, and the novice acquires them through training as part of his preparation for group-membership.

This group activity constitutes "normal science," which to Kuhn "means research firmly based on one or more past scientific achievements." For Kuhn, the scientific method starts with scientists noticing the achievements of other scientists. Their expert intuition then suggests a way to build on those achievements. They try a new combination. Whether that combination produces further achievements is unpredictable, but once new achievements happen, other scientists study those achievements and build further on their success.

And so Sir Isaac Newton, the founder of modern physics, declared, "If I have seen farther, it is by standing on the shoulders of giants." Those giants included Copernicus, Kepler, Galileo, Viète, Wallis, and van Schooten. They were the equivalent of Napoleon's "great captains." It was their achievements, not their ideas, that Newton built on for his own success.

We find a similar view from Sir Peter Medawar, winner of the 1960 Nobel Prize in medicine:

> Everything that a scientist does is a function of what others have done before him: the past is embodied in every new conception and even in the possibility of its being conceived at all.[22]

Medawar echoes Roger Bacon, one of the founders of the scientific method in the thirteenth century:

> At first one should believe those who have made experiments or who have faithful testimony from others who have done so . . . experience follows second, and reason comes third.[23]

This is the true scientific method. Ray Kroc and Steven Jobs were good scientists, because they adopted a new course of action upon discovering the specific achievements of other scientists: the McDonald brothers and Xerox.

But how do you know what is an achievement and what is not? Kuhn tells us that scientists rely on "evidence," or "persuasion rather than proof." Scientists know that they never prove anything. Instead, they try to provide enough evidence to persuade their fellow scientists to accept their results. Mathematics is the only branch of knowledge that yields "proofs"—i.e., in which perfect logic reigns. Science, in contrast, requires measuring what happens in the real world, an approximate task at best.[24]

And so we are back to imperfect information, where we began. Expert intuition cuts through the "fog of science" to pick out certain pieces of evidence and not others, and resolution helps you carry through despite the lack of proof. Sometimes the evidence doesn't even fit your existing equipment, so you adjust the equipment to fit the evidence. Then you give the new measurement a new name, often that of the first scientist to use it: an ohm, a watt, a curie, or a volt. These measures represent new combinations of past measures (such as wavelength, time, mass, or temperature) to suit the results at hand.

Kuhn tells us that normal science gives way to revolution when a new achievement overturns past theory rather than simply adding to it. But even here Kuhn stresses continuity with the past:

> Novelty for its own sake is not a desideratum in the sciences as it is in so many other creative fields. As a result, though new paradigms seldom or never possess all the capabilities of their predecessors, they usually preserve a great deal of the most concrete parts of past achievements.

In practical terms, then, even great revolutions in science build on the past. For example, Copernicus showed that the planets go around the sun, not the earth. Yet his breakthrough led to little change in the daily work of most astronomers. He gave new calculations for only seven heavenly bodies: the sun, the moon, and the five known planets. For the multitude of stars, the old calculations remained intact. The stars are so far away that it hardly matters whether you measure their movement from the sun or from the earth. Naval academies still taught "celestial navigation" using the old calculations—with the earth at the center of the universe—until computers took over navigation in the late 1990s.

The continuity of past achievement in science is the basis of expert intuition, and that intuition also speeds achievement. Like Napoleon, scientists choose battles that they can win, or, as Kuhn puts it, the scientist aims "to concentrate his attention on problems that he has good reason to believe he will be able to solve." But the same is not true for scholars of the social world, including business. Kuhn notes this contrast between natural and social scientists:

The latter often tend, as the former almost never do, to defend their choice of a research problem . . . chiefly in terms of the social importance of achieving a solution. Which group would one then expect to solve problems at a more rapid rate?

Social scientists, like Jomini, choose those battles that they judge it most important to win. Thus, they set their goal first and then look for ways to reach it. Natural scientists, like Napoleon, choose battles that their expert intuition tells them they have a chance to win. Successful business strategists do the same thing, as later chapters show.

East Meets West

Last but not least, we can find a strain of expert intuition in both Western and Eastern philosophy.

In the West, expert intuition shows up in pragmatism. The *Oxford English Dictionary* gives this definition of *pragmatism*:

> Theory that advocates dealing with social and political problems primarily by practical methods adapted to the existing circumstances, rather than by methods which have been conformed to some ideology.

That is, a pragmatist chooses a strategy based on its chance of success, not on whether it fits a certain theory. Expert intuition applies this kind of pragmatism to strategy of all kinds, not just political and social problems.

The clearest statement of pragmatic philosophy comes from William James in the early twentieth century.[25] In *Pragmatism*, James wrote that the Pragmatic method is "fully armed and militant" against "rationalism." Pragmatism has no "dogmas" or "doctrines," but rather chooses among dogmas and doctrines at will. And James uses a vivid image for how the choice happens: Pragmatism "lies in the midst of our theories, like a corridor in a hotel."

For any particular problem or situation, you stroll up and down the corridor, looking into each room. When you see a theory that you can use, you enter that room. You may pass by a theory, but you never argue against it: You might need it later, in another situation. So for James, Pragmatism is "completely genial" and "will entertain any hypothesis" and "consider any evidence":

> Any idea upon which we can ride . . . any idea that will carry us prosperously from one part of our experience to any other part . . . is true for just so much, true in so far forth, true instrumentally . . . truth in our ideas means their power to "work."

Once again, von Clausewitz, Kuhn, and James agree on the role of theory. A theory is neither true nor false. It is right or wrong for a particular situation. Good theories come from past achievement: The fluid theory of electricity had Franklin's results to back it up. So you choose what past achievements to draw on depending on the situation. Whatever works: that's the pragmatist creed.

Even the best theory is just an approximate statement based on many real cases. It can never cover all cases, so it is never exactly true. Franklin's fluid theory of electricity was right for the moment, in that he used existing equipment and terms that fellow scientists of the day might understand. Today we know that electricity is not a fluid at all, but rather charges of stationary mass. Yet Franklin's idea endures: We speak of electric "current," as if electricity really does flow. So some of Franklin's theory still works, and some of it doesn't. The situation has changed. A pragmatist changes with it.

A recent intellectual history, *The Metaphysical Club* by Louis Menand, portrays Pragmatism as the dominant philosophy of the United States as it became a great power at the start of the twentieth century. Pragmatism enabled the country to reconcile new scientific discoveries, many different religions, and the mix of political ideas that generations of immigrants brought over, especially from Britain and France. Which ideas should the country adopt? The answer: all of them, depending on the situation.

Menand tells us that the founders of Pragmatism included the great jurist Oliver Wendell Holmes, who applied the same philosophy to law. While other judges used logical principles to decide cases, Holmes did the opposite. For him, the principles came after. Menand quotes him:[26]

> It is the merit of the common law that it decides the case first and determines the principles afterwards.

You might think that pragmatists lack principles, but that's not so. They accept all principles as possibly useful, and they pick which ones to apply according to the situation. For Holmes, the "life of the law" is not "logic" but "experience"—that is, precedent. Some unforeseen combination of what worked in the past will work in the present for a particular situation. Holmes was a great intellectual who loved theories, but he found them of little use in his courtroom:

> All the pleasure in life is in general ideas but all the use of life is in specific solutions which cannot be reached through generalities any more than a picture can be painted by knowing some rules of method. They are reached by insight, tact, and specific knowledge.

Note that Holmes uses the word *tact*. The *Oxford English Dictionary* defines it as, "The sense of touch; and figuratively, a keen faculty of perception or discrimination likened to the sense of touch." So we have yet another name for expert intuition: an expert's "touch."

These days, we find this image applied most often in high crafts and sports of skill: a violin maker or a tennis champion is said to have a certain touch. As it turns out, yet another philosophical tradition speaks directly about such physical expertise, as well as applying it to strategy of all kinds. That philosophy takes us to the other side of the world from James and Holmes, and far back in time: to China in 450 B.C.

That is the approximate date of the *Tao Te Ching*, which is the founding text of Taoism. The title means "The Book of the Way." So Tao is "the way." Little is known about the author, who is remembered by the name Lao Tzu, or "Old Master." The *Tao Te Ching* is very short, poetic, and mysterious in many parts. Yet some of the mystery drops away if we read it through the eyes of expert intuition.

For example, in expert intuition, you give up what you want in exchange for what you can achieve. So the Tao says,

> Free from desire, you realize the mystery.
> Caught in desire, you see only the manifestations.

To see what you can achieve calls for presence of mind, where you expect the unexpected. At an unforeseen moment, a coup d'oeil cuts through the fog to show you what action to take. So the Tao says,

> Do you have the patience to wait
> Til your mud settles and the water is clear?
> Can you remain unmoving
> Til the right action arises by itself? . . .
> The master doesn't seek fulfillment.
> Not seeking, not expecting,
> She is present, and can welcome all things.

You don't go into a situation knowing what theory to apply. You choose the theory depending on what you find. So the Tao says,

> A good scientist has freed himself from concepts
> And keeps his mind open to what is.

Fight only battles that you see a way to win. Pass up battles that you don't see a way to win. So the Tao says,

> Yield and overcome
> Bend and be straight.

The *Tao Te Ching* applies to strategy of all kinds, including the conduct of your personal life. Later in the same century, around 400 B.C., we can see the influence of the Tao on *The Art of War*, by Sun Tzu:[27]

Those skilled in war cultivate the Tao and preserve the laws and are therefore able to formulate victorious strategies.

Sure enough, Sun Tzu does not tell us to identify our "objective points" and march our armies to them, as Jomini does. Instead, we should choose battles when we see a way to win them, as Napoleon did:

> Experts in war depend especially on opportunity and expediency. . . .
> To refrain from intercepting an enemy whose banners are in perfect order, to refrain from attacking an army drawn up in calm and confident array—this is the art of studying circumstances.

By fighting where you can win and holding back where you can't, you conform to circumstances instead of trying to bend them to your will. That may seem weak, but it's the source of the greatest strength:

> Now an army may be likened to water, for just as flowing water avoids the heights and hastens to the lowlands, so an army avoids strength and strikes weakness. . . . Subtle and insubstantial, the expert leaves no trace.

As a basic philosophy, Tao has many elements in common not just with pragmatism but also with its Asian neighbor, Buddhism. In fact, Tao and Buddhism merged in China in the early centuries A.D., to form "Chan" Buddhism. Chan then spread to Japan as Zen.[28] In Japan, Zen became the favorite discipline of the high crafts and especially the martial arts. The *do* in Judo, Tai-Kwan-Do, Kendo, Aikido, and other fighting disciplines is the Japanese word for *Tao*.

Japanese samurai all practiced Zen. In *The Book of Five Rings*, Miyamoto Musashi, a famous samurai of the seventeenth century, instructed his pupils in the Zen of expert intuition. Above all, it's an art of the eyes:[29]

> It is necessary in strategy to be able to look to both sides without moving the eyeballs. You cannot master this ability quickly. Learn

what is written here: use this gaze in everyday life and do not vary it whatever happens.

This is another version of presence of mind. You look straight ahead, but you see everything around you. You have to see everything because you cannot predict what information will be most useful. You enter battle with no expectations about what will happen, where to look, or what you will find. So you look everywhere, at all times. Yet you can't move your eyes around constantly; it would make you dizzy. Thus, you don't move your eyes at all, yet you see everything at once.

And as you fight, you look for success, however small. Then you build on that success:

> The strategist makes small things into big things, like building a great Buddha from a one-foot model.

Like Sun Tzu, Musashi tells you to conform to circumstances and to avoid battles that you don't see a way to win. The result is a "natural" flow of events:

> The Way of strategy is the Way of nature. When you appreciate the power of nature, knowing the rhythm of any situation, you will be able to hit the enemy naturally and strike naturally.

Above all, strategy depends on expertise. An expert sees what a novice can't. Expert intuition takes practice and study:

> When you attain the Way of strategy there will not be one thing you cannot see. You must study hard. . . . Develop intuitive judgment and understanding for everything.

Today, the "zen" of a craft or sport or other skill commonly means an expert presence of mind, just like the presence of mind that von Clausewitz described. In a coup d'oeil, "the right action arises by itself."

You give up your goal to get your goal.

To overcome, you yield.

This is the art of what works.

An Eye for Business

In this chapter, we saw how the four key elements of expert intuition—coup d'oeil, resolution, examples from history, and presence of mind—are found in military strategy and many other fields of life. But what about business?

Rumor has it that most business decisions are made by "gut instinct," otherwise known as intuition. Most companies try to replace this gut instinct with analysis, or systems, or some kind of orderly decision making—all to no avail. Intuition still rules. Yet our lessons from other fields offer a different path. Instead of trying to stamp out intuition, we can study it, use it, and make it better in all our business decisions.

Above all, we now know the difference between ordinary intuition and expert intuition. In ordinary intuition, you just have a feeling about something. In expert intuition, you draw on what worked before. The more you know about what worked before, the better your expert intuition.

In business, as in war, in science, or in any other field of endeavor, you don't know what battle you can win until you see a way to win it. You don't know what problem you can solve until you see a way to solve it. You don't know what goal to set until you see a way to reach it. And you "see a way" by combining what works from past experience—yours and anyone else's.

And so we now turn to applying the art of expert intuition to our main subject: business success.

**CHAPTER
3**

The Art of Success
Expert Intuition in Business

T HE PREVIOUS CHAPTER presented the four key elements of
the art of what works that von Clausewitz first identified: coup
d'oeil, resolution, examples from history, and presence of mind.
We then found these elements again in different forms in modern
research on expert intuition, in science, and in Eastern and
Western philosophy. We now apply these four elements to business strategy.

We have many studies to draw from that indicate the exis-
tence of expert intuition in business. We will take just a sample.
In each of the studies, we look for our four elements in the cases
the authors cite and in the explanations they provide. Again and
again we find the same story: The art of what works is the key
to success.

Adaptive versus Creative Response

Paul Allen and Bill Gates went to high school together in Seattle.
There they worked with computers, as two of the many ama-

teurs around the country who built and programmed their own machines. Their biggest success was a traffic-counting program they wrote for a microcomputer they had made themselves.

After high school, Allen dropped out of college and went to work for a computer company in Seattle. In December 1974, he went to visit Gates at Harvard. On the way, he picked up the latest issue of *Popular Electronics*. There on the cover was the Altair, the world's first mass-market microcomputer, made by MITS of Albuquerque, New Mexico. Up to that time, computer owners had programmed their own computers. In the article on the Altair, MITS announced that it wanted to provide a single operating system with every machine. The company invited amateurs and professionals alike to try their hand at writing such a program.

First Allen and then Gates had the same coup d'oeil: to adapt their traffic-counting program for the Altair. It was written in BASIC, a simplified language that two Dartmouth professors had invented 10 years before. Dozens of other programmers set to work too, and many of them used BASIC. But Allen and Gates won the race. Allen traveled alone to MITS headquarters to run the program. It made a single calculation: 2 + 2 = 4. MITS gave them the contract.

And so Microsoft was born.

In *Hard Drive*, James Wallace and Jim Erickson quote Gates on the future of the software industry at that time:[1]

> When Paul Allen and I saw that picture of the first Altair computer, we could only guess at the wealth of applications it would inspire. We knew applications would be developed but we didn't know what they would be. Some were predictable—for example, programs that would let a PC function as the terminal for a mainframe computer—but the most important applications, such as the VisiCalc spreadsheets, were unexpected.

Note how Gates cites predictable software applications: those in which a PC was an add-on to a mainframe computer. But unexpected applications made the PC a mini-mainframe all by itself. Microsoft, of course, made its fortune on the unexpected rather than the predictable strategy for PCs.

Gates and Allen were never great programmers, but they expected the unexpected with great presence of mind. Their coup d'oeil combined past achievements to make a stand-alone Altair program. One of the key past achievements came from MITS itself: Gates and Allen had no hand in making the Altair hardware. Yet they built on their unexpected combination with great resolution, in defiance of the predictable path of software applications. As in Musashi's *The Book of Five Rings*, they turned a 1-foot model into a giant Buddha.

Gates and Allen were artists of what works.

We find the same distinction between predictable and unexpected business achievements in the work of the great Austrian economist Joseph Schumpeter. In a classic 1947 article, "The Creative Response in Economic History," Schumpeter called a predictable strategy an "adaptive response." He called the unexpected strategy a "creative response." For Microsoft, the adaptive response would have been to write programs that would connect PCs to mainframe computers. Instead, the company made a creative response: to help turn the stand-alone Altair into a whole new industry.

For Schumpeter, the adaptive response comes from "traditional" economic theory, whereas the creative response comes from "entrepreneurship." Solid analysis led Xerox to hand over its PC advances to Apple. To Xerox and most of the rest of the industry, including Gates and Allen, more computing power meant better mainframes. Gates and Allen switched sides not because of superior industry analysis but because their program for the Altair—their creative response—worked.

Schumpeter did not think the creative response overturned the traditional theory of economics. He thought that "from the standpoint of the observer who is in full possession of all relevant facts," the creative response "can always be understood *ex post*; but it can practically never be understood *ex ante*: that is to say, it cannot be predicted by applying the ordinary rules of inference from the pre-existing facts." Economics is always right, but only after the fact. It cannot predict the future.

Schumpeter describes the coup d'oeil and resolution of the entrepreneur that make up a creative response:[2]

The entrepreneurial performance involves, on the one hand, the ability to perceive new opportunities that cannot be proved at the moment at which action has to be taken, and on the other hand, will power adequate to break down the resistance that the social environment offers to change.

The resolution or "will power" of Gates and Allen pertained to specific achievements, not to a theory. After their success with the Altair, they strove to repeat the same core elements for each new generation of mass-market microcomputers. As Gates explains in *Hard Drive*, their post-Altair strategy closely resembled their Altair achievement:

> Microsoft's goal was to write and supply software for most personal computers without getting directly involved in making or selling computer hardware. Microsoft licensed the software at extremely low prices.

Before the Altair, companies charged a lot of money for computer programs, as they were one-of-a-kind products. But now, with a mass machine, Microsoft could charge a low price because it could simply adapt what it already had, rather than writing a new program for every new mass-market machine that followed the Altair:

> It was our belief that money could be made betting on volume. We adapted our programming languages, such as our version of BASIC, to each machine. We were very responsive to all the hardware manufacturers' requests. We didn't want to give anyone a reason to look elsewhere. We wanted choosing Microsoft to be a no-brainer. Our strategy worked. Along the way, Microsoft BASIC became an industry software standard.

Microsoft believed that money could be made in this way because the strategy had worked for the Altair. The belief—or theory or goal—followed the specific achievement.

Schumpeter thought that the creative response was everywhere:

> To see the phenomenon even in the humblest levels of the business world is quite essential though it may be difficult to find the humble entrepreneurs historically.

Yet Schumpeter thought that entrepreneurial behavior might decline because "the economy would progressively bureaucratize itself" and "the element of personal intuition and force would be less essential than it was." But even in large firms, he noted that there were "different colors to entrepreneurship," including "setting up" or "organizing." That is, you might not have a superior product, but your coup d'oeil might show you a way to run the business that would allow you to keep costs low and profits high. That too is a creative response.

Note that Schumpeter does not say here that the creative response comes from past achievements. He does that in a later article, "Change and the Entrepreneur,"[3] where he says that new "combinations" rather than original inventions are the key product of an entrepreneur—the way Jobs saw "combining" as the key to creative success, and the way Gates and Allen combined BASIC, their previous traffic program, and the Altair machine to make their new strategy.

In a third article, Schumpeter tells us that innovation leads to imitation. For "as soon as the success is before everyone's eyes," we find that "everything is made very much easier." Thus, "with much diminished difficulty," the success can now "be copied, even improved upon, and a whole crowd invariably does copy it." So one entrepreneur leads to another, as they build on each other's success.[4]

If we put Schumpeter's three articles together, we find three of the four elements of expert intuition that von Clausewitz cited: coup d'oeil, resolution, and examples from history. All that's missing is presence of mind. In a way, this is the easiest element to miss, for the creative response begins with coup d'oeil, and presence of mind precedes it. That's why we find presence of mind more in philosophy than in economics: It is a state of mind rather than a phenomenon that you can observe.

Schumpeter wrote more than 50 years ago. Do his views still hold up today? For that we turn to a recent study of successful entrepreneurs. Sure enough, we see the same elements of expert intuition that Schumpeter praised so highly.

Creative Imitation

From its start in 1979, *Inc.* has been the leading U.S. magazine on entrepreneurship. In 1981, the magazine created an "*Inc.*-500" list of the fastest-growing privately held companies in the country, based on growth rates over the previous 5 years. For his study *The Origin and Evolution of New Businesses*, Amar Bhidé interviewed founders of companies from the 1989 *Inc.*–500 list. He narrowed the list to companies founded in the previous 8 years in order to capture the earliest phase of a company's creation, and he ended up with a total of 100 companies to study.

Bhidé's study stands out in the strategy literature for two reasons. First, most books on business strategy give you principles to follow without providing much evidence that the principles work. Bhidé, in contrast, presents the empirical results of actual strategy in action.[5]

Second, when other studies do report on actual strategy, they do not single out those strategies which are successful. They tell you what companies do, not how they succeed. Bhidé, in contrast, studied not just strategy but successful strategy. Like Napoleon, he studied not just captains, but the "great captains," in the same way that von Clausewitz studied Napoleon, the most successful captain of all, Kuhn studied successful scientists, and Klein studied successful decision makers.

These two features of Bhidé's study—empirical results and success—turn out to be rare in the strategy literature. That makes his results all the more precious for our main subject: the art of what works.

Bhidé found that only 6 percent of successful entrepreneurs claimed to have started with unique products or services. The *Inc.* founders he interviewed typically imitated someone else's ideas, and any innovations they made were incremental or easily replicated.

These results overturn the conventional wisdom on how innovation happens. The entrepreneurs that Bhidé studied were very creative, but they built on something that already worked. This takes us back to the distinction between the definitions of creativity as "making something" and as "making something new." What Bhidé is describing is creative imitation, which would be impossible if creativity required novelty.

The majority of the entrepreneurs who Bhidé studied "replicated or modified an idea encountered through previous employment" (71 percent), while many others "discovered their ideas serendipitously" (20 percent). Very few "followed a systematic approach to identifying and evaluating opportunities" (4 percent). This sounds very much like expert intuition, where you suddenly see a new combination of past achievements to suit a new situation.

Yet Bhidé does not quite say this. His entrepreneur carries forward someone else's idea, not someone else's achievement. Still, we infer that the idea was a good idea that had some evidence of success. Otherwise, why imitate it? This does not mean that the prior achievement worked completely—especially when the idea comes from a previous job, you might see a way to do it better and go off on your own to do so.

Bhidé then tells us that in imitating the previous idea, "any innovations were incremental or easily replicated." Such was certainly the case with McDonald's, Microsoft, and Apple—so much so that Jobs felt "guilty." When Bhidé says "easily," he means conceptually easily. That is, modifications of the original idea are easy to figure out, but it still requires very hard work to make them succeed. The original coup d'oeil might or might not include the eventual alterations, but in either case the resolution must follow.

Bhidé only hints at coup d'oeil in his description of how the entrepreneurs identified and evaluated their opportunities. We see coup d'oeil in the 20 percent who "discovered their ideas serendipitously." Yet even the 71 percent who found their idea at a previous job benefited from a form of serendipity. When you took that previous job in the first place, you did not foresee taking a particular idea from it and going off on your own. Even if you said to yourself, "I'm going to learn this business and then go off on my own," you did not have a specific idea at that time. The specific idea strikes you or dawns on you while you are doing the job. It comes to you in a coup d'oeil.

So Bhidé's entrepreneurs follow von Clausewitz—and they also reject Jomini. Bhidé found that 41 percent of the entrepreneurs had no business plan at all and 26 percent had just a rudimentary plan. A mere 5 percent worked up financial projections for investors, and only 28 percent wrote up a full-blown business plan.

Remember that making the *Inc.*-500 list requires 5 years of sustained growth. More than two-thirds of Bhidé's entrepreneurs accomplished this great feat without a written plan. They did have another kind of plan, however—the unwritten kind. Jomini tells you to plan on maps, while Napoleon saw a plan in his eye.

You do not have to write down a plan to have a good one. The *Oxford English Dictionary* defines *plan* this way: "A formulated or organized method according to which something is to be done; a scheme of action, project, design; the way in which it is proposed to carry out some proceeding." This sounds like a strategy. By that definition, Bhidé's entrepreneurs certainly had a plan. What they lacked was a plan on paper. So in one sense, they were great planners: A "scheme of action" came to them in a coup d'oeil, and they followed through with resolution. In another sense, they were poor planners: They failed to write their plans down.

We will return to these two different meanings of *plan*—a strategy versus a written document—in a later chapter on strategic planning. For now, let's see what Bhidé himself says about the lack of formal planning by his entrepreneurs: It's something they grow out of.

Bhidé tells us that entrepreneurs start out without much money, they don't make much at first either, and it's not certain that they ever will, so they can't afford the time or expense of formal planning. That's why only 4 percent do formal research before they start their business. This lack of planning plus the high uncertainty means that the entrepreneurs must "adapt to unexpected problems and opportunities." Since they have little money and no "long-term strategy," that adaptation is "opportunistic or myopic."

For Bhidé, therefore, adapting to unexpected problems and opportunities is a bad thing. Formal planning can overcome it, but entrepreneurs can't afford that. As the business grows, however, they make enough money to pay for planning, and the company becomes large enough and certain enough to make planning a worthwhile investment. That's why "corporations are more likely than individual entrepreneurs to find opportunities after a systematic search, to conduct extensive research and formulate careful plans, and to stick to their plans once an initiative has been launched."

So big companies do not act like entrepreneurs—and Bhidé thinks that's a good thing:[6]

> This seemingly regimented approach does not reflect the incompetence or the bureaucratic tendencies of corporate executives, as their critics sometimes claim. Rather, it is a necessary consequence of the resources they control and the constraints they face.

Bhidé sees formal planning as a good and a necessary thing for a company. In Schumpeter's terms, Bhidé seems to say that a firm grows from creative response to adaptive response. This is only right and proper: Everyone grows up sometime. But still we miss that frisky child—as start-ups turn into corporations, we mourn the loss of expert intuition.

Yet, must it be so? Or is there a way to stay, like Peter Pan, forever young?

Let's remember that Bhidé's book is an empirical study of successful entrepreneurs. For the corporate picture, he reverts to a statement of common practice, not an empirical study of success. Perhaps he would find the same thing on the corporate side if he studied corporate behavior the way he studied his entrepreneurs. After all, he overturned the conventional wisdom on entrepreneurship. Maybe he would do the same thing with corporate planning.

Without such a study from Bhidé, we must look elsewhere for evidence on expert intuition in larger firms.

And, sure enough, we find it.

Build on What Works

Built to Last, by James Collins and Jerry Porras, was one of the leading studies of business strategy in the 1990s. In the fog of the dot.com and telecom booms, where the new pushed out the old every day, millions of readers peered through the fog to learn from *Built to Last* what worked in the past. Like Bhidé, Collins and Porras studied achievement. They looked at U.S. companies that had "lasted"—that is, that remained successful throughout the twentieth century.

Their initial list of companies came from a survey of 700 CEOs in August 1989. They asked each CEO to name 5 "highly visionary" firms, and then they took the top 20 of those named. From the 20 they knocked out 2 that were founded after 1950. The remaining 18 had a long history of success behind them. Their average founding date was 1897.

Collins and Porras plotted stock prices for the 18 firms, and found that for the visionary firms the "stock fund would have grown . . . over fifteen times the general market." So the CEOs had guessed right. These were very successful companies indeed.

Built to Last aims "to identify the underlying characteristics and dynamics common to highly visionary companies (and that distinguish them from other companies) and to translate these findings into a useful conceptual framework." Among the many lessons that come through, two stand out. First, successful companies have "Big Hairy Audacious Goals." Second, they "Try a Lot of Stuff and Keep What Works."

At first glance, this seems to be a combination of Jomini and von Clausewitz: You set goals, but you also do what works. But which comes first? In their conceptual framework, Collins and Porras put the goals first. That tilts them toward Jomini. But in the actual cases, what works comes first. That tilts them back toward von Clausewitz.

Here, for example, they seem to favor expert intuition:

> In examining the history of the visionary companies, we were struck by how often they made some of their best moves not by detailed strategic planning, but rather by experimentation, trial and error, opportunism, and—quite literally—accident. What looks in hindsight like a brilliant strategy was often the residual result of opportunistic experimentation and "purposeful accidents."

Collins and Porras give three leading examples of this "opportunistic" strategy in action. Let's look at each example in turn, to see how expert intuition comes through in the details of the case.

Johnson & Johnson

Johnson & Johnson was started in 1886. It made sterile, ready-to-use medicated bandages that vastly reduced the infection rate from surgical procedures.

Then in 1890, a doctor complained of skin irritation from the bandages. Fred Kilmer, the company's director of research, sent the doctor a packet of Italian talc. The doctor liked it.

Kilmer then proposed that Johnson & Johnson include a small can of talc with some of its bandages as part of the standard package. Customers liked the talc and asked to buy it separately. That surprised the company, but it quickly agreed. The powder became a major product line, one that is famous to this day. Collins and Porras cite the official company history: "The Johnsons got into the baby powder business quite by accident."

This was surely a creative rather than an adaptive response, but was it really an accident? It might have looked like one to the company as a whole, but how did it look to Kilmer himself? The company was surprised, but he was not. He had a coup d'oeil and the resolution to follow it through. The company had the good sense to follow his lead rather than stick to its previous plan. Yet expert intuition rather than "accident" is a better way to describe the path of success.

Accidents happen to people. They are not something people do. But successful strategy is something you do, something that starts with coup d'oeil.

Marriott

J. W. Marriott founded his company in 1927 as a root beer stand. Ten years later, he had a chain of 9 successful restaurants, which he planned to expand to 18 over the next 3 years. Then, on a regular tour of his chain, he found a surprise at restaurant number 8.

This restaurant was next to Hoover Airport in Washington, D.C. Passengers were stopping at the restaurant to stock up on food to carry onto the plane. This was not the kind of information that showed up in reports to headquarters, so Marriott found out about it only by chance, when he went there. The store manager explained that the airplane trade was growing bigger each day.

Overnight, Marriott figured out what to do. The next day he went straight to Eastern Air Transport. Then and there he worked out an arrangement for the restaurant to deliver box lunches right to the planes, as part of ordinary flight preparation. The service grew quickly—to 22 flights a day in just a few months. Over the years it spread to more than a hundred airports. It led Marriott to look for other opportunities in food service beyond his original restaurants. The result was a major business that led to hotel food, and then to hotels themselves.

Collins and Porras praise Marriott for skipping a research and planning phase. He "could have bogged down in long meetings and strategic analyses to decide what to do." Instead, "Marriott made an incremental shift in corporate strategy by quick, vigorous action taken to seize upon a stroke of unexpected good luck." This is a clear case of von Clausewitz over Jomini. We can even pinpoint the night of Marriott's coup d'oeil.

As Schumpeter says, you can explain a creative response *ex post*, but you can't predict it *ex ante*. Collins and Porras seem to agree: "The step looks brilliant in retrospect, but in reality was simply the result of an opportunistic experiment that happened to work out." Yet they also diminish Marriott's achievement: It was not really brilliant at all. He was just lucky.

So again, as in the case of Johnson & Johnson, Collins and Porras suggest that success happens by chance. In expert intuition, it comes from skill and will, which Marriott showed in abundance.

American Express

American Express began in 1850 as a specialized transport company for money and financial documents. In the early 1880s, the U.S. government introduced postal money orders, but they were easy to forge. In 1882, Marcellus Berry of American Express figured out how to prevent forgery and began issuing the company's own money orders. They were a huge success. You could buy and cash the orders not at post offices, but at a far larger number of American Express offices, railroad stations, and even general stores across the country.

In 1891, the company president went on vacation to Europe. He carried the usual letters of credit. On his return, he stormed into Berry's office to complain about the letters. Collins and Porras quote him as saying, "The moment I got off the beaten track they were no more use than so much wet wrapping paper."

So Berry went to work again. The previous time, he had improved on the postal money order. This time, he combined the money order with an ordinary checkbook. The result was the first traveler's check. You prepaid for a book of money orders and countersigned each one like a check when you used it. The company already had a system for selling and redeeming money orders. It now adapted this system for this new but related product.

The Express Money Order became the American Express Travelers Cheque. And because there was a much longer lag between the prepayment for the travelers checks and their use, American Express found that it was holding the money longer and thus making more interest income. Collins and Porras report: "Unintentionally, AmEx had invented the 'float.' . . . A mere $750 at the beginning, the float would eventually top $4 billion by 1990, generating $200 million in revenue."

So Collins and Porras conclude:

> In what started as just another incremental, opportunistic step, the travelers check further evolved American Express toward financial services. AmEx didn't plan to become a financial services company. Nonetheless, it became one.

Once again, Collins and Porras praise the company for deviating from its "plan," but reduce what happened to "just another incremental, opportunistic step." We imagine that Marcellus Berry might have seen it differently. He knew that his invention was a huge step. Right from the first, he saw within the 1-foot model the giant Buddha to come.

In these three examples—Johnson & Johnson, Marriott, and American Express—*Built to Last* offers solid evidence that companies beyond their start-up phase can continue to discover and carry out a successful strategy based on past achievements through expert intuition. Kilmer, Marriott, and Berry are the principal heroes of these tales, yet in each case the company as a whole deserves great credit too, for adopting rather than opposing the new strategy.

And that is what *Built to Last* is really about. Most of the other chapters describe how a company stays open to unexpected success and adjusts accordingly to take advantage of that success, not just once but again and again over the decades. So we find that the book carries Bhidé's insights concerning small entrepreneurs up to major corporations.

Yet in some respects, Collins and Porras explain things in terms that are very different from expert intuition. Their examples fit, but some of their concepts don't. We note especially their concepts of experimentation, trial and error, opportunism, and accident. These come not from expert intuition but from a very different source: natural evolution.

Collins and Porras offer this quote from Charles Darwin's classic work *Origin of Species*:

> To my imagination it is far more satisfactory to look at [well-adapted species] not as specially endowed or created instincts, but as small consequences of one general law leading to the advancement of all organic beings—namely, multiply, vary, let the strongest live and the weakest die.

This is what Collins and Porras mean by "Try a Lot of Stuff and Keep What Works." From the point of view of the art of what works, this is half right. Yes, you "try a lot of stuff," but not as a mass of random experiments. Few scientists experiment randomly. They try something that they think will work because their expert intuition tells them so. If it doesn't work, they study the result until their expert intuition tells them to try something else. Kilmer, Marriott, and Berry did not conduct experiments—

they tried something that they thought would work in a particular situation.

And, yes, you "keep what works," but that is only the start of what you do next. Your coup d'oeil shows you a course of action, and your resolution commits you to follow it. Johnson & Johnson, Marriott Corporation, and American Express did not just "keep" the new achievements—they forcefully turned them into major businesses.

By way of summary, Collins and Porras rephrase Darwin's quote "so it might read like this":

> It might be far more satisfactory to look at well-adapted visionary companies not primarily as the result of brilliant foresight and strategic planning, but largely as consequences of a basic process—namely, try a lot of experiments, seize opportunities, keep those that work well (consistent with the core ideology), and fix or discard those that don't.

Again, from the point of view of the art of what works, this is half right. It's true that "strategic planning" does not explain success, but "brilliant foresight" does—in the form of coup d'oeil, which is foresight based firmly on hindsight. And "try a lot of experiments" is not the same as "seize opportunities." Again, our three heroes—Kilmer, Marriott, and Berry—did not experiment, but they did seize opportunities.

As for "keep those that work well," the art of what works has two things to say. One we have already noted: that keeping an achievement is the least of it—you have to get behind the achievement in a big way to make it a major success. But the second point is how Collins and Porras believe companies decide what to keep: They keep things that are "consistent with the core ideology."

This is their main distinction between the natural world and business. They see that "species in the natural world do not consciously choose what variations to select; the environment selects." But companies are made up of humans. We make conscious selections. In the natural world, evolution "has no goal or ideology other than sheer survival of the species." Not so in the human world. Visionary companies stimulate evolutionary progress toward desired ends in a process that Collins and Porras call *purposeful evolution.*

Here we veer back toward Jomini, where your "purpose" or "desired ends"—your goal—precede your course of action. In expert intuition, you see a course of action first. That decides your goal. Your core ideology changes, too.

The lack of a prior goal is fundamental to expert intuition, as well as to Darwin's theory of evolution. If you toss that out, the theory fails. This is also a main point of Kuhn's last chapter, "Progress through Revolutions," in *The Structure of Scientific Revolutions.*

In the art of what works, you select achievements not on the basis of their conformity to a core ideology or prior purpose but on the basis of their potential for further success. Marriott, for example, had a huge coup d'oeil—overnight he "saw" a whole new business, not just an incremental, experimental, opportunistic step. And did he even have a "core ideology" at that point? More likely, he judged that airline catering was close enough to the restaurant business that he and his company knew enough to succeed at it. That gave him a new core ideology—food or travel services, instead of just restaurants. This new ideology came after the coup d'oeil, not before.

But even if *Built to Last* goes astray in its evolutionary model, its intentions are worthy: to counter the rigidity of strategic planning in large companies with a flexible evolutionary strategy. We will return to the distinction between evolutionary strategy and the art of what works in a later chapter on strategic planning. For now, we conclude that the best way to "build to last" is not to experiment and select, but to look for and build on what works.[7]

Creative Structure

So far, our examples of expert intuition in established firms have involved developing new products or services. But remember Schumpeter's comment on the creative response in large companies. He noted that there are "different colors to entrepreneurship," including "setting up" or "organizing." So the art of what works in large companies can also take the form of creative structure. Let's look at some examples.

Our primary source for creative structure is a classic work of business history, Alfred Chandler's *Strategy and Structure*. Chandler wrote in the early 1960s, when American companies were mushrooming in size. He looked back to the era before World War II, when just a few firms had achieved such scale. Chandler studied how they did it, as a lesson for modern companies that were going through the same thing. As you grow, "complex administrative problems" make you adjust your structure. Chandler looked for lessons in the earlier period, asking what structures had been used to administer great enterprises of the day.

Here we consider the choice of structure as an act of strategy. You have to decide on a course of action, even if that action concerns your structure. In contrast, Chandler and many other writers restrict the term *strategy* to your choice of product, service, or market. Then structure follows. One of the great lessons of Chandler's book is that "strategy follows structure." That's fine. But the art of what works embraces both the original strategy and the choice of organizational form. Our definition of strategy is wider than Chandler's: It's how you decide on any course of action and changes along the way. So how you decide on a structure can also be a strategy.

Chandler himself says that executives "faced with complex problems" can use a structure to solve them. For those problems, their course of action was to choose a particular structure. So in Chandler's cases, the structure was a means to an end, a solution to a problem—in other words, a strategy.

Chandler selected four "great enterprises" that had all adopted the same structure early and well: a single general office with several decentralized operating divisions. When faced with the complexity brought about by scale, they all found a similar solution. The four firms were DuPont, General Motors, Standard Oil (New Jersey), and Sears. At the time Chandler studied them, these four firms were thriving. So, like Bhidé and *Built to Last*, Chandler studied success.

Let's look at each company in turn, to see if expert intuition played a role in its achievements.

DuPont

DuPont began in 1804 as a maker of gunpowder. It quickly dominated the American market and branched out to other explosives. World War I helped the company grow even more. But during the war, DuPont branched out further, to other products that used some of the same ingredients as explosives. It went from one product line to many, almost overnight.

The result was an administrative nightmare. Profits started to suffer. Chandler cites a report that noted, "The more paint and varnish we sold, the more money we lost."

Right after the war, in 1919, DuPont's Executive Committee appointed a subcommittee to study the problem and propose solutions. The subcommittee's members came from the company's four "grand divisions"—Production, Sales, Treasurer, and Development—plus the old Explosives Manufacturing Department. This subcommittee then appointed a sub-subcommittee to do the actual work.

First the sub-subcommittee wrote a detailed report on the problem. Then, Chandler tells us, "They made a detailed study of outside experience." So like Isaac Newton, they stood on the shoulders of giants.

The company knew little about marketing; it was used to selling explosives by the ton. Now many of its products came in packages. So the sub-subcommittee interviewed an expert, a "Mr. Boyd" of Curtis Publishing in Massachusetts. Boyd came to DuPont headquarters in Delaware to explain how advertising and merchandising worked.

Now that it knew a little more about the subject, the sub-subcommittee looked more widely. It made a list of companies "with market activities comparable with their own" and interviewed executives from eight of them: Armour, International Harvester, Johns-Manville, Scoville, Alcoa, Procter & Gamble, Colgate, and the U.S. Tire Company.

From these interviews, the sub-subcommittee arrived at a major insight: Each company had "a single controlling head over their manufacturing and sales departments."

Coup d'oeil.

The sub-subcommittee knew that "none of these companies had so diversified a product line" as DuPont. That was the point: It wanted to see how a company with a narrower product line worked. DuPont's single sales department could not handle so many different product lines.

After 6 months of study, the sub-subcommittee recommended dividing the company in two, with each half being responsible for both manufacturing and sales for its own product lines, like the companies they had studied. A single general office would provide nonproduct services, like development and finance, to both.

The Executive Committee rejected the proposal.

But more committees followed. Finally, as of 1927, DuPont "was beginning to move toward a de facto structure based on product divisions rather than functional departments."

In the DuPont case, Chandler gives us a striking example of coup d'oeil by committee. The new strategy came from the past achievements of other firms. It took years of resolution, but in the end it won the day.

General Motors

General Motors shows us two stages of creative structure. First, GM's founder, William Durant, created the general office. Then his successor, Alfred Sloan, made it work.

Durant started out in 1886, making horse-drawn carriages. He developed an assembly line and specialized manufacturing plants to feed it. That made him the country's largest carriage maker. In the early 1900s, he switched to cars, entering the car business by buying out the failing Buick company in 1904.

At the time, Olds was the country's leading carmaker. It produced the first low-cost automobile, the Runabout, using the same assembly-line methods that Durant used. In 1908 (the same year that Henry Ford produced his first Model T), Durant bought out Olds. That made him the country's largest carmaker. He called the new company General Motors.

Chandler describes how Durant succeeded at GM, noting that the policies he used to build the company were the same ones that he already had tested and proved at Buick and in the carriage business.

So Durant was an artist of what works. He carried forward his past achievements in a new combination to fit the new situation.

Durant gave GM a small general office and let the operating divisions run their own show. It was the opposite of the old DuPont structure, where the central office was far too large. So where DuPont set out to reduce its central office and give the divisions more power, Durant faced the opposite problem: He had to give the central office more power over the separate divisions. The two companies would end up in the same position, but they came to it from opposite directions.

But Durant refused. He kept his central office so small that it was unable to keep up with the growth of the company. Despite booming sales, debt and cash flow problems mounted. Finally the GM board stepped in. It looked for alternatives, and it found one in 1920, when Alfred Sloan proposed a new structure. The company accepted it, and in 1923 Sloan replaced Durant.

Sloan had started out at Hyatt Roller Bearing, where he became president in 1899. Hyatt served a few large automobile manufacturers. When Durant bought Hyatt in 1916, he made Sloan head of GM's United Motors, which made parts and accessories for the other GM divisions. United was a bigger version of Hyatt, except that it also made parts other than bearings, and it made parts only for GM cars. In addition, it was made up of several different companies. While the heads of other GM divisions just ran their own factories, Sloan had to coordinate production from many sources and delivery to all the divisions.

Chandler tells us that Sloan solved the problem by building a general office to coordinate and expand the activities of the different operating companies. Thus, he developed a general office just for United Motors. When the crisis came in 1920, Sloan saw a chance to expand the same structure to all of GM.

Sloan's 1920 plan for GM followed two basic principles:[8]

1. The responsibility attached to the chief executive of each operation shall in no way be limited. Each such organization headed by its chief executive shall be complete in every necessary function and able to exercise its full initiative and logical development.
2. Certain central organization functions are absolutely essential to the logical development and proper control of the Corporation's activities.

The first principle continued Durant's previous achievements in acquiring different car manufacturers and running them along the same lines as Buick. The second principle followed Sloan's own achievements in setting up a general office for United Motors. Sometime in 1920, Sloan had a coup d'œil about how to combine these two prior achievements for GM as a whole.

And there may have been a direct precedent for the combination: DuPont's proposed reorganization plan.

Pierre DuPont was chairman of the GM board. He took over as president from Durant during the 1920 crisis. He orchestrated a bailout with funding from the DuPont company and J. P. Morgan. Meanwhile, over at DuPont, the sub-subcommittee's reorganization plan was presented in May 1920 and came up again in November of that year. Pierre's brother Irénée rejected it both times. Back at GM, Pierre accepted the Sloan plan "within less than a month" of an emergency GM meeting, also in November 1920.

Sloan cited no sources for his plan. Chandler thinks that there was no link between the DuPont and GM plans, even though both plans "called for autonomous operating divisions and a general office consisting of general executives and staff specialists." According to Chandler, Pierre and Irénée DuPont did not consider the two plans "in any way comparable" because GM's problem was too little centralization, whereas DuPont's was too much.

But elsewhere, Chandler presents the two plans as very comparable indeed. He gives us four different companies—DuPont, GM, Standard Oil, and Sears—that ended up with a similar general office structure. So why would the DuPonts and presumably Sloan think that such similar plans were not "in any way comparable"?

Perhaps the reason was the lawsuit.

DuPont's bailout of GM led to the "General Motors-du Pont Antitrust Suit." For Sloan to admit that he had studied the DuPont plan before the bailout would only have added fuel to the fire. If there had been no legal fears, perhaps Sloan would have come right out and cited DuPont's plan as a precedent for his own.

Standard Oil

John D. Rockefeller founded Standard Oil in 1870. It grew rapidly, capturing so much of the U.S. market that the government broke it up into several separate companies in 1911. Standard Oil (New Jersey) was the largest and most diverse of those companies.

To handle its complex operations, "Jersey" made decisions by committee. Representatives of the different operating companies within the larger firm sat on every committee. There was a committee for every activity that cut across the various operating companies: "for transportation, pipelines, production, manufacturing, export trade, domestic trade, and for the purchase of supplies." Over time, the committees made more and more decisions involving greater and greater detail, such as "the amount of crude oil to run per day in a specific refinery or the amount of kerosene a branch office or sales subsidiary should sell."

Walter Teagle inherited this structure when he became president of Jersey in 1917. As long as business was good, the structure seemed to work. Then a slump in demand in the mid-1920s showed its weakness: Despite all the committees, there was very little coordination. On a trip out west in 1925, Teagle found the oil wells still pumping far beyond storage capacity or demand.

The solution?

Another committee.

But this one, the Coordination Committee, was different. Teagle gave it a staff: the Coordination Department. The model was the Export Trade Department, which since 1912 had effectively replaced the committee covering this area. The new Coordination Department really started to coordinate, and it slowly put the other committees out of business.

Chandler notes that Teagle did not make a study of the problem or present the new committee and department as a solution to the overall structural problem. The committee and department were an immediate response to the problem of overproduction that he had seen out west. In these terms, it looks like a coup d'oeil.

The new department, headed by Orville Harden, succeeded beyond its original purpose. It did not just solve the problem out west, it quickly became the most effective link among all the company's different units, for everything. As Chandler tells us, "It was soon furnishing the data so necessary for planning for the company as a whole."

Teagle singled out the achievement of the Coordination Department and contrasted it with the old committee structure: "I have a horror of too large committees as they never accomplish much but spend endless time in talking." He formed other new departments—for shipping, production, and development—at headquarters and kept them free of committee interference. Last but not least, Teagle noted that in the company's own affiliates, and among its competition, nobody ran things by committee.

So in 1927, 2 years after the departments took over from the committees, Teagle changed the company's structure. Over 6 months, he replaced the committees with departments at headquarters "headed by a single executive." The Coordination Department became in effect the general office.

Chandler cites the precedents for this change: the success of those few departments that were headed by individuals, including the Export Trade Department and the Coordination Department; the success of the central Coordination Department itself, which meant there was less need for other coordinating committees; and the experience of other oil companies, including Jersey's own affiliates.

In 1927, Teagle and his staff brought these past achievements to bear in a single reorganization plan. We don't know whether his original coup d'oeil of 1925 took in the whole company. The coup d'oeil of 1927 certainly did so.

Sears

Sears began in 1886 as a seller of watches through the mail. It quickly branched out into other items. Its famous catalogue came to dominate the mail-order business in the early twentieth century.

In 1925, Sears moved into retail too, with 8 stores. In 1926, the company added another store. In 1927, it opened 16 more. Then in 1928, it added 167 new stores, and in 1929, it added 155.

What happened in 1928 to turn Sears so strongly toward retail?

That was the year that Robert Wood became president. Wood had graduated from West Point in 1900 and spent 10 years working on the Panama Canal as an army quartermaster. Chandler tells us that from that position, Wood became "the good right arm" of the canal's builder, George W. Goethals. Then Wood served in World War I, where again he succeeded as a quartermaster. Despite his youth, he rose quickly through the ranks to become the "director of purchasing and storing all army supplies except ordnance and aircraft." On his way up, he mastered all aspects of "supply, purchasing and transportation."

It was the perfect training for heading a department store chain. So after the war, Wood joined Montgomery Ward, a competitor to Sears in the mail-order business. Right away, Wood tried to push Ward into retail. He noted that small towns were growing fast, more and more farmers owned cars, and everyone had more money to spend. It was time to build retail stores in small towns. As Chandler tells us, Wood pointed out to Theodore Merseles, Ward's president, in October 1921 that chain stores like J. C. Penney were already beginning to exploit this small-town market.

Wood had operated a huge network of stores for the army, and he saw how to do the same thing for Montgomery Ward:

> With its existing branch houses as distributing points, its highly developed purchasing organization, and its long-established reputation, Montgomery Ward could easily compete with, Wood insisted, the chain stores in any market.

But Merseles had already tried retail. Earlier that year, Montgomery Ward had set up outlet stores in its mail-order plants and opened two outlets away from the plants. The stores failed. This was not at all what Wood had in mind: He envisioned a vast network of stores, like the one he ran in the army. But Merseles's mind was made up. He "paid little attention to Wood's proposals."

Wood moved to Sears in 1924. There he ran the "retail office," even though Sears had no retail stores. But Wood had plans for plenty of them. Chandler reports that again he ran into "strong opposition from the older mail-order executives, who were more interested in expanding their established business." Still, Wood managed to open a few stores in the 1925–1927 period. And when he became president in 1928, he took Sears squarely into the retail business.

We can see that Wood had a big coup d'oeil at Montgomery Ward. His resolution took him to Sears, where he finally was able to follow through on it.

Now came the push for a decentralized structure. Despite good profits, the old centralized structure was holding Sears back. Retail stores plus mail order, across the whole country, made for a complex puzzle indeed. The problems mounted until "Wood decided, in May 1929, to defer further expansion."

Wood called in a consultant, George Frazer, and appointed five executives to a committee, including Alvin Dodd as the retail expert. What did that committee do? Like the DuPont sub-subcommittee, the Sears group looked for what worked in other firms. They stood on the shoulders of giants.

Their principal object of study was "the structure of J. C. Penney and other chains." This marked the final triumph of retail over mail order: Sears was imitating retail chains. The result was a "district organization" of regional offices and a general office at headquarters.

Sometimes old structures die hard. The new structure took 20 years to implement. Yet in the end, district offices became the heart of the decentralized structure that the general office oversaw.

So, like GM, Sears found its structure through two coups d'oeil. At Montgomery Ward, Wood saw how to reorganize a mail order company into a retail chain. Then, Frazer, Dodd, and the others saw how to imitate the success of J. C. Penney and other retail chains through a district organization.

This ends our review of Chandler's four cases. He surely succeeded in his worthy cause: to show U.S. executives how in a variety of situations a central office can solve the problem of diversification and scale. Chandler found this a question of national urgency:

> The coming of this new strategy and with it the new structure is of paramount importance to the present health and future growth of the American economy.

Chandler's book is a classic demonstration of the art of what works. Thanks to his study, "the builders of the new organizational structures could look to the model created by du Pont, General Motors, Jersey Standard, and Sears." These are the giants—stand on their shoulders. That's what Chandler's book is about.

So expert intuition finds support not only in Chandler's cases, but also in his overall aim. As you look to the model of the central office, do what Chandler's examples themselves did. They studied the experience of their industries, both their own and of other companies, to see what worked. Then they built on that past achievement in their own course of action.

The Art of Japanese Business

Two decades later, the structure that Chandler studied fell on hard times.

By the early 1980s, companies from Europe and Japan had overtaken U.S. companies in many major products and markets. The leading example was the automobile industry. The United States built big, expensive cars that guzzled gas and fell apart, while Japan built small, cheap, durable cars with good gas mileage. Many critics blamed the centralized general office, which took its eye off the market and fell in love with its own plans.

As a result, many businesses looked to Japan for guidance. One of the key studies that executives turned to was *The Mind of the Strategist*, by Kenichi Ohmae. It explains how Japan after World War II had succeeded in achieving the highest growth rates in the history of the world.

Ohmae sees the source of "successful business strategies" in Japan as "a particular state of mind" rather than "rigorous analysis." He writes:[9]

> In what I call the mind of the strategist, insight and a consequent drive to achievement, often amounting to a sense of mission, fuel a thought process which is basically creative and intuitive rather than rational.

Ohmae's "insight" and "consequent drive to achievement" match the coup d'oeil and resolution of von Clausewitz. And Ohmae's "state of mind" seems like von Clausewitz's "presence of mind." In addition, Ohmae sees strategy in business as similar to strategy in other fields:

> Great strategies, like great works of art or great scientific discoveries, call for technical mastery in the working out but originate in insights that are beyond the reach of conscious analysis.

So far, Ohmae seems to endorse presence of mind, coup d'oeil, and resolution. What about examples from history? Sure enough, he puts "new combinations" at the center of strategic thinking:

> Coming up with new combinations is very simple. One simply scans through existing combinations of things and tries putting them together mentally in different ways.

Ohmae also cites Schumpeter: "An Austrian economist once said that anything new in this world is a combination of known elements." And we see the role of analysis in resolution, after coup d'oeil: "Once the strategist has hit on the idea for a new combination, it is time for the analyst to step in and test it out for market potential and current feasibility." And note how Ohmae calls new combinations "simple," the way Steven Jobs called them "obvious."

Ohmae was not the only one to see expert intuition as the key to Japan's business success. Ryuei Shimizu, author of *The Growth of Firms in Japan,* saw it too. Shimizu conducted the largest and deepest study of Japanese business ever done, covering the years 1966 to 1977. Sixteen separate research projects made up the study, with Shimizu as leader of all the projects. They surveyed 5207 firms, interviewed the presidents of 64 firms, and interviewed all 1200 employees of one firm about morale.

Shimizu touches on strategy in a chapter called "Top Management." The leading ability for decision making is "intuitive sensitivity" or the "sixth sense"— *kan* in Japanese:[10]

> The president's sixth sense does not rest on inference through logic or the accumulation of facts. Kan forms the very basis for the recognition of problems and is the first step in decision-making.

Intuition can be "sharpened by study," comes from "a diversified store of information accumulated in their memories," and comes with a "strong sense of curiosity," which is "not an innate trait but has been learned through the cumulative reinforcement of repeated experiences."

This sounds very much like expert intuition. Shimizu says that it even extends to the "recognition of problems." That is, you do not identify a problem through analysis and then try to solve it. First you see a problem you can solve.

Shimizu notes that strategic decision making in a changing environment requires risk: "The ability to take risks requires spiritual courage, boldness or decisiveness."

This sounds like resolution.

Shimizu also notes a particular feature of "the Japanese way of thinking that contributed to post-war growth": The Japanese "make judgments *on a case by case basis* and have the ability not to worry about the *no functional relationship* among individual things."

This sounds like pragmatism.

Shimizu makes special note of a result from his study for 1974:

Firms placing weight on the president's sixth sense rather than on objective information in strategic decision-making always showed better achievements. Many founder-presidents are found in small firms and have supposedly developed a highly attuned intuitive sense through experience.

So here we have empirical evidence that the "sixth sense" yields better business results.

Ohmae and Shimizu provide plenty of clues about expert intuition as a key to Japanese business success. American companies mostly missed these clues, but they did get the point about planning. Maybe they did not turn to von Clausewitz, but they did give up on Jomini.

Here is Ohmae on planning:

Detailed long-range planning coupled with tight control from the center is a remarkably effective way of killing creativity and entrepreneurship at the extremities of the organization, the individuals who make it up.

Japanese firms rely instead on "individual or group contributions and initiatives for improvement, innovation, and creative energy":

The whole organization looks organic and entrepreneurial, as opposed to mechanistic and bureaucratic. . . . Actually, in my opinion, many Western corporations already suffer from too much strategic planning.

This is the heart of the message that U.S. executives took from Japan. They set out to slash bureaucracy and promote innovation. But Ohmae also makes a related point that received less attention: how Japanese executives rise. Even graduates from the best schools begin on the shop floor. They learn the business from the ground up:

This emphasis on actual experience underlies the pragmatism and provides the basis for the seemingly long-term orientation of

Japanese executives, in contrast to the short-term analytical mentality of the West.

Deep experience feeds expert intuition, or pragmatism, and allows for a "long-term orientation," if not detailed long-range plans. And it helps keep coup d'oeil tied to resolution. If you separate muscle from brain, you can't follow through on your strategy.

All in all, Ohmae and many other writers helped U.S. corporations reduce bureaucracy and promote individual creativity throughout the 1980s and 1990s. We might see this as one great coup d'oeil, with American industry seeing Japan's achievement and trying to do the same. Ironically, it seems that in the recent decades, Japan moved in the opposite direction—creeping bureaucracy helped to bring about a recession that continues to this day.[11]

The GE Way

Among the many American successes in emulating the Japanese, General Electric stands out. It grew to become the world's most valuable corporation through the 1990s, with steady profits and an increasing stock price. Profits rose from $1.5 billion in 1980 to $12.7 billion in 2000, while the share price rose 21 percent per year over that same period, a rate that was 50 percent higher than that of the S&P 500. Jack Welch, the CEO from 1981 to 2001, became the world's most famous businessman. GE's success even contradicted the common wisdom that conglomerates make for the worst bureaucracies of all.

Sure enough, expert intuition played a key role in GE's success.

We have available to us published accounts of Welch's years at GE from Noel Tichy and Robert Slater. Tichy ran GE's in-house business school, the Crotonville Institute, in the mid-1980s. Slater is a business journalist who wrote a series of books on GE during the 1990s, with Welch's full cooperation. Tichy's and Slater's accounts together give us a full picture of the nearly two decades of Welch's tenure as head of GE.

Tichy notes that in the late 1970s and early 1980s, "Japanese companies were boosting productivity by 8% annually," while

GE's productivity growth "rarely topped 1.5%." From auto-mobiles to laptop computers, consumers favored Japan's "exciting new products." But before Welch, GE seemed unable to change. As Tichy tells us, "Promoting innovation at GE felt like getting a root canal." There were controls for everything, from "detailed monthly budget approvals" to a mammoth strategic plan every year that ate up "six to eight months of preparatory research and analysis."

Good ideas did come up, but someone who had a good idea had to "entomb" it in a lengthy report and submit it to formal review by GE's strategic planners, who "vetted budgets and most operating decisions." These "inquisitions" killed off most ideas. For those that made it through the gauntlet, it was usually too late: "its moment of opportunity often had passed."

So before Welch, GE was a company of Jomini planners. They fixed their objective points and set the troops marching. It seemed to matter little to them that their army was losing the war.

Then along came Welch. He wanted to make the new GE "systematically foster the creation of new ideas," the way the old GE had "promoted the manufacture of products." And so "the bureaucracy had to go."

To make this change, Welch built on past achievement. First, he imitated Japan. Second, he drew from two successful GE companies that he had worked for on his way up.

GE Plastics and GE Financial Services had grown fast and had stayed free of the bureaucracy that crippled other GE businesses. Plastics was "a red-hot start-up venture" that already had "over $1 billion in sales." In Financial Services, you could invest $10 million on Monday and by Friday, if you thought the investment looked bad, "you close the window and go home." As Welch explained, "Everybody should work in a fast-growing business like Plastics or Financial Services. . . . A lot of managers don't know what a good business looks like."

So Welch's expert intuition carried over to GE as a whole his earlier experience of what a good business looks like. But what did this mean as an overall strategy, beyond slashing bureaucracy?

At the end of his first year as CEO, Welch gave his first speech to a Wall Street audience:[12]

> If I could, this would be the appropriate moment for me to with-draw from my pocket a sealed envelope containing the grand strategy for the General Electric Company over the next decade. But I can't . . . tie a bow around the many diverse initiatives of General Electric. . . . What will enhance the many decentralized plans and initiatives of this company isn't a central *strategy*, but a central *idea*—a simple core concept that will guide General Electric in the eighties and govern our diverse plans and strategies.

That central idea was "planful opportunism." Instead of a "GE-style strategic plan," you set "only a few clear, overarching goals." That leaves people "free to seize any opportunities they saw to further those goals." Tichy tells us that Welch cited a military source for the idea:

> Welch operated that way instinctively, but the notion crystallized in his mind in the late 1970s, after he read Johannes von Moltke, a nineteenth-century Prussian general influenced by the renowned military theorist Karl von Clausewitz.

Von Moltke was a student of von Clausewitz at the Prussian War School. It was von Moltke who led the Prussian army to victory over the French in 1870–1871.[13] Thanks to von Clausewitz, von Moltke fought like Napoleon, and that was the secret of his success. So Welch's core concept of "planful opportunism" leads straight to the art of what works.

Slater picks up the story from Tichy in the 1990s. He reports that "Welch pushed for an open and informal GE" in his first years as CEO. Then, in the mid-1990s, he switched to "the need for GE employees to learn from one another—and from outsiders."

Planful opportunism gave way to an even simpler idea: "plagiarize." The overarching goals that Welch ended up setting were hardly goals at all. He wanted each GE company to either be first or second in its sector or get out of that sector. Because GE could raise money easily or acquire other companies, it was easy enough to attain scale in a sector. But profits were something else. That's where imitation came in: You found what made money for others and did the same thing yourself.

Welch saw finding and spreading what works as the chief job of a CEO. Slater notes how Welch described one of his primary goals:[14]

> My job is to find great ideas, exaggerate them, and spread them like hell around the business with the speed of light. . . . And to put resources in to support them. Keep finding ideas. That's the job of just about all of our CEOs.

Welch's view of a top executive overturns conventional wisdom, and even the popular notion of Welch himself: A leader is a tough guy who knows all the answers and makes people do what he wants. Instead, Welch's notion of imitation calls for great humility. He doesn't have the answer—someone else does. Go find it.

Or, as Welch puts it,

> The operative assumption today is that someone, somewhere, has a better idea; and the operative compulsion is to find out who has that better idea, learn it, and put it into action—fast.

So where do you look? Everywhere. Welch argues that an idea can come from any source:

> So we will search the globe for ideas. We will share what we know with others to get what they know. . . . Be open to all ideas . . . no matter where they come from.

These quotes give only a fraction of Welch's words on the subject. Welch exhorted his troops to "plagiarize" again and again through the years.

Welch's first method for finding and spreading good ideas was Work-Out, modeled directly on Japan's *kaizen*. In the late 1980s, an ongoing series of meetings around GE encouraged employees to raise problems with their bosses and offer solutions. Some of these meetings took place at Crotonville, with Welch attending as one of the bosses. Work-Out continues to this day.[15]

The second method was Best Practices. In 1988 Welch assigned a team of 10 "to develop a list of companies worth emulating, and then to study their achievements." The team picked nine companies, including Ford, Hewlett-Packard, and two big Japanese multinationals, and spent a year studying the companies on-site. Tichy reports that although GE's team absorbed a lot of minutiae, it kept an Olympian perspective as it sought an answer to the question of what the secret of success was.

This is a pure case of the art of what works. Study success, to see what elements you can use yourself.

The team's report summarized the secrets of success that it found, and provided detailed cases, too. Tichy reports: "No less valuable to GE than these overarching ideas were the mind-blowing stories of these companies' achievements." After hearing the team's presentation, Welch became an instant convert. From this began Crotonville's Best Practices course for spreading what works throughout the company.

Thanks to Best Practices, Work-Out, and other Crotonville methods, GE shifted from spreading ideas to spreading successful ideas. For GE, a good idea or a best practice is something that shows evidence of prior success.[16] Under Jack Welch, GE stood on the shoulders of giants, both inside and outside the company, again and again and again. And above all, Welch himself identified this method as the secret of his own success.

The Erratic Goddess

In their studies of GE, Tichy and Slater both use the word *revolution*. That's what Welch brought to GE.

Such were the times. In the 1980s, U.S. businesses needed to make drastic changes in order to get back on track. Company after company declared its revolution. But while GE built on past achievements, many other revolutionaries took a different path. They followed their imagination—the "erratic goddess" that von Clausewitz wanted to ban from the battlefield.

The leading example of imagination driving strategy was the dot.com boom. At the time, many commentators urged other companies to follow the lead of the e-commerce revolutionaries.

For example, in *Leading the Revolution*, Gary Hamel tells that "the real story of Silicon Valley is not 'e' but 'i,' not electronic commerce but innovation and imagination." Hamel is a leading expert on business strategy who helps shape the way businesses see the future. In his praise of e-commerce, he also reflected a popular view of the time:[17]

> What distinguishes many of the dot-com companies is not their technical prowess . . . but their imagination. They are young, hungry, and totally devoid of tradition. It is the power of "i," rather than "e," that separates the winners from the losers in the twenty-first-century economy.

Here again we have the notion that creativity means something new. Sure enough, Hamel praises the dot.coms as "totally devoid of tradition." But if we take the other view of creativity, that it involves new combinations of things that worked in the past, then a lack of tradition is a very bad thing.

For it is in tradition that we find prior achievements to build on. Tradition might contain bad things, too, those you don't carry forward. But you can't succeed at strategy without knowing what worked in the past.

Hamel, on the other hand, turns strategy into a mental exercise that is entirely free of the past. He offers this challenge:

> Pick a company you care about—one you think deserves to be more successful than it is—and try to imagine a breakout business concept.

Remember that von Clausewitz said that good theory has many constraints, based on its actual examples from experience. But for Hamel, a business concept has no constraints:

> The great advantage of a business concept is that it is infinitely malleable. It is, at the outset, only an intellectual construct. So pretend you're a kid again—with a very big Lego set, one that allows you to remake the very foundations of commerce. This isn't some meaningless exercise. This is mental training for industry revolutionaries.

For a time, the imagination of the dot.com revolutionaries did seem to "remake the very foundations of commerce." But in the end, the foundations of commerce won out. The majority of e-commerce companies imagined themselves into oblivion, and dragged down much of the stock market with them.

The dot.com revolution, and Hamel's enthusiasm for it, is an extreme example of imagination as a business strategy. But imagination remains a topic of serious business study. The literature on imagination continues to grow: We cite especially *Creativity in Context*, by Teresa Amabile, and a group of *Harvard Business Review* articles published as *Breakthrough Thinking*.[18]

But as von Clausewitz, Klein, and many others tell us, expert intuition and imagination are two very different things. Let's take a look at one of Hamel's examples to see precisely how.

Hamel tells the story of Motorola versus Nokia. Motorola led the world in cellular telephones until 1997, but it "missed the shift to digital wireless technology by just a year or two." That brief window gave Nokia its chance to forge ahead. In the 1980s, Nokia was known for its snow tires and rubber boots. Suddenly, it was one of the fastest-growing high-tech companies in Europe, leaving Motorola in its wake. Motorola was slow to catch on to the move to digital phones, and it has paid a heavy price for its ambling ways.

Nokia shot past Motorola suddenly, in just that 2-year window. How did Nokia do it? Apparently it had more imagination.

But let's take a closer look.

First, Nokia had the advantage of location. The far north of Finland, where it was based, may seem remote, but that turned out to be a boon. In 1987, 13 European countries joined together in the Global System for Mobile Communication (GSM) to develop a common digital standard for wireless telephones. Finland was one of the 13. Thus, Nokia was in and Motorola, an American company, was out.

Thanks to GSM, Europe's mobile system outpaced America's. A Nokia phone placed the first GSM call in 1991. As of 1993, there were a million customers in the GSM network. That was the year in which Motorola produced its first digital phone. So the competition, Nokia versus Motorola, really began in 1993.

How does Nokia explain its success from 1993 on? We find out in a *New Yorker* profile of Nokia's phone designer, Frank Nuovo, by Michael Specter. Here we learn that the leader in cell phones has always had more than a third of the market. In 1993, that was Motorola. In 2001, it was Nokia. Specter tells us, "In fact, Nokia's sales are greater than those of its three closest rivals combined: Motorola, Ericsson, and Siemens."

What happened?

The head of production, Eric Anderson, tells this story:[19]

Originally, we had one phone — the phone Frank designed. And we tried to make it that one perfect phone. By 1993 . . . I realized that making one perfect phone wasn't going to work for us. We needed to make many perfect phones, and they needed to be different.

Here we have a creative insight on Anderson's part: Nokia needed a whole line of phones, not just one. But where did that insight come from? Was it just his imagination?

Here is how Anderson explains it:

There is a bar in Salo. Rikala, it's called. It's a seedy place, and Nokia engineers went there on Friday nights. They would get there and take their big phones off their belts, slap them down on the bar, and they would drink beer and eat peanuts until 4 A.M. Then one of the engineers would say, "Oh my God, which is my phone?" How would they know? They all had the same damn phone in the same color with the same ring.

There in the bar, the Nokia engineers first had the experience that other cell phone users around the world would later have: all cell phones looked alike. The scene at the Rikala bar, where a very high percentage of the customers had cell phones, looked like the future. But it wasn't an imaginary future, dreamed up in someone's head. It was the real future, right there in the Rikala bar.

Anderson explains what the engineers did next:

So they went out and painted the phones themselves with high-quality car paint. It isn't so glamorous, but that's where the route to color and fashion phones began.

So that was how Anderson got the idea for a line of phones instead of just one. The engineers painted their phones and so were able to tell them apart. They were satisfied customers for the new line of phones that they had just invented. Either the engineers or Anderson or someone else at Nokia had a coup d'oeil—that other customers might like colors, too.

Anderson draws on a theory to explain this breakthrough:

> Any growing market will segment—it's an economic law of nature. First, you have a heavy black mobile phone. Then a red and green one.

The tendency to segment is common knowledge in business, with many famous examples, such as General Motors and its various styles and colors of automobiles versus Henry Ford's single model, in black. But Anderson knew many other theories, too. He picked the theory to draw on only after the coup d'oeil. As Kuhn said, the theory comes after the achievement.

GSM grew to 30 million customers by 1996—30 times the number in 1993. With great resolution, Nokia rode that wave to become Europe's most valuable company by the end of the millennium, selling a whole line of colorful fashion phones.

Motorola never had a chance.

Creative Success

In this chapter, we studied many different examples of business success. We heard from Schumpeter and Bhidé on entrepreneurs, *Built to Last* and Chandler on big businesses, Ohmae and Shimizu on postwar Japan, Tichy and Slater on GE, and Nokia on itself. In every case, the art of what works made the difference. There are countless other examples that we could highlight as well. But science tells us to consider the negative case too. Does expert intuition ever lead to failure?

Of course.

Expert intuition is no guarantee of success. Even when you do everything right, you still may fail. Napoleon did everything right at Waterloo—but it rained that morning. He had to wait for the ground to dry to start the battle, because he needed to roll his artillery forward. That gave the Prussians time to arrive and reinforce the English. And so Napoleon lost.

But a study of success gives us examples to learn from and emulate. As von Clausewitz says, "Examples from history make everything clear, and furnish the best description of proof in the empirical sciences." And remember what Jack Welch said: "A lot of managers don't know what a good business looks like." So this chapter shows what good strategy looks like, by bringing prior achievements to bear through expert intuition.

Of course, there are many studies that explain business success without any reference to expert intuition. We turn to some of those other explanations in the next chapters. There we find that the art of what works leaves plenty of room for other theories of success. Whatever theory, model, tool, or technique you wish to apply to business strategy, you can add expert intuition to make it better. It's another form of creative combination, and a key to creative success.

PART
II

The Advantage
of
Expert Intuition

Plan-to versus Can-do
The Art of Strategic Planning

W E TURN NOW to other views of business strategy. Our aim is to understand their strengths, to see how they differ from the art of what works, and to show what they gain when we add elements of expert intuition to them. We do not have to choose between the art of what works and these other views. Instead, we combine them, to provide a stronger light to cut through the fog of strategy.

The Triumph of Planning

We start with the most popular school of strategy: strategic planning. As we saw, Jomini stands out as its first scholar, but strategic planning started long before Jomini. We can trace it back to ancient civilizations, when they reached a scale of activity that was beyond the scope of a single leader. Planning helped them manage that activity.

The first planner in history that we know by name lived in ancient Egypt around 2600 B.C. His name was Imhotep, and he was the Pharaoh's right-hand man. He lived in a time of peace after centuries of struggle between the Nile Valley and the Nile Delta. Imhotep organized the Pharaoh's army, administration, and public works. His most famous achievement was Egypt's first pyramid. It went up at Saqqara, right where the Valley meets the Delta, to mark the union of the two regions.

The Saqqara pyramid is the oldest surviving building in the world. It stands out among the 97 pyramids of Egypt for its unusual shape. Instead of being a smooth triangle like later pyramids, it's a series of stone steps. You see the same shape in organizational charts for bureaucracies to this day: the pharaoh at the top, then a few vice-pharaohs, then more sub-pharaohs, down to the workers slaving away at the bottom.[1]

Statues show Imhotep holding papyrus, so we know he wrote things down. But papyrus crumbles to dust over centuries, so none of Imhotep's writing has survived. We don't know exactly what he wrote. We do know, however, that down through the ages Egyptian scribes prayed to Imhotep before they dipped their pens in ink. And to this day, the step organization and writing things down go hand in hand. One level gives orders in writing to the level below, which reports back in writing, up and down through the pyramid.

Imhotep was a commoner. He rose through the ranks as a result of his skill, not because of his noble birth. In the centuries after him, it took a long time for step organizations to favor skill over birth. For example, Napoleon rose quickly through the ranks of the French army partly because its noble officers had fled the French Revolution.

The great sociologist Max Weber heaped great praise on step organizations that fill their ranks by merit.[2] Such an organization, he argued, offers "the highest degree of efficiency" and exceeds all other forms of organization "in precision, in stability, in the stringency of its discipline, and in its reliability." The result is "a particularly high degree of calculability of results for the heads of the organization and for those acting in relation to it." And this applies to all sectors of human endeavor, because such an organization "is formally capable of application to all kinds of administrative tasks."

No wonder the Saqqara step structure has survived so long: It works. And it works through plans. There is a "high degree of calculability of results" because you write down what results you want. Step by step, everyone knows what part to play in order to get those results. As you proceed, you write down what happens. That report informs the next cycle of planning. And this procedure continues on and on through the year and through the decades, as it has been done through the centuries from Imhotep's time to this day.

In a modern classic, *The Practice of Management*, Peter Drucker restated these principles as management by objectives, or MBO:[3]

> Each manager, from the "big boss" down to the production fore-man or the chief clerk, needs clearly spelled-out objectives. These objectives should lay out what performance the man's own man-agerial unit is supposed to produce.

MBO is the guts of strategic planning. It fills in the step pyra-mid with Jomini's "objective points" for every level. It includes not just vertical objectives, but horizontal ones as well—not just pharaoh to sub-pharaoh, but among sub-pharaohs too.

As Drucker explains:

> They should lay out what contribution he and his unit are ex-pected to make to help other units obtain their objectives. Finally, they should spell out what contribution the manager can expect from other units towards the attainment of his own objectives.

So MBO wraps you in objectives, up and down and across. But we ask: Where do these objectives come from? In expert intu-ition, they come from a coup d'oeil that shows you a path to suc-cess. Your objective—what you want—comes from what you can do. But in MBO, your objectives come from what the company wants. Objectives should always be derived from the goals of the business.

Jomini again.

In the 1980s, when many American industries broke up their planning departments to spur innovation, strategic planning did not go away. Instead, it spread more deeply through the organization, just as Drucker suggests. Now every department plans, not just headquarters. Strategic planning lost the battle but won the war.

In many companies today, every person plans. You write down your goals for the year, and your performance rating depends on how well you meet those goals. There are a variety of guides to help you put such a system in place, such as *The Strategy-Focused Organization*, by Robert Kaplan and David Norton; *The HR Scorecard: Linking People, Strategy, and Performance*, by Brian Becker, Mark Huselid, and Dave Ulrich; and *Make Success Measurable!* by Douglas Smith.[4]

So goal setting down through the pyramid has become a common business practice, but does it make for success? Our study of expert intuition suggests that it doesn't. A winning goal comes not from above, but from coup d'oeil. Yet to follow von Clausewitz rather than Jomini, you do not have to give up the pyramid itself. Napoleon kept the step structure of the French army, but he did not succeed through strategic planning. Jack Welch kept the step structure of General Electric, but he abandoned strategic planning. And so on through our examples of success.

We saw from Bhidé's entrepreneurs that having a good strategy does not always require a written plan. The reverse is possible too: You can have a written plan without a good strategy. That is, you can write down your goals and activities in great detail but have no idea of how to succeed in achieving your goals.

For these reasons, W. Edwards Deming opposed classic strategic planning. Deming was probably the most important figure in the turnaround of U.S. industry in the 1980s. He launched the American quality movement. It started on June 24, 1980, when he starred in an NBC White Paper documentary. The program was called, "If Japan Can . . . Why Can't We?"

Deming was an artist of what works. His main tool was statistical quality control. He learned it from Walter Shewhart of Bell Labs in the 1930s, used it in American industry in the 1940s, taught it to the Japanese in the 1950s, saw the Japanese add quality circles to Shewhart's methods in the 1960s, and taught the Japanese version to American industry in the 1970s. Before the 1980s, not many listened.[5]

In *Out of the Crisis*, Deming singles out MBO for special criticism. To transform the "Western style" of management, "managers must be leaders." For that,[6]

> Focus on outcomes (management by numbers, MBO, work standards, meet specifications, zero defects, appraisal of performance) must be abolished, leadership put in place.

As an expert in statistical quality control, Deming loved numbers. But he hated the way MBO used them. He believed that MBO led to an evil in which everyone in management or research received a rating every year. That rating system led to something more akin to management by numbers, or, worse, management by fear.

For Deming, numbers give you information, and you analyze that information in order to figure out what to do. That allows you to set a numerical goal. But MBO gives you the numerical goal before you figure out what to do. Without a blueprint for reaching the objective, numerical goals often have effects opposite to the desired outcome.

Deming especially hated the abuse of averages. For example, a company notices that half its factories or workers are producing at a below-average rate, so it sets a goal for these laggards of meeting the average. Deming would throw up his hands.

By definition, half of anything falls below average. That's what *average* means. Different factories and different workers face different situations, so of course their production will vary. Computing average production does not in any way set a goal for anybody. Thinking that it does is a huge mistake. Instead, you should study everyone, above or below average, to see how to improve people's particular situations.

At times, you can see Deming lose patience. He ends up fairly shouting on the page, as if pushing his finger into the chest of a manager who just won't listen:

> Do you manage by objective? If yes, how much is this mode of management costing you? Do you understand what is wrong

with this practice? What are you doing to replace it with better management?

In fact, many managers did listen to Deming. The data-intensive Six Sigma system that Motorola, General Electric, and other major companies adopted in the 1980s and 1990s came out of Deming's work.

But despite the spread of Deming's methods, old habits die hard. For example, in 2000 and 2001, Lucent Technologies gave its staff the goal of increasing sales and earnings by 20 percent. However, it gave them no means to do it. The number came out of the air—or, rather, it came from what stock analysts thought would keep Lucent even with other companies in the sector.

The staff protested, but the goal stayed. So the staff met the target the only way they could: by giving their customers discounts and credits that pushed losses into the following year. Before 2000 was over, Lucent admitted the problem. Its stock price collapsed.[7]

So writing down goals does not show you the path to success. Neither do numbers. Study the numbers. Then comes coup d'oeil. Then you plan.

Strategic Flexibility

In the 1990s, strategic planning met another avid critic. In *The Rise and Fall of Strategic Planning*, Henry Mintzberg gave planners a taste of their own medicine when he noted that[8]

> Planners have been so busy calling on everyone else to collect data and to be objective that they have seldom gotten around to doing so about their own activities.

Mintzberg asked: Does planning pay? To find the answer, he looked at three kinds of evidence: survey, anecdotal, and intensive research. His conclusion was that planning "does not pay in general," although it does help larger organizations to take advantage of their size by "the systemic programming of strategy." But the advantage comes from size, not from planning. For Mintzberg, planning is "a failed effort, a terribly costly one."

So Mintzberg thinks planning does not work. He gives many reasons why, and sums them up in a "grand fallacy":

> No amount of elaboration will ever enable formal procedures to forecast discontinuities, to inform managers who are detached from their operations, to create novel strategies. Ultimately, the term "strategic planning" has proved to be an oxymoron.

We find ourselves back where we started, with imperfect information. "Formal procedures" cannot "forecast discontinuities." That is, analysis cannot cut through the fog of business to predict the future.

As an alternative, Mintzberg quotes our old friend Herbert Simon on intuition:

> The effective manager does not have the luxury of choosing between "analytic" and "intuitive" approaches to problems. Behaving like a manager means having command of the whole range of management skills and applying them as they become appropriate.

So in *The Rise and Fall of Strategic Planning*, Mintzberg endorses intuition. In his later work, however, he drops it.

In *Strategy Safari*, Mintzberg and his coauthors, Bruce Ahlstrand and Joseph Lampel, present 10 different schools of strategy. Three of them favor analysis: the "design" school, the "planning" school, and the "positioning" school. Intuition shows up in the "cognitive" school, as "flashes of insight." But we don't know enough about how intuition works to do much good:[9]

> Hence we must conclude that the cognitive school, while potentially the most important of the ten, practically may well now be the least.

Well, at least intuition is potentially the most important. For the present, however, Mintzberg endorses the "learning" school instead:

> If the world of strategy is really as complex as implied by the cognitive school, and thus overwhelms the prescriptions of the design, planning, and positioning schools, then how are strate-

gists supposed to proceed? Our sixth school suggests an answer: they *learn* over time.

In the learning school, you don't cut through the fog of war; rather, you feel your way through it. You bump into things, change course, make mistakes, and find your way forward bit by bit.

Mintzberg traces the learning school back to a 1959 article, "The Science of Muddling Through," by Charles Lindblom.[10] And then in 1980 came *Strategies for Change,* by James Quinn. For Mintzberg, that was the "takeoff" for the learning school.

Quinn shows top executives "selectively moving people toward a broadly conceived organizational goal." Then, in a "continuing, pulsing dynamic," the goals can change too:

> Constantly integrating the simultaneous incremental processes of strategy formulation and implementation is the central art of effective strategic management.

The core idea here is flexibility. You start out with a goal. You take action. That leads to new information. You change your action, or even your goal. That leads to more information. And so on, until you either succeed or give up.

For the most part, Mintzberg and Quinn have won. These days, almost every book on strategy tells you to be flexible. Here's a recent example, from the *Financial Times Guide to Strategy,* by Richard Koch:[11]

> Strategy should not be over-planned. Ideally, it should emerge as part of an iterative process of thought, hypothesis, experimentation, success, and renewed experimentation.

Koch even brings in intuition:

> The process should combine analysis and intuition, and should be open-ended. There should never be a "final solution;" the strategy should always evolve, and continually deepen.

So now we might ask: Is flexible strategy the same as the art of what works? Let's take a closer look.

Note the sequence that Koch lays out. What comes first? Thought. Then hypothesis and experimentation. Look what comes fourth: success.

In the art of what works, success comes first. It launches strategy. You study success in similar situations, and that shows you the path to take.

Koch's sequence follows a common view of the scientific method. Doesn't it start with thought? No. As Kuhn, Bacon, and other scientists tell us, science starts with the successes of other scientists. You study what worked in the past, and a coup d'oeil shows you what path to take next.

Once again, we are back to the question of where a goal comes from in the first place. In *Strategic Leadership*, Sydney Finkelstein and Donald Hambrick ask it this way:[12]

> From where does the company's strategy come? . . . Is it an incremental variation of the company's prior strategy? Which in turn raises the question, from where did *that* strategy come?

Although Koch points to thought, his fellow scholars of the flexible school don't care very much where the strategy starts. It will only change anyway, right? You end up at the right place, no matter where you start from.

We find one reference to the contrary. In *Strategic Flexibility*, Kathryn Harrigan counsels companies to follow the lead of Mao Tse-tung, who conquered China against all odds:[13]

> Mao would not fight unless he saw an opportunity to seize an advantage. Mao's strategy was . . . fighting only when the chances of success were high, thereby avoiding battles he could not hope to win.

So Mao fought just like Napoleon, and Harrigan, like von Clausewitz, counsels companies to do the same. Take action only when you see a chance for success.

But overall, the school of strategic flexibility does not care much how strategy starts, and it does not tell you when to change your goal or activities. It tells you to be flexible, but it does not tell you how to do that. It does not offer guidance on when to keep to your current strategy versus when to change, or on what makes a good change versus a bad.

Expert intuition, in contrast, offers concrete counsel on all these fronts. It seems just as flexible, but the standard for change—for a new goal, a new path—is much, much higher. You change when you see a chance to combine what worked in the past.

To see the contrast, let's take one of Mintzberg's examples.

Honda Takes Off

In *Strategy Safari*, Mintzberg tells a story of "emergent" strategy in action: Honda motorcycles in the American market. Let's see what the art of what works might add.

Our story starts in the 1970s. The British government hired the Boston Consulting Group (known as BCG) to tell it why British motorcycle firms lost the American market to the Japanese in the early 1960s. BCG reported that the "basic philosophy" of Japanese manufacturers made all the difference. Their "high volumes per model," plus "capital intensive and highly automated techniques," yielded "high productivity."

Mintzberg notes that the BCG report "was about experience curves and high market shares and carefully thought-out deliberate strategies." But is that how it really happened?

Mintzberg cites a 1984 article by Richard Pascale, who interviewed the Honda managers themselves.[14] Pascale gives a very different view from that of BCG. The Honda managers told him that, in fact, they had no strategy other than seeing if they could sell something in the United States.

Honda started in Los Angeles with big motorcycles, because that was what Americans rode. Britain too made big bikes, which sold well in the United States. But the Japanese bikes broke down. Americans drove motorcycles much faster and for much longer distances than the Japanese back home.

But what about small bikes? You found them all over Japan, but Honda did not try to sell them in the United States. The managers told Pascale that while small motorcycles were a smash success in Japan, they didn't seem to be the right match for the U.S. market, where everything was bigger and more luxurious.

But the managers used the small bikes themselves around town. They were much cheaper and more convenient than the larger bikes or a car:

> They attracted a lot of attention. One day we had a call from a Sears buyer. While persisting in our refusal to sell through an intermediary, we took note of Sears' interest. But we still hesitated to push the 50cc bikes out of fear they might harm our image in a heavily macho market. But when the larger bikes started breaking, we had no choice. We let the 50cc bikes move.

That was the managers' great coup d'oeil. The rest is history. The small Honda bike swept America. From there, it was an easy step for Honda to sell big bikes too.

Note that the managers said they "had no choice." But of course they had a choice. There were many other paths they could have taken. They could have asked the factory back home to improve the big bikes. They could have lowered the price of the big bikes. And so on. Selling the small bikes looked like the only possibility thanks to the strength of their coup d'oeil. A coup d'oeil does that. It makes you feel that you have no other choice.

Mintzberg notes as well that British motorcycle sales in America continued to fall during the 1970s and 1980s—after the BCG report. Thus, the report did not help the British compete with the Japanese. To Mintzberg, the report tells you to "lock yourself in your office and do clever competitive analysis." But of course, "Honda never would have produced its strategy that way."

Mintzberg first made his Honda case in a 1990 article for the *Strategic Management Review*. Michael Goold, one of the authors of the BCG report, replied 2 years later in the same journal.[15] He commented on Mintzberg's advice to "try something, see if it works and learn from your experience":

> For the manager, such advice would be unhelpful, even irritating. "Of course, we should learn from experience," he will say, "but we have neither the time nor the money to experiment with endless, fruitless non-starters."

Here we have to side with Goold. Honda did not "try something" in Los Angeles and "see if it works." Mintzberg tells the British to "buy a pair of jeans, and start riding around Des Moines, Iowa" as an experiment. But the Honda managers in Los Angeles did not experiment with the small bikes. They rode them around town on errands. They were not trying to sell them to see if it worked.

Once again, we note the difference between experimentation and expert intuition. The Honda managers had the presence of mind to see that the small bikes were working, even though they were not trying to sell them. Mintzberg titles the Honda section, "Learning from Mistakes." But that's backwards. Honda learned from success, not from mistakes. It found eager customers for its small bikes. That's what gave Honda its strategy.

Like Koch, and like Collins and Porras in *Built to Last*, Mintzberg thinks that "experiment" and "trial and error" make up the scientific method. But the real scientific method is "trial and success." When something works, you go where it takes you.

The Honda people had the presence of mind to expect the unexpected. When they saw that customers wanted small bikes, they had a coup d'oeil. Resolution overcame their doubts that small bikes would ruin their image in America.

In other words: the art of what works.
So what do we say to the British in 1975?
BCG says: market and production analysis.
Mintzberg says: experiment and learn.
Expert intuition asks: what works?

Surely there was something that the British were doing right, or there was something that their competitors were doing right that they could do too. A successful strategy emerges not from analysis or experiment, but from what works.

So the art of what works adds a key element to strategic flexibility. Honda had a plan going into Los Angeles: Sell big bikes. The Honda managers admit that they had "no strategy" beyond that. Then they saw the success of the small bikes, and that showed them a winning strategy. Then they made new plans.

The Honda managers were artists of what works.

What's a Good Plan?

Despite assaults from Deming, Mintzberg, and many others, strategic planning is still a growth industry. There are dozens of strategic planning guides available to help you in your planning, and more appear every year. That's well and good. Expert intuition does not eliminate planning; it just changes how you do it. Let's look at some recent planning guides to see how to make the adjustment.

We start with *Business Planning*, by Wesley Truitt.[16] Here we find a classic outline, descended from Jomini but much improved. First comes a "vision statement," which leads to the "goal, mission, and strategy statement." Then you do a resource audit, assess your overall business environment, and assess your competitors. Next come your "specific objectives and operating plans," then control and review, then implementation.

We can see that Jomini's core sequence remains intact: "objective points" and then "marches of armies." Goals precede the means to attain them. Sure enough, in Truitt's outline, we do not find out what the means are until late in the game, under specific objectives, operating plans, and implementation. The vision, goals, and mission come first.

We find a similar outline in the Baldrige National Quality Award.[17] Begun in 1987, this official program of the American government was designed to reward companies that gave up their old ways and caught up with the Japanese. The Baldrige instructions include strategic planning, in two parts. "Strategy Development" describes "how your organization establishes its strategic objectives." "Strategy Deployment" describes "how your organization converts its strategic objectives into action plans." Once again, we see the Jomini sequence.

Most guides to strategic planning follow the same outline. Yet some do not. Let's look at an example that comes closer to expert intuition.

In their *Encyclopedia of Model Business Plans*, Wilbur Cross and Alice Richey provide more than 60 model business plans drawn from real life.[18] This alone fits the art of what works: The best start for your business plan is to find a model for creative imitation.

Cross and Richey give a model outline that is very different from traditional strategic planning. Right off, they note that a business plan is not a tool for finding your strategy. Instead, a business plan gives "information and statistics required by others who are evaluating a proposed venture, most often to determine its potential for financing and support." That's what Bhidé found. His entrepreneurs seldom wrote plans, except when they were seeking funding.

So for Cross and Richey, planning does not equal strategy. You write a plan in order to get money, not in order to figure out what to do. For them, you should already know what to do before you start to plan.

So far, so good.

Their plan outline asks for a description of the venture, classification of the business, its products or services, its locations, the economic environment, the market for its products or services, a description of management, the personnel on hand or to be recruited, the competition, and the financing request.

Note what's missing: There is no vision, mission, goals, or objectives. These traditional elements of strategic planning do not appear on Cross and Richey's list. How can a plan do without them?

Let's look at their first model plan to see.

Coastline Pool Consortium

The Coastline Pool Consortium of West Charleston, South Carolina, wrote a plan to ask Anchor Bank for funding. After basic information on the consortium, there is an "Organizational Summary." There we find that the consortium is a "closely knit organization" of "six product/service businesses" related to swimming pools. The consortium handles the "joint sale of products, services, materials, and consultation" and "collective advertising, promotion, accounting and public relations" for all six. The members founded the consortium "with the conviction that a mutual commercial enterprise" would do better than each member on its own.

Here we have a model of clarity concerning what the business does, and why. Yet the plan never once uses the words *vision, mission,* or *goal.*

But where did the members' "conviction" come from? Did they do research and analysis to decide on a strategy? From Bhidé's study, we doubt that. Sure enough, in the second section of the consortium plan, "Collaborative Growth," we find that they built on what works:

> Coastline Pool Consortium originated in 1984 when two of the present members, Whitecap Pools and Waterway Accessories, joined forces in an advertising campaign to promote the installation and use of pools and related products.

The plan then quotes the president of Whitecap on the success of that joint activity:

> We discovered that we could stretch the advertising dollar almost twice as far and yet each could double the consumer response to individual ads and commercials. We also found that we could slice administrative and staff costs through this kind of cooperative effort, and in many cases receive from each other sound sales and marketing advice that we might not have thought of on our own.

Based on this success, they added a third partner, and "the idea of a consortium began to grow."

In other words, the art of what works. Again we recall Musashi's *Book of Five Rings*: "The strategist makes small things into big things, like building a great Buddha from a one-foot model." For the consortium, what worked on a small scale led to something bigger. The coup d'oeil came not in a flash, but as an "idea" that "began to grow" in the fertile ground of success.

The consortium plan goes on to tell us that the members discuss their long-term strategy every time they add a new member. Their annual report includes the results of the discussion, to give everyone a picture of the consortium's "entrepreneurial vision," and thus to enable people to "understand the benefits, impacts, and challenges of their respective business operations and responsibilities."

So the strategy kept evolving as new members joined, and the consortium spelled out the new strategy every year in its annual report. Yet still it had no plan. That came later, when the consortium decided to ask for a loan from Anchor Bank.

In the rest of the consortium plan, we learn about the consortium's competition, its marketing and sales, and its operations, and we are given a financial analysis. All in all, the consortium plan offers a striking example of a simple, clear statement that explains a strategy based on what works.

The Coastline Pool Consortium business plan is an easy model for others to imitate, in part or in its entirety. And yet, it's a small plan. What about big plans? The Baldrige Award goes to big companies that dwarf the Coastline Pool Consortium.

In large firms, a written strategic plan keeps everyone working together. Without it, won't people all go off in different directions? A small operation like the Consortium can do without a mission, vision, and goal statement, but what about Lucent Technologies? If not its "20 percent plan," then what? Lucent has 56,000 employees in more than a dozen countries around the world. If it doesn't set a common goal, doesn't it risk ending up with 56,000 different strategies?

The Lucent Web site in 2002 offered an answer to this question. The Web site referred to a "strategic focus," a "strategic direction," and a "strategic thrust." All three of these terms seem to mean the same thing: not a specific goal to reach or plan to follow, but a general strategy statement. Here it is:[19]

> Our strategy is to use our core technology strengths in optical, data and third generation (3G) wireless—along with our unique capabilities in network software and worldwide services—to offer segment-specific solutions for integrated wireline networks and mobility networks focused on the individual needs of the largest leading service providers around the world.

With this strategy statement, it is then up to each part of Lucent to develop the details of its own plan.

We see in this Lucent example a major trend in strategic planning: Headquarters sets an overall strategy, and divisions then work out specific plans. It's a form of strategic flexibility from top to bottom. That is, the top does not change its strategy. It just keeps that strategy loose enough to allow different units to develop their own flexible plans.

Let's take a closer look at this trend, to see again what the art of what works might add to it.

Strategic Intent

For *The Change Masters*, Rosabeth Kanter studied dozens of American companies in the early 1980s.[20] While others looked to Japan for guidance, Kanter searched for good practices within the United States itself. She found good news, but mixed with bad:

> Even when a few hardy internal entrepreneurs succeed in producing innovation, officials in the company may not know what to do with it—or even *about* it.

But in successful organizations, "leaders select strategy in part from among solutions developed from grass-roots efforts, rather than defining it in advance and thus constraining innovation." Kanter urged other firms to do just this, to make an "American corporate renaissance."

And it happened. Hundreds of companies slashed their central planning departments, eliminated management layers, adopted Japanese methods for raising quality, and spread their own good practices. Information technology certainly helped, especially in the 1990s. By the turn of the millennium in 2000, America was back on top.

But as we noted earlier, strategic planning did not go away. It loosened up and permeated the firm down to each employee's performance appraisal. Headquarters no longer defined strategy for everyone "in advance," as Kanter found in the early 1980s. Instead, it gave them a strategic direction, or focus, or thrust, and let them devise their own plans. Yet Kanter hints at something more: perhaps that strategic direction should come from below in the first place.

Let's go back to the Marriott example, to see how this might play out.

What if Marriott had already been a major corporation, and Wilbur Marriott had not visited restaurant number 8? What if the manager of the restaurant had had the coup d'oeil himself? Suppose he goes to the airline and works out a tentative contract to serve food on airplanes, then submits the proposal to headquarters.

What should headquarters say? We hope it doesn't say, "No. We operate restaurants." In Kanter's terms, that would "constrain innovation in advance." That is, you can innovate in restaurants but not in anything else. Instead, we want Wilbur Marriott or someone else from headquarters to go to restaurant number 8, check out the deal, and say instead, "Yes. Let's start a new line of business."

The army calls this leading from the front. Wherever the original coup d'oeil comes from, the general has to see the strategy from the ground. There is no other way to judge the value of the strategy or to understand what the rest of the organization has to do to make it succeed. And yet, even at the front, the general cannot go around giving commands to each and every soldier. Hence the search for a method to communicate a general idea of strategy to the troops, like Lucent's strategic direction, or thrust, or focus, or "intent."

"Strategic Intent" is the title of an influential 1989 article by Gary Hamel and C. K. Prahalad.[21] It makes the case that the top should make a general strategic statement, like Lucent's new strategy, which everyone else then implements in a flexible way.

But that's not an excuse for laxity. Strategic intent requires an "obsession with winning at all levels of the organization." It "sets a target that deserves personal effort and commitment." The top must set "clear milestones" and "review mechanisms" that "track progress" and "give recognition and rewards" to "reinforce desired behavior." When it does so, the "challenge" becomes "inescapable" for everyone.

But wait. This sounds like ordinary strategic planning again. You set milestones—Jomini's "objective points"—and you make them "inescapable" for everyone. What's different about strategic intent?

Flexibility. Hamel and Prahalad explain that strategic intent is flexible as to means while being clear about ends. It leaves room for improvisation. Achieving your strategic intent requires enormous creativity.

So in classic strategic planning, the top decides on both the ends and the means, and the bottom implements the means. In strategic intent, the top decides on the ends, then the bottom decides on the means.

Still, Jomini rules. Strategic intent lets the bottom decide on the means (the "marches of armies") but the means still follow the ends (the "objective points"). It's still a form of strategic planning, where the goal comes first.

In expert intuition, the means precede the ends. The coup d'oeil can come from anywhere, top or bottom, but the top must decide to follow it through. The top then communicates both ends and means to the bottom. Thus, the coup d'oeil drives what everyone does, top and bottom alike. It's a strategic *path* with both ends and means, not a strategic *intent* with only ends.

Strategic intent comes in many variations. We saw how Lucent used the idea under different names. And we also find a version that comes closer to expert intuition in *Reinventing Strategy*, by Willie Pietersen, a former CEO. Pietersen calls his version of strategic intent "the winning proposition."

In his business career, Pietersen developed a "strong sense of pragmatism." So he asks of any business idea, "Does it work?" He does not quite invoke expert intuition directly. But his view of strategy touches on several elements of the art of what works.

For Pietersen, the winning proposition answers this question:[22]

> What will we do differently or better than our competitors to achieve greater value for our customers and superior profits for our firm?

Note that this is not a statement of goals. The key question is what a firm will *do*. It asks about means, not ends. Or, rather, the ends are general in the extreme: "value for our customers" and "superior profits." Thus, the winning proposition is less a statement of strategic intent than a strategic path to follow. This is very similar to the key question of Napoleon's strategy: "What battle do I fight to defeat the enemy army?" Therefore, the winning proposition comes close to coup d'oeil. It tells you what to do, what actions to take in order to win.

Pietersen goes on to explain that a winning proposition indicates "what choices management must make—that is, what they will actually *do*"—to achieve better value and higher profits. This emphasis on strategy as action rather than strategy as goal comes close to the art of what works.

Pietersen comes even closer in a vivid example from baseball. He tells us that "to score more runs" is not a winning proposition:

> The real question is *how* you intend to do that. A great baseball coach doesn't simply run up and down the sidelines shouting, "Score runs! Score runs!" but instead offers some specific how-to strategies that make effective use of the talents of the team.

We recall Deming scolding managers for imposing number goals on their employees without a "road map" showing how to reach them. Pietersen gives an example of just such a baseball road map that a coach might give:

> "Lenny, I want you to lay a bunt down the third base line. Then, Wally, your job will be to hit to the opposite field and move Lenny down to second base so Keith can drive him home with a base hit." That's what a winning proposition is like.

Pietersen's "how-to" strategy comes closest to coup d'oeil in his discussion of insight. That's where a winning proposition comes from. Insight "means seeing the underlying truth first or seeing it better." It's an "Aha!" moment, when "all of a sudden people begin to make connections or see answers they had never noticed before."

Last but not least, Pietersen is the rare strategy expert who puts "vision" after coup d'oeil. For him, "Vision . . . is best viewed as an extension of your winning proposition." So first you see what to do, then you have your vision, like Marriott. He saw a way to succeed at airline catering, and then came the vision of a food service company over and above his existing chain of restaurants.

So even though Pietersen's version of strategic intent does not cite expert intuition directly, it comes very close indeed.

Core Competence

Prahalad and Hamel are the source of yet another version of flexible strategic planning. In a 1990 article, "The Core Competence of the Corporation," they announce a new strategy for the decade to come. In the 1980s, companies set out to "restructure, declutter, and delayer." But in the 1990s, companies will face a different standard:[23]

> They'll be judged on their ability to identify, cultivate, and exploit the core competencies that make growth possible—indeed, they'll have to rethink the concept of the corporation itself.

Here we have revolution again. Out with the old, in with the new. In the old concept of the corporation, an autonomous business unit made decisions about its own products. In the new concept of core competencies, products draw on the strengths of the whole corporation:

> Core competencies are the collective learning in the organization, especially how to coordinate diverse production skills and integrate multiple streams of technologies . . . that empower individual businesses to adapt quickly to changing opportunities.

You can't depend on products, because they come and go. Core competencies last longer. They carry you from product to product, and even spawn "unanticipated products." So long-term success comes from building core competencies "at lower cost and more speedily than competitors."

Hamel and Prahalad cite the example of Canon. There you find core competencies in precision mechanics, fine optics, microelectronics, and electronic imaging. Its various business units all draw on the same pool of competencies for an ever-changing mix of products: electronic cameras, a color video printer, a laser imager, a cell analyzer, and so forth. The autonomous business units lend one another skilled staff as needed to develop the next line of products.

At first glance, core competencies sounds like the art of what works. You build on what worked in the past, in new combinations, to suit the new situation. You modify Product A to get a Product B. But still we wonder: Where did Product A come from? How does a core competency start?

We don't know. Prahalad and Hamel tell us about competencies that a company already has and can build on, not about how it gets those competencies in the first place. To find your best competencies, you "take inventory of skills and look forward to applying them in nontraditional ways." Then you conduct three analytical tests: Does the core competency provide "potential access to a wide variety of markets," does it "make a significant contribution to the perceived customer benefits of the end product," and is it "difficult for competitors to imitate"?

The inventory and tests of core competencies seem simple enough. But what about that middle step? How do we look forward to applying core competencies in "nontraditional ways"? For that, business units need to work as a team. For example, at NEC Corporation "divisional managers come together to identify next-generation competencies."

But how? What exactly do you look for?

Prahalad and Hamel don't tell us.[24]

Here, expert intuition can help. You look for what works, not as a competency but as an activity that has elements of success. Again, when Mr. Marriott discovered that restaurant number 8 was selling food to airline passengers, he realized that his company could develop a core competency in food service in general, not just running restaurants. He did not identify the core competency first and then go out and look for applications, like airline catering.

So Prahalad and Hamel have it backwards. Core competencies do not lead to new products. Instead, new products make you realize your core competencies. The coup d'oeil precedes the vision. Otherwise we're back to plain strategic planning, where your goal is to apply your core competencies and the activity is a new product or service. The activity comes first—you see what to do—and that tells you the skills and whatever else you need in order to do it. And you look everywhere in your own or other industries, not just at what you're doing yourself. What works can come from anywhere, not just from your current competencies.

Creative Planning

From our review of strategic planning, we see that flexibility does not solve the problem of which comes first, goals or the means to reach them. Flexible action toward your goal still begs the question of where the goal comes from in the first place. A good strategy is not something that you plan to do; it's something that you can do, based on coup d'oeil. First you see what you can do to succeed. Then you plan.

But what if it's just too late? You're a sub-pharaoh, and the pharaoh gives you a goal. In most companies, you have to accept it, even if it's not based on coup d'oeil. Don't reject it; that would not be very pragmatic. You'd be choosing a battle you had no way of winning.

So go ahead and take on the goal. Then ask: Has anyone ever succeeded in reaching a goal like this? That will lead you to elements that are worth imitation, at least in part. It may not get you all the way there, but at least it's a start. If, along the way, you see a path to a better goal that leads to more success for the company, tell your boss. Who knows? Even if it's not in the plan, the better way might strike your boss as something worth putting in.

For some sub-pharaohs, creative planning is one of their specialties. They don't see the path themselves, but they know how to work it into the plan. That might explain some of the cases that Kanter picked out in which successful strategy comes from below. In big companies especially, creative planning can help a coup d'oeil make it to resolution.

CHAPTER
5

Change versus Charge
The Art of the Learning Organization

I N THE LAST CHAPTER, we saw that strategic planning fits with the art of what works when the plan arises from expert intuition. In this chapter, we look at another popular school of strategy to see what the art of what works might add to it.

The idea of the "learning organization" arose in the 1990s to help companies change as the business environment changes, not just once or twice, but over and over again. You do not simply modify your old plans; you toss them out and trust in teamwork instead. But the art of what works trusts in something else: coup d'oeil. Can the learning organization live with expert intuition, or must the two go their separate ways?

The Fifth Discipline

In *Strategy Safari*, Henry Mintzberg presents the "learning school" as emergent strategy, where you change your plans as you learn by doing. In the same book, his coauthor, Joseph Lampel, offers another view of learning, in which the "holy grail" of strategy is "cumulative learning and constant self-renewal." A company "learns from experience" yet does not get "trapped" in that experience, and it "can leverage this learning in the marketplace." Lampel concludes:

> This so-called "learning organization" represents the fullest expression of the learning school. It strives to make organizational learning central rather than an accidental activity which often goes unused.

While Mintzberg's emergent strategy reacts to new events, the learning organization goes much farther. It constantly draws in new information, spreads that information around, and uses it to change everything the company does. Lampel sees the learning organization as the "antithesis of the old bureaucratic organization." Instead of bureaucracy, you find decentralization, open communication, teamwork, collaboration, "risk taking, honesty, and trust":

> Indeed, the picture that emerges has an uncanny resemblance to the utopian visions of social reformers at the turn of the century, and may prove just as difficult to create and sustain in practice.

So the "utopian vision" of the learning organization is very difficult to put into practice. But where did it come from? Who drew the picture?

It was Peter Senge who launched the learning movement with *The Fifth Discipline* in 1990. During the 1990s, hundreds of businesses and other organizations around the world declared themselves learning organizations. But Senge spoke most directly to those big American firms that had become bogged down in bureaucracy and let the Japanese overtake them. The learning organization offered another way.

Senge offers five "disciplines" that a company must take up if it is to become a learning organization. First comes personal mastery, for "personal growth and learning." The second, mental models, entails "surfacing, testing, and improving our internal pictures of how the world works." The third, team learning, means "aligning and developing the capacity of a team to create the results its members truly desire." The fourth, shared vision, answers the question, "What do we want to create?" And the fifth, systems thinking, "is a conceptual framework" to "make patterns clearer, and to help us see how to change them effectively."

For each discipline, Senge cites a few examples. But overall, he presents a utopian picture—not what is, but what should be. Building a learning organization has no "there," no "ultimate destination." There is only "a lifelong journey."

In this utopian world, Senge takes us very far from the art of what works. Instead of new combinations of past achievements that show you a path to success, Senge offers five ways to learn, forever. Strategy in a learning organization comes not from a coup d'oeil, but from the shared vision of team members throughout the system who open their minds through personal mastery and mental models.

In expert intuition, a vision is a course of action to take. You see it by coup d'oeil. In the learning organization, a vision is the end goal, a picture of where you want to end up. It's Jomini's "objective point" again. Senge thinks that a shared vision of the end goal is the key to success through the ages:[1]

> If any one idea about leadership has inspired organizations for thousands of years, it's the capacity to hold a shared picture of the future we seek to create.

Senge tells us that great organizations feature "goals, values, and missions that become deeply shared throughout the organization." For IBM, this is "service." For Polaroid, it's "instant photography." For Ford, it's "public transportation for the masses." For Apple, it's "computing power for the masses." Senge tells us that, despite their drastic differences in content and kind, these organizations bind people together around a common identity and sense of destiny.

But is it true that shared vision gave IBM, Polaroid, Ford, and Apple their greatness? The art of what works sees the opposite: Greatness produced the shared vision. Success came first, or at least a coup d'oeil that showed the way to success. That's what holds people together. That's what created the vision, the common identity, the sense of destiny.

Once again we are back to the question of where the goal—or vision or objective—comes from in the first place. Senge says that no formula for "how to find your vision" exists, but he knows how to build a shared vision. It takes "ongoing conversations where individuals not only feel free to express their dreams, but learn how to listen to each others' dreams." You unearth shared "pictures of the future." That makes for "genuine commitment and enrollment rather than compliance." It's counterproductive to "dictate a vision," period.

We saw that emergent strategy is flexible strategic planning. The learning organization goes one step further, to participatory flexible strategic planning. All join in with their "dreams." Through "dialogue," you arrive at a shared dream. The result is your strategy.

This method is the opposite of Leonardo's advice to "want what you can do." Senge says instead that you should do what you want, as long as others want it too. It's like Jomini with the chairs in a circle and everyone holding hands.

Senge offers a variety of tools for building a learning organization: systems drawings and archetypes, dialogue sessions, computer models, and team discussion. His *Fifth Discipline Fieldbook* presents these tools in greater detail. Of the five disciplines, he seems to favor the fifth, systems thinking, in both the amount of text devoted to it and the number of tools available. After all, Senge has a Ph.D. in systems design, and this discipline is the title of the book.

In systems thinking, we see a glimmer of intuition. You bring to light the "underlying systemic structures" that are otherwise hard to explain. The more you practice systems thinking, the more you find that your "intuitions become explicable":

> Eventually, reintegrating reason and intuition may prove to be one of the primary contributions of systems thinking.

This sounds very promising, but we hear no more about intuition and systems thinking. Perhaps this is because intuition gives you an answer quickly. *The Fifth Discipline* seems more like an endless search for an answer, where the journey counts more than the arrival. You're not really after answers, because often "the most important problems that managers confront" have "no single, best solution." The only way to deal with such problems is "genuine openness":

> The best definition of the love that underlies openness is the full and unconditional commitment to another's "completion," to another being all that she or he can and wants to be.

Here we have the key to Senge's success: He promises a workplace in which people help one another to develop and thrive, while the company does better, too. No wonder his book is so popular.

But still we ask: Does it work?

A dozen years have passed since *The Fifth Discipline* came out. Is that enough time for results? In a 1994 interview, Senge said, "If it isn't working, we should stop and do something else."[2] So do we know yet if the learning organization is working?

In 1996, Senge helped create the Society for Organizational Learning to "advance the state of the art" in building learning organizations. The society's Web site tells us about an "Assessment Initiative." It began with a workshop for 33 participants in January 1998. In December 1998, Stella Humphries wrote a progress report that reviewed the workshop and presented assessment questions, such as "How can we show others that something really changes?" We find nothing more on assessment after 1998. And no one else has reported on the success of learning organizations.

So we do not know if the learning organization works. Still, we cheer Senge on, and we hope that his dream comes true. Meanwhile, we add to his fifth discipline a sixth sense: coup d'oeil.

Great Groups

In *Organizing Genius*, Warren Bennis offers another view of the learning organization. Bennis first wrote on the subject in a 1965 essay, "Beyond Bureaucracy."[3] Like Senge, he points to a better world of the future, one in which hierarchy crumbles and people love their jobs.

Bennis tells us that a "pyramidal structure" is fine for "routinized tasks," but that it can't adapt when the environment changes. Therefore, he predicts the "demise of bureaucracy" and the "collapse of management as we know it." In the future, "fantasy, imagination, and creativity will be legitimate in ways that today seem strange." Bureaucracy fit an earlier time, but

> In today's world, it is a lifeless crutch that is no longer useful. For we now require structures of freedom to permit the expression of play and imagination and to exploit the new pleasures of work.

Such is the dream of the learning organization. Yet here we are, nearly 40 years after Bennis wrote these words, and the "pyramidal structure" endures throughout the world. But Bennis did not give up.

In *Organizing Genius*, he tries another assault on the fortress, this time with case studies. He tells the tale of six "Great Groups" that fought bureaucracy and won.

Bennis starts with a motto: "None of us is as smart as all of us." Right away we see where strategy comes from: the good ideas inside you. Put together many "yous," and you get more good ideas.

The art of what works says the opposite: Good ideas come from outside you. You see what works, and that shows you the path to success. If that's "smart," fine. So our motto says: "No one of us is as smart as all of us seeking what works."

Bennis titles his first chapter "The Death of the Great Man." He wants to topple the pharaoh. Out with the Great Man, in with the Great Group. Still, every group must have a leader. In a Great Group, "people with rare gifts" work together "as equals." One of them "acts as maestro, organizing the genius of the others":[4]

> He or she is a pragmatic dreamer, a person with an original but attainable vision. . . . Typically, the leader is the one who recruits the others, by making the vision so palpable and seductive that they see it, too, and eagerly sign up.

Here, Bennis comes closer to the art of what works. An "attainable vision" sounds like a battle that you see a way to win. You make that vision, or the way you will win that battle, "so palpable" that others "see it, too." But where does the vision come from? To Bennis, vision is a talent of "superb people" with original minds, who see things differently and have skills that help solve important problems and discover interesting things. They want to do the new, next thing—not rehash the old.

We're back to that erratic goddess, imagination. But this is an easy mistake to make. If you don't know what to look for, expert intuition can seem like a gift of the gods rather than something that is based on the past achievements of ordinary human beings. It's magic, until you know the secret.

So perhaps the Great Groups that Bennis cites did succeed through the art of what works. Let's look at three of his cases, to see.

The first is Apple Computer and the Macintosh. We have already seen how Jobs had his coup d'oeil on a visit to Xerox. Bennis puts this episode at the heart of his tale. So the Great Group at Apple had its big breakthrough thanks to expert intuition.

A second case is the Manhattan Project at Los Alamos, New Mexico.[5] There, Robert Oppenheimer put together a Great Group to build the first atomic bomb before Nazi Germany could beat them to it. So how did this Great Group start?

Enrico Fermi was one of several scientists, including Albert Einstein, who alerted President Roosevelt in writing that Hitler could exploit current scientific knowledge on atomic energy to build a bomb. As a result, Roosevelt authorized the Manhattan Project. It started in September 1942, with Fermi in charge. Oppenheimer took over in October, to free Fermi for work in his lab at the University of Chicago. In November, Oppenheimer selected Los Alamos, New Mexico, as the main research site. On December 2, Fermi created the world's first chain reaction. Four days later, construction began at Los Alamos. The Great Group arrived there 3 months later, in March 1943.

What gave the Great Group its vision? Fermi's success 3 months before. And the speed of Fermi's achievement meant that he mostly used current knowledge. Oppenheimer's team did the same, as they solved the giant puzzle of turning Fermi's device into a bomb. They succeeded in only 2 years.

So the Manhattan Project was a classic case of the art of what works.

Our third case is Disney. Bennis tells us that the story of how Disney's classic *Snow White and the Seven Dwarfs* was made is a paradigm of a Great Group at work, creating something wonderful and new. And it all started with a vision.[6]

Snow White was certainly wonderful—it was the first full-length animated film. But was it so new? And where did the vision to make it come from—Walt Disney's imagination or past achievement?

Bennis reports that Disney had the vision on a trip to Europe in 1928. In Paris, he found a movie theater showing "successful programs" of Mickey Mouse cartoons, "one after the other, without any feature film." That gave him the idea of making an animated feature film. He wanted to do more than put together a string of short cartoons. That had been done. Instead, Disney wanted to create a wonderful, full-length animated feature. That was new, and he was positive that distributors would pay handsomely for it.

Right away, we see success: An audience is paying money to sit through a full-length animated show. Disney wanted to do it again and again, to build on that success. Distributors paid much more for full-length films than for short cartoons, so here was a way to make more money. In fact, Disney lost money for years on cartoon shorts. The first one to turn a profit was *Three Little Pigs* in 1933.

But wait: If Disney had a vision of *Snow White* in 1928, why did it take him so long to make it? *Snow White* came out in 1937. In 1928, he had enough short cartoons to equal the length of a feature film. In just a few months, he could have made a long film with exactly the same technology. Why did it take him 9 years to make *Snow White*, from the vision in 1928 to its completion in 1937?

It didn't. Disney's vision of full-length films might have come in 1928, but the vision that led to *Snow White* came in 1934. It was a classic coup d'oeil, based on past achievement.

Disney first tried to make a full-length film in 1931: *Alice in Wonderland*. He gave that up in 1932 when an English studio came out with a live-action version. It would have been too much competition. Disney's *Alice* would have combined a real-live Alice with animation for everything else. That was the formula that he had used in *Alice in Cartoonland*, a series of shorts that he made between 1923 and 1926. Was that the vision Disney had in Paris, to turn his *Alice* shorts into a full-length film? If so, the quality of the film would have been quite low. It was only in 1988, with *Who Framed Roger Rabbit*, that the Disney studios solved the technical problems of combining animation and live characters.

Thus Disney might have had a vision for a low-quality *Alice* film in 1928, but he certainly did not have a vision of making *Snow White*. *Alice* and *Snow White* were very different. There was no live character in *Snow White*, and the technology to make *Snow White* did not exist in 1928, or even in 1931.

It was only in 1932 that a technical breakthrough greatly improved Technicolor. Right away, Disney bought the exclusive rights to use the new process in animation. He added a whole color department, including crew, materials, and laboratory. The Technicolor company itself owned the only other color lab in Hollywood and rented it out film by film to live-action studios. Its monopoly lasted until 1949, when Eastman Kodak produced a rival product.

So before 1932, Disney had no vision of producing a film like *Snow White*. In 1931, he had set out to combine animation and live action in his first full-length feature, whereas *Snow White* was all animation. And it was the Technicolor breakthrough in 1932 that took Disney into color production.

In 1932, Disney made his first full-color animation short, *Flowers and Trees*. It won an Academy Award. Again: success. Disney had mastered full-color animation in less than a year. He built on that success with more color shorts.

At about the same time, in 1932, Disney started using a new technique for planning out stories: the storyboard. One of his cartoonists, Webb Smith, adapted it from cartoon strips. Disney's shorts now included color and sound, singing and dancing, so the task of developing all the pieces and keeping them together had become daunting. With a storyboard, artists made preliminary drawings of every scene and clipped them on a board in sequence. It was like a newspaper cartoon strip—the industry in which both Webb and Disney had started their careers. So Disney adapted an old craft to planning out animated films.

Suddenly, a complicated story was easy to follow. That meant that the story line could become more complex. Disney's first storyboard short was *Father Noah's Ark* in 1933. Right after this, in 1934, he wrote a memo to announce the technique to the whole studio. That was the year the studio began to work on *Snow White*.

Coup d'oeil.

Snow White combined all Disney's previous achievements: synchronized sound and action, Technicolor, singing and dancing, and a complex story line developed on a storyboard. Thanks to his Paris visit, Disney knew that at least some audiences would pay to sit through a full-length cartoon. And the *Snow White* story was hardly new: It was a successful fairy tale that had remained popular through the ages.

During 1937, the last year of work on *Snow White*, Disney tried using a multiplane camera in a cartoon short, *The Old Mill*, to give scenes greater depth. It worked. That was the last element Disney added in making *Snow White*.

From its first release at the end of 1937, the film was an instant success. It took Disney from the brink of bankruptcy to being a major Hollywood studio. He went on to repeat the formula year after year. Full-length animated features became his signature product.

Disney was an artist of what works.

As we see from Apple, the Manhattan Project, and Disney, the art of what works takes nothing away from the insights that *Organizing Genius* offers. We simply add the element of expert intuition to complete the picture of what explains success. The same is true with other books that promote teamwork over command and control, such as *Stewardship*, by Peter Block, or *The Radical Team Handbook: Harnessing the Power of Team Learning*, by John Redding.[7]

Work as a team—that's good advice. But also, successful teams follow what works.

Knowledge Management

In his work on the learning organization, Senge stood on the shoulders of giants. He names several prior sources, especially *Organizational Learning*, by Chris Argyris and Donald Schon.[8] But those sources were technical studies, whereas Senge was writing for a wider audience. And he came after American business had its coup d'ocil about Japan. There is an old saying: "When the student is ready, the teacher appears." Senge appeared at just the right time.

Yet much of what Senge proposed was very hard to do. Dialogue, team learning, and shared vision take a lot of time and great skill to do well. So most companies adopted the easiest parts: Train all your employees in a wide range of subjects, and circulate information widely so that everyone can take what he or she needs from it. The training department became a "learning center" with a much bigger budget. And "knowledge management" brought learning to everyone's desk through the magic of computer technology.

The field of knowledge management also arose at just the right time: It caught the wave of the Information Age. In the 1990s, American companies spent more on information technology than on any other type of investment. With the rise of the Internet, companies built intranets to connect everyone, everywhere, all the time, about everything.

Knowledge management promises to solve the problem of strategy. Thanks to better information, you can lift the fog of war. Everyone's strategy improves.

Or does it?

In 1998, the *California Management Review* dedicated its spring issue to "Knowledge and the Firm." It reviewed the evidence on knowledge management: whether better information has led to learning that makes for better strategy.

In one of the articles, "The State of the Notion: Knowledge Management in Practice," Rudy Ruggles reports on a 1997 survey of 431 U.S. and European companies.[9] The survey asked these companies how they manage knowledge, how they would like to do so better, and what stops them from doing that.

Overall, the survey showed poor results for knowledge management. Ruggles reports that "only 13 percent thought that they were adept at transferring knowledge held by one part of the organization to other parts." Almost all of the companies surveyed—94 percent—thought that "it would be possible, through more deliberate management, to leverage the knowledge existing in my organization to a higher degree."

So what's the problem?

The survey gives two big obstacles to successful knowledge management: "changing people's behavior" (56 percent) and "culture" (54 percent). But here we see a paradox: To make knowledge management work, you have to convince people to use it. But if it doesn't work, why should they use it?

We see a possible answer in a second article, "If Only We Knew What We Knew: Identification and Transfer of Internal Best Practices," by Carla O'Dell and C. J. Grayson.[10] Now we're talking. Instead of flooding the company with all kinds of knowledge, let's single out what works.

But even this is not easy. O'Dell and Grayson cite a 1994 study for the International Benchmarking Clearinghouse on "what prevents the transfer of practices across a company."[11] The number one barrier was "ignorance on both ends of the transfer":

> At most companies, particularly large ones, neither the "source" nor the "recipient" knew someone else had knowledge they required or would be interested in knowledge they had.

You hear it all the time: "I didn't know you needed this" or "I didn't know you had it." Worse, best practices "took an average of *27 months* to wind their way from one part of the organization to another." That's more than 2 years. By then, the information is probably out of date.

But O'Dell and Grayson also cite cases of companies doing it right. Their leading example is Chevron Refining. Chevron's senior managers for operations picked "six highest priority areas" and formed a team to deal with each one. One study found that, based on a comparison of practices, each best practices team was able to identify more than $10 million in potential improvements. Process masters then helped plants adapt those practices.

So what did Chevron do next? It expanded the program beyond refining, to all areas of its business. It did so by holding best practice team meetings every other month or more often, under a common charter. Between meetings, the team members were linked and worked electronically, and they had the resources and support they needed from Chevron.

The refining group succeeded in finding what works, so its method spread to the rest of the company. And that succeeded too. More than $650 million in savings has been generated by a network of more than 100 Chevron people who share ideas.

Over time, Chevron expanded its search for best practices to other companies in the industry and even other industries. It looked for *"any practice, knowledge, know-how or experience that has proven to be valuable or effective within one organization that may have applicability to other organizations."*

In other words, what works.

Chevron stands out as a learning organization that figured out how to use information technology to transfer knowledge. The best practices teams not only communicate electronically, but put everything they find in a "Best Practices Sharing Database." And it all depends on expert intuition:

> The database recognizes that no single "best-practice" is suitable for every circumstance. Each end-user will use unique criteria to judge what is best for each business.

It's up to you to find what combination of best practices suits your own situation. Thus, you see new combinations of past achievements: That's what makes coup d'oeil.

The Achievement Network

Chevron's definition of a "best practice" exactly matches General Electric's definition of a "good idea." Sure enough, we find at

General Electric a similar method for finding and using what works. GE's scale and success exceed even Chevron's, so let's take a look at GE, too.

GE officially became a learning organization in 1994, with the appointment of Steven Kerr as one of the world's first Chief Learning Officers. Kerr inherited Work-Out and Best Practices. Work-Out brought all levels of staff together to identify and work on problems, and Best Practices documented successes both in other companies and inside GE. Under Kerr's guidance, these methods continued to develop, spread throughout the organization, and take new forms.

One new form stands out. It developed from the Trotter matrix, which in turn came out of Best Practices.[12]

Lloyd Trotter was head of Electrical Distribution and Control at GE in the early 1990s. As part of Best Practices, he listed the elements that made for a good electrical factory and asked each factory to score itself on each element. Trotter then put the scores together in a matrix, using the elements for the rows and the factories for the columns. The scores—from 1 to 5—went in the boxes. Thus, a factory might merit a 2 on one element and a 4 on another. The Trotter matrix showed all the scores for all the factories and elements on one page.

If you had a low score on one element, Trotter made you visit a factory with a high score on that element to find out how that factory did it. If you had a medium score on an element, maybe you just needed to improve what you were doing, or maybe you too should visit a factory with a high score. If you had a high score, you had to explain the secret of your success to the managers whose factories had lower scores who came calling.

The matrix worked so well that GE asked Trotter to extend it to all GE factories. And under Kerr, the matrix took on a life of its own at GE's Crotonville Institute.

After staff reductions in the 1980s, GE grew again to over 300,000 employees in the 1990s. The top 10 percent spent at least 2 weeks at Crotonville. Kerr encouraged each of GE's 20 companies or departments within those companies to send people in teams, with a real business problem that the company or department really wanted to solve. If you came as an individual, Crotonville put you in a mixed team and gave the team a real business problem that cut across GE. Each team used the Trotter matrix to solve its problem.

Like Trotter, the teams listed the elements that made for a good solution: What did you have to do well in order to solve the problem? Those elements were used for the rows. The columns were the places to look for prior success with these elements. Most of the time the columns were simply the 20 GE businesses, but they might also be a subset of companies, certain departments from all the companies, or other companies outside of GE. It depended on the team's understanding of the problem and its choice of elements.

Then the team went on a treasure hunt to fill in the matrix. Its first source was right there at Crotonville. Kerr spread the basic Trotter matrix across GE, beyond the factories to all departments, and verified all high scores to make sure that the high-scoring groups were worth emulating. Thus, there were stacks of matrix results on file at Crotonville that the team could consult. The team members also had their own knowledge of GE and other companies to draw on for leads.

As the team started filling in its own matrix, it might find that it needed to change one or more of the elements in the rows to give a better picture of the problem. Or it might add locations to search in the columns. Or it might even recast the problem itself.

Ideas that worked in other situations started filling the matrix, until the team had a coup d'oeil—that is, until it saw a course of action to follow. That's when the team stopped. It then wrote up a report and presented it right there, at the end of its Crotonville stay, to the other teams and sometimes to a panel of visiting GE executives.

These discussions might result in the team's changing or abandoning its proposal. But if the discussions were positive, the company or department team went back home and presented the proposal there. The mixed teams kept in touch remotely to shepherd the proposal through whatever approvals it needed. And the teams kept going until their course of action succeeded or failed. That is, they followed their coup d'oeil with resolution.

In addition, the all-GE Trotter matrix came to feed Work-Out sessions as employees noticed success elsewhere and proposed to their bosses that they try the same thing. Top management meetings went through business quickly and then spent most of the time learning about outstanding best practices that came from a Trotter matrix, Work-Out, a Crotonville team, or some other source. And GE's top management made sure that everyone actively sought out other groups' successes and spread their own.

Jack Welch sometimes sat in on the Crotonville panels that reviewed a team's Trotter matrix. Even when he was absent, he was there in spirit. Slater quotes Kerr on how Welch helped him out:[13]

> So Welch says moving ideas is really simple. You wonder why you wouldn't learn from, say, the plastics business, because Welch has convinced you that some "best practice" is there, and you feel bad if you don't find it.

When Kerr traveled out of Crotonville to visit the GE companies, he met Welch's spirit there too:

> Sometimes these leaders have said to me, "I have a best practice, and Jack Welch is coming to visit. Help me move the best practice around the company. I don't want to get caught with it alone when Jack arrives." The point is that the manager understands there will be no reward for having a good idea, only in sharing it with others.

In a later chapter on tools and techniques, we will study Kerr's version of the Trotter matrix in greater detail. For now, we conclude that the learning organization model can offer excellent guidance for deciding on and implementing strategy. But Kerr's version of the model is very different from Senge's ideal of the learning organization: It has no systems analysis, no dialogue, no alignment.

Kerr did involve everyone in the GE "system" at some point, but not to sort out their conflicting views, to develop a common vision of the future, or to learn everything about everything. Instead, everyone learned what worked. That kept the information that circulated down to a manageable volume. And you knew exactly what to do with the information when you got it: consider trying it yourself.

Instead of ongoing dialogue, there was rapid communication on a narrow but vital topic: what worked. And instead of company-wide alignment, there was group action on specific projects based on past achievement. GE did not row in a single direction, but in many directions at once, with units building on what worked in their own department, company, or team. Each group went along with a particular strategy not because dialogue had produced a shared vision of the future, but because the group saw that the strategy had a firm basis in past achievement.

We use this case as an example of a complete learning organization based on what works—like Napoleon's "campaigns of the great captains." Note too that Kerr's activities resemble Kuhn's description of a scientific community, where scientists pay close attention to the achievements of other laboratories and adjust their own work accordingly.

GE's size helped. It cut down Kerr's per-employee costs, and it ensured that there were plenty of worthwhile achievements to find. Smaller companies might not be able to do exactly what GE did. Yet the learning organization aims above all to help large companies overcome the ills of bureaucracy. Strategy based on expert intuition is much easier when you're small. But GE shows that it can work on a larger scale too, without being crushed by the bureaucracy.

GE's version of the learning organization focused so much on what works that we might want to call it an "achievement network" instead. Achievement was both GE's subject of learning and the direct use for what they found. And the search for what works ends up being a network activity because it crosses so many organizational boundaries. From learning organization to achievement network: Welch, Kerr, and the Trotter matrix made that shift for GE.

Organizational Change

We turn now to another variant of the learning organization: "organizational change." It too arose as a field in the 1990s as companies tried to change direction in one big push, using the concepts and tools of the learning organization. Thus, organizational change stands out as an explicit attempt to apply learning to strategy.

In a 1995 article, "Leading Change: Why Transformation Efforts Fail," John Kotter gave a gloomy report on the many organizational change projects that were underway at that time.[14] He followed with a book, *Leading Change*, to help companies do better at organizational change.[15] There are many guides to organizational change, but Kotter's stands out as perhaps the most popular. Let's look at what he says.

Kotter offers a series of steps to create major change. First you establish a sense of urgency. Then you put together a "guiding coalition." Next comes vision and strategy. You communicate the change vision, empower "broad-based action," get "short-term wins," consolidate your gains, and make more progress. Finally, you "anchor" the change in company culture.

Senge's fifth discipline, systems thinking, comes in during Kotter's second step. The guiding coalition includes all the key people who need to be involved in order to make the whole system change. In the third step, we see vision and strategy. We learn that the "leadership" creates the vision, which is "a sensible and appealing picture of the future." This fits Senge again, because the vision gets shared in the fourth step, where we find: "If employees have a shared sense of purpose, it will be easier to initiate actions to achieve that purpose."

The leadership also creates the strategies, which are "a logic and a first level of detail to show how a vision can be accomplished." But again we ask Finkelstein and Hambrick's question: Where does the strategy come from? A vision can lead to hundreds of possible strategies. How do we choose among them? We don't know; Kotter tells us nothing more about strategy.

But wait: In the fifth step, empowering broad-based action, we see that strategy hardly matters. Everyone takes the vision and runs with it. People are empowered. A key to empowering broad-based action is "aligning systems to the vision." That means that you adapt performance evaluation, compensation decisions, promotion decisions, and recruiting and hiring systems to "support the transformation," because "unaligned structures block needed action."

In Kotter's book, we get a clearer picture of something that is lurking in the work of Senge and Bennis and the learning organization in general: Strategy hardly matters. The key is vision, plus a flexible organization that lets teams of people do what they see fit in order to make that vision come true. If you try to tell people what to do, you're a bureaucrat. A dictator. A pharaoh.

Kotter concludes with a look at the future. He predicts that a "strategy of embracing the past will probably become increasingly ineffective over the next few decades." So what are you to do? You should "start learning now how to cope with change" to "help our organizations in the transformation process." In spite of the risks, you should "leap into the future," and you should do so "sooner rather than later."

So the end product of the learning organization is not strategy or success, but change. Constant change, on and on into the future.

In the learning organization, you line up the troops—no, don't line them up; invite them to assemble in free-form groups of their own making.

Then call out: Change!

With expert intuition, a coup d'oeil shows you what to do. Then you line up the troops and call out: Charge!

The word *charge* has three meanings here. First, a charge is a call for quick and vigorous action by everyone. Second, it is an electric charge, a spark of excitement. Third, a charge means marching orders: Your charge is the piece of the action that it's up to you to do well. Expert intuition tells you what that is.

As we saw in this chapter's examples, coup d'oeil solves the basic problem of the learning organization: how to get everyone working together in a new direction, not just once, but whenever we need to. Senge, Bennis, and Kotter all give good advice. We just add to it the art of what works, to give learning and change an extra charge of success. Become an achievement network—that's the best change of all.

Forces versus Sources
The Art of Competitive Strategy

IN THE LAST TWO CHAPTERS, we saw how the art of what works complements two of the leading schools of strategy. Flexible strategy makes strategic planning more adaptable as circumstances change, while the learning organization calls for full participation by everyone in the system or group. Expert intuition adds to both schools. It tells you when and how to be flexible, and it gives everyone guidance on when and how to participate.

We turn now to a third major school of strategy: competitive strategy. Here you cut through the fog of business with economic analysis of your industry, of your competitors, and of your own competitive position. Once again, we study the strengths of competitive strategy, how it differs from the art of what works, and what expert intuition might add to it.

Five Forces and Three Strategies

In 1980, with the publication of *Competitive Strategy*, Michael Porter both founded and named a new school of strategy.[1]

Over the next two decades, competitive strategy became the dominant type of strategy taught at the world's leading business schools. As a result, companies now hire economists, either on staff or as consultants, to perform their competitive analysis. If you look in annual reports and on company Web sites, you will find many references to competitive advantage, competitive position, and the competitive analysis that drives the firm's decisions. And the Baldrige Award criteria, under "Strategic Planning," ask you to address key elements of competitive strategy: "your competitive environment and your capabilities relative to competitors" and "your supplier/partner strengths and weaknesses."

All thanks to Porter, more than 20 years ago.

Soon after *Competitive Strategy*, Porter published two companion volumes that carried forward his principles: *Cases in Competitive Strategy* and *Competitive Advantage*.[2] *Cases* offers a wealth of detail on 26 companies in 18 different industries; it is designed to serve as a "case book" for teaching with *Competitive Strategy*. And while *Competitive Strategy* devises economic principles that you apply in an outward direction to analyze your competitors, *Competitive Advantage* applies the same principles inward, to your own "value chain" of supply, production, and distribution.

Porter wrote *Competitive Strategy* as a contribution to strategic planning. He notes that "each functional department" in a firm would go its own way if it were "left to its own devices." Companies need strategic planning to provide an "explicit process of formulating strategy" that makes sure that the policies, if not the actions, of those functional departments "are coordinated and directed at a common set of goals." Porter then offers an "explicit process": competitive analysis.

But wait. Mintzberg disputes the merit of strategic planning as a means of coordinating departments, and many companies turned away from elaborate strategic planning in their drive to compete with Japan and Europe. So why did competitive strategy catch on?

Because Porter adds something unusual to strategic planning. He wants to give managers "a subtle understanding of industries and competitors." The "strategy field has offered few analytical techniques for gaining this understanding," so Porter sets out to fill that gap. At the same time, "economists have long studied industry structure," but they have done so to help governments set tax and regulatory policies, whereas Porter wants to use industry studies to help companies develop strategy.

Here is the secret of Porter's success. As planning fell out of favor, companies replaced it with economic research. Out with the planners, in with the economists, for better strategic planning.

And Porter is right. There was little economic research behind most strategic plans. Let's look at a classic work in the field, *A Concept of Corporate Planning*, by Russell Ackoff. Here we learn from this work that planners should "picture changes that might take place, assess their significance to the firm, and consider ways in which they might be exploited." Ackoff gives a real-life picture, drawn from the strategic plan of an unnamed food company:[3]

> The small car will be coming into vogue just as women are decreasing the frequency of their shopping trips and increasing the amount purchased per trip. The cars will be too small to carry all that is purchased. For these reasons, then, we can expect an increase in home delivery.

A "little further into the future," a computer will "keep a record of a household's purchases, analyze them," figure out what the household needs, and "deliver without an order being placed," the way "heating-fuel distributors" are already doing:

> O.K.; so there is going to be an increase in home delivery. . . . We can wait and see and adapt to it when it comes or we can find out how to make something of it. . . . At a maximum it offers us an exciting and potentially profitable direction for relevant diversification and expansion.

What's wrong with this picture?

It's rampant speculation.

The company is just guessing. There's no research to back up its plan.

So Porter's book is as the first practical guide to using economic research for strategic planning. He leads you through it, step by step.

The first step is "The Structural Analysis of Industries." Competition in an industry boils down to "five basic competitive forces."[4] In competitive strategy, you "find a position in the industry" where you can "best defend" against these five forces or "influence them" in your favor.

Porter's five forces are current competitors, potential entrants, substitutes, suppliers, and buyers. These forces are not all equally relevant for every situation, so you study some more than others. For example, "In the ocean-going tanker industry the key force is probably the buyers (the major oil companies)" and "In the steel industry the key forces are foreign competitors and substitute materials."

And each force has subforces. For example, the force "potential entrants" includes the "barriers to entry" of economies of scale, product differentiation, capital requirements, switching costs, access to distribution channels, cost disadvantages independent of scale, and government policy.

For each subforce, Porter gives us a brief description and some useful tips. For example, the "switching costs" for intravenous (IV) kits come from the different methods that each kit uses "for attaching solutions to patients" and for "hanging the IV bottles." So "great resistance from nurses" and "new investments in hardware" raise the switching costs.

Porter gives examples like this for all the subforces, through the five main forces. That's all well and good. But what does this have to do with strategy? We give "the bulk of the analytical and strategic attention" to "the nature of competition [in] a particular industry." So we know all about IV kits, but how do we decide whether to go into that sector or not? We know about the sector, but we don't know what to do about it. After analysis, what?

Porter tells us to use our competitive analysis to "cope successfully with the five competitive forces and thereby yield a superior return on investment for the firm." Again, that's fine. But how do you cope? Coping means taking action. After your analysis, how do you decide what action to take in order to beat the competitive forces?

Porter tells us that each firm has a different answer, "reflecting its particular circumstances." That's fine. So the action that I take is different from the action that others take. But that still leaves me with dozens of possibilities. How do I choose which one?

Porter narrows down the choices to three "internally consistent generic strategies" for creating a position that can be defended in the long run to enable the company to outperform the competition: overall cost leadership, differentiation, and focus. These three strategies can be used alone or in combination. Note where these strategies come from: They are "internally consistent." In other words, they are a product of logic. They don't come from the five forces or from empirical evidence on what works.

To get these three generic strategies, you divide all products into two kinds: (1) low-cost or "standard" and (2) high-cost or "unique." And you consider your targeted customers as being either (A) the whole market or (B) a particular market segment. Thus the first generic strategy, overall cost leadership, involves selling low-cost products to the whole market (1A). The second generic strategy, differentiation, involves selling a line of high-cost products to the whole market (2A). And the third generic strategy, focus, involves selling either low-cost products or a line of high-cost products to a particular market segment (1B + 2B).

Porter tells you to choose one of the three generic strategies and stick to it. If you don't, you're "stuck in the middle," which is "an extremely poor strategic situation." You don't have enough "market share, capital investment, and resolve" for "the low-cost game." You're not different enough for the higher-cost market, and you don't have the focus to go after a particular market segment with either low- or high-cost products.

This sounds very logical. But is there evidence to support it?

Like Senge in *The Fifth Discipline*, Porter relies on theory and principles rather than evidence. In *Competitive Strategy*, we find mini-examples, like the IV kits for hospitals and a long paragraph each on Timex and Prelude Corporation. But even these cases serve to illustrate particular points, as the IV story illustrates switching costs, rather than to provide empirical support for Porter's overall method.

So we must look elsewhere to find out whether competitive strategy works.

Does It Work?

In a 1997 research paper, "Competition and Business Strategy in Historical Perspective," Pankaj Ghemawat reviews the literature from the field of industrial organizations, or "IO," on Porter's five forces.[5] Here's what Ghemawat found.

If you break the five forces down into 47 key points, only 6 of those points show positive results. For the other 41, we just don't know. Ghemawat concludes that even though these 41 points do not match IO research, "they reflect the experience of strategy practitioners, including Porter himself."

So Ghemawat tells us that the five forces come not from direct empirical evidence, but from the expert intuition of Porter and others. On the one hand, this fits the art of what works. On the other hand, if you can't point to the evidence, current or past, you're asking others to take it on faith that you're right.

We find more research on competitive strategy in a 2000 article, "What Have We Learned about Generic Competitive Strategy? A Meta-Analysis," by Colin Campbell-Hunt. A meta-analysis is a study of studies. You take research results from many sources and use advanced statistics to see what they say collectively. Campbell-Hunt used 17 studies that were done between 1983 and 1994 and covered more than 6,000 companies around the world.

Campbell-Hunt tells us that the "dominant paradigm of competitive strategy is now nearly two decades old." It fits "Kuhn's account" of a paradigm because it has so penetrated research, theory, and business practice that it has become "the received wisdom" taught in textbooks. And yet there has been little "normal science" about competitive strategy, where you find a "dialogue" between "fact and theory."

In other words, Porter's theory has taken over the field, but we still don't know if it works. So Campbell-Hunt tries his hand at finding out.

The result?[6]

There is no clear evidence here that no-distinctive-emphasis designs are any more or less capable of above-average perform-

ance than other archetypes . . . "stuck-in-the middle" designs may
be superior to strategic specialization.

By "distinctive-emphasis," Campbell-Hunt means that a strategy falls into one of Porter's three categories. By "no-distinctive-
emphasis," he means that it doesn't. Thus, his results show that
Porter's three generic strategies do not produce greater success
than other strategies. Campbell-Hunt concludes:

> These propositions encourage a reconceptualization of the no-
> distinctive-emphasis design, from its current status as the "lemon"
> of competitive strategy, to an "all-rounder" design that is well
> adapted to a specified set of competitive conditions.

But how can that be? It seems so logical that you should concentrate on either high- or low-cost products for either the whole
market or a market segment, rather than spread yourself around.
But Campbell-Hunt's results do not argue against concentration.
Porter picks two elements to concentrate on: product cost and
market segment. But there are many other elements that a firm
could concentrate on. Those other elements might be just as important, or more so.

For example, one such element is product quality. High-quality
products might fit into any of Porter's three generic strategies.
Maybe high quality is the key to successful strategy. Perhaps low
cost of operations is key, whatever your market or product mix.
Most likely, a mix of elements fits your situation. Porter's two elements are important, but so are all the others.

Let's look at a third study of the results of competitive strategy,
this time from Porter himself.

In a 1987 article, "From Competitive Advantage to Corporate
Strategy," Porter reports the diversification record of 33 major
U.S. companies from 1950 to 1986. He calls it "a sobering picture."
The firms were not just stuck in the middle. They went here and
there, all over the place.

We find that each of the 33 companies "entered an average of
80 new industries and 27 new fields." This is a staggering figure.
That's more than two new industries per year for every company.
How did these companies find time to do anything else? Worse,

they made these entries mostly through acquisitions. And the acquisitions failed:[7]

> My data paint a sobering picture of the success ratio of these moves. I found that on average corporations divested more than half their acquisitions in new industries and more than 60% of their acquisitions in entirely new fields.

Note how Porter measures success: retention. If you take on a new company and then get rid of it, that's failure. Porter says that "shareholder value" is not a good indicator because there's no way to compare. You can't know what shareholder value might have been without diversification. And so Porter makes his "own measure of diversification success" by noting how many of the units it developed or acquired the company retained. That's "as good an indicator as any."

On the one hand, this seems like a good guess. Adding units and then dropping them would seem to be bad business. On the other hand, Porter's data can't tell us whether this is true. He can tell us about the adding and dropping, but not about the business results. But let's accept Porter's judgment: He's the scientist who knows this field, and he thinks retention is a good measure. In other words, let's trust his expert intuition.

Note too what Porter leaves out. There's nothing about the five forces or the three generic strategies. In this article, Porter just wants firms to concentrate. He almost doesn't care what they concentrate on.

Once again, he throws in good advice along the way. For example, his data show that a company's own start-ups fare better than acquisitions, like a tree sprouting new branches instead of the trauma of grafting them on:

> When a company has the internal strength to start up a unit, it can be safer and less costly to launch a company than to rely solely on acquisition and then have to deal with the problem of integration.

Start-ups are better than acquisitions: This is a very useful result. But it has nothing to do with competitive strategy's five forces or three generic strategies.

Porter calls his worst offenders "portfolio managers" rather than "strategists" because they treat companies like simple investments that are to be added or dropped rather than made productive. Here he refers to a strategy model by the Boston Consulting Group that tells you to add and drop companies according to how much cash they yield and how mature their market is.[8] In contrast, Porter gives two cases of successful diversification that show a very different path to success.

Porter's first case is Hanson Trust of Great Britain. As a "conglomerate with units in many industries," you might think that it's a classic "portfolio manager" of the type that Porter disdains. But like "one or two other conglomerates," Hanson has a real strategy. It buys up a mature company with "low growth," a "market leader" that has bad management but is "rich in assets." Hanson pays a low price, fixes up the company, and sells it. Then it buys another. Each unit is approached with a modus operandi that has been perfected through repetition. Hanson has become one of the best restructurers.

We don't know how Hanson first hit on its winning formula, but it uses that formula again and again. It is an artist of what works. So even though Hanson adds and drops businesses, its results are very good.

Porter's second case is Marriott.

He picks up the story with Marriott's jump into airline catering. That led to food-service management for institutions, hotels with restaurants, and airport merchandise shops. Porter highlights Marriott's "6,000 standardized recipe cards" and standard hotel procedures that help keep everything on track. He then notes a few ventures in which Marriott failed: gourmet restaurants, where standard menus don't work, and cruise ships and theme parks, where entertainment counts more than efficiency.

From *Built to Last*, we already know about Mr. Marriott's coup d'oeil that kicked off the company's first diversification. From there, it continued to build on success. When it tried something that was too far afield, it failed. Even in Porter's telling, it comes through that Marriott management remained an artist of what works.

Again, these two cases—Hanson and Marriott—show Porter's great insight into what makes for business success. But we find nothing about the five forces or the three generic strategies. So what does competitive strategy offer, beyond Porter's own insights case-by-case?

Competitive Intuition

From Porter's 1987 article, we see that competitive strategy and the art of what works are quite compatible—if we skip the five forces and three generic strategies. Thus, we can return to *Competitive Strategy* for its examples rather than for its theory.

For instance, we learn that "fragmented industries" deprive "centralized production or marketing" of its usual "economies of scale." We even find cases of "diseconomies," where centralization "weakens rather than strengthens the firm." Examples include solar heating, garbage collection, and liquor stores. Yet technology can consolidate an industry; for example, feedlots allow a few big beef growers to gain ground at the expense of small ranchers.

Yet despite all this industry analysis, we still don't have a strategy.

Let's take a closer look at what Porter says about fragmented industries. To "formulate strategy," you follow these steps. First, you identify "the structure of the industry and the positions of competitors." Then you determine why the industry is fragmented. You ask whether the fragmentation can be "overcome," and if so, how. You calculate whether "overcoming fragmentation" will be "profitable," and where to position the firm in order "to do so." And if "fragmentation is inevitable," you find "the best alternative for coping with it."

These are fine steps. They ask good strategic questions, but they don't give you answers. We can analyze the industry forever, but the analysis still doesn't tell us what to do. Porter comes closest to giving answers when he says that fragmentation might "be overcome through innovation or strategic change." That's true. But competitive analysis cannot yield those things. Schumpeter would call that a creative response. It comes from coup d'oeil, not economics.

As Schumpeter noted, economic analysis can always explain a creative response after the fact. You can never use it to explain a creative response before the fact. And strategy calls for a creative response.

Hamel and Prahalad agree. In *Competing for the Future*, they note how "a strategy textbook or marketing handbook" will talk about "competition within extant markets":[9]

> The tools of segmentation analysis, industry structure analysis, and value chain analysis are eminently useful in the context of a clearly defined market, but what help are they when the market doesn't yet exist?

And in *The Innovator's Dilemma*, Clayton Christensen gives cases of new technology creating new markets while industry leaders lost out by concentrating on old markets. Similarly, in *Creative Destruction*, Richard Foster and Sarah Kaplan show that even the most successful companies must find new markets all the time in order to stay on top.[10]

We can again trace these insights—from Hamel and Prahalad, Christensen, and Foster and Kaplan—back to Schumpeter. To the articles we cited earlier, we add Schumpeter's essay "The Process of Creative Destruction."[11] For economists, new products and new markets make all the difference. Without them, profits over time tend to zero. With them, you get a "price premium," at least until your competitors catch on and then catch up. Then profits tend to zero again until the next innovation.

And as we have seen time and again, successful innovations come from what works.

This takes us back to our original problem of strategy. Thanks to imperfect information, you can't predict the future. Porter tries to cut through the fog of business with economic research and analysis. In *Strategic Leadership*, Finkelstein and Hambrick credit Porter's success to a "yearning of strategy scholars to demonstrate that their domain was as analytically rigorous as any other."[12] The "movement toward relatively quantifiable and concisely modeled conceptions of strategy" left "the fuzziness and multi-dimensional nature of executive behavior" to other fields of study.

But those extra dimensions and fuzziness are part of the fog of strategy. They are just as important as the numbers. Finkelstein and

Hambrick review dozens of studies of what executives actually do, and find different combinations of analysis and other factors. They see four kinds of executives: Visionaries, Coaches, Administrators, and Strategists. The Administrator comes closest to competitive analysis, while the Strategist comes closer to the art of what works.

Their Administrator is a "Sensation Thinker," while the Strategist is an "Intuition Thinker." "Sensation" means that you take in all the data you find, whereas "intuition" means that you select among what you find. The Administrator tends to be fact-oriented, impersonal, practical, and orderly, while the Strategist is possibilities-oriented, impersonal, ingenious, and integrative. Administrators rely on verifiable data, whereas Strategists "pursue more radical, innovative strategies."

So the Administrator uses competitive strategy for analysis, and the Strategist uses intuition for action.

But can you combine competitive strategy and expert intuition? Or must you choose between Administrators and Strategists? We're back to the question of two modes of thought, two sides of the brain, analysis versus intuition. And once again we answer that expert intuition draws on both.

Grounded Research

Remember the problem that Porter set out to solve: "Economic research has not addressed itself to the concerns of business managers." Competitive strategy offers one solution: the five forces of industry analysis. But analysis does not equal strategy. Can we use the five forces in a different way, to feed expert intuition?

Let's look for guidance in a classic research method. *The Discovery of Grounded Theory*, by Barney Glaser and Anselm Strauss, grew out of "an embarrassing gap between theory and empirical research."[13] Social scientists tried to close the gap by "testing theory" with empirical research. But that's backwards: Where did the theory come from in the first place? So "grounded theory" means that you conduct your empirical research first. That's how you find your theory.[14]

Glaser and Strauss were sociologists, but their work applies to all "social phenomena—political, educational, economic, industrial, or whatever":

> Our basic position is that generating grounded theory is a way
> of arriving at theory suited to its supposed uses. We shall con-
> trast this position with theory generated by logical deduction
> from *a priori* assumptions.

This sounds like von Clausewitz, who counsels you to leave
your theories behind as you step onto the battlefield. Or like
William James, who walks the corridor of pragmatism and
reaches into different rooms for different theories as needed. And
some of our key sources used grounded research, especially Klein,
Bhidé, and Collins and Porras. That is, they found their results
and then looked for theories to explain them.

We remember how Nokia "discovered" the theory of segmentation by seeing segmentation happen before their eyes. And we
wonder how Ray Kroc could have found McDonald's by applying
any theory at all.

Like many theories in economics, competitive strategy was
"generated by logical deduction from *a priori* assumptions," as
Porter tells us. To apply it, you use vast quantities of data. But a
study of data is not where the theory came from in the first place.
Grounded theories, in contrast, "take hard study of much data" in
order to generate theory.

So how does grounded theory work?

Basically, you study everything— statistics, interviews, records
of all kinds. You analyze the data one way, then another, and then
you go back for more data. Over time, your grounded theory
emerges from the data. After all, "the root source" of any good
theory is "the sensitive insights of the observer himself." And
where do those insights come from? Anywhere, anytime, anyhow.
In the shower or on the treadmill. At home, at work, or at play.[15]

This is the "Aha!" moment that Pietersen describes. Yet Glaser
and Strauss do not quite show us coup d'oeil. For them, the insights "can be derived directly from theory," can "occur without
theory," or "may appear just as fruitfully near the end of a long
inquiry as near the outset." We don't learn the precise mechanism
of how an insight happens, like the combination of past achievements in expert intuition.

But Glaser and Strauss do say that theory follows insight, like
Kuhn, von Clausewitz, and James. You "transform insights into

relevant categories, properties, and hypotheses," using "all the usual strategies for developing theory." So Glaser and Strauss are not antitheory. They just put it in the right order.

Grounded theory shines a new light on Porter's work. We can look at his insights separate from his theory. He has done so much industry analysis that we need to do less ourselves. Therefore, we can treat his work as part of our research. His insights spark our insights, to help us discover our strategy.

For example, in *Competitive Advantage* we learn that Crown Cork and Seal combines cans and "highly responsive service" for "select customer industries." Its R&D department does little product research, but instead aims "to solve specific customer problems on a timely basis, and to imitate successful product innovations rapidly."

So if you're working on R&D, keep Crown in mind. You might want to copy what it does, or at least some part of it. That's not quite five forces or three generic strategies, but it's useful all the same.

In another example from *Competitive Advantage*, we learn that a substitute may not just take share from competitors, but can also "raise or lower overall industry demand." Radial tires not only replaced bias-ply tires but also cut the market for new tires because they last so long. Sony's popular Walkman took share from plain cassette players but "surely expanded the market for cassette players at the same time."

So if you have a substitute, it might raise or lower industry demand. Study radial tires and the Walkman to see which case it resembles more.

In a third example, from *Cases in Competitive Strategy*, we learn that Hospital Affiliates International (HAI) set out to buy or build hospitals with the intention of running them. Then Tulane University made a study of its new teaching hospital. It found that similar hospitals elsewhere "suffered an average operating loss of $2 million per year." Tulane looked for a professional management contract instead, to keep costs down. HAI won the bid. An HAI executive reports:

> Tulane was the first nationally known hospital affiliated with a medical school to use an outside management company. The

industry awareness HAI gained by this is what established our reputation in the contract business.

HAI shifted its goals. Over the next 4 years, it "added about nine new hospital management contracts per year," and even stopped building its own hospitals for a while. So if you're a start-up, look for opportunities to sell your services instead of owning everything yourself. You might want to emulate HAI.

In another example from *Competitive Strategy*, we learn that you can afford to outbid competitors on an acquisition if you have "distinctive assets or skills" that will improve your future returns. Other bidders drop out of the bidding. You pay more, but you make more from the purchase than they could. That's how Campbell's acquired Vlasic and Gould acquired ITE.

So if you're bidding for a company that suits your skills, study Vlasic and ITE to see at what point other bidders dropped out. In the high pressure of bidding, it helps to have some sort of guide from past experience, even if it's not your own.

These are just four examples among hundreds. As you read Porter's work, you get a guided tour through a vast terrain of corporate strategy. Carry a sack. Along the way he tosses off precious nuggets that can serve you well in the future. You just don't know exactly when, or where, or how. It's a form of grounded research. Take everything in, to feed your expert intuition.

These competitive sources do not replace competitive forces. Porter's original insight was right: Planning needs economic research. It's vital that you study your current competitors, new entrants, substitutes, your suppliers, and your buyers. But you don't really know who they all are until you have your coup d'oeil. For example, Marriott thought that his competition was other restaurants until he saw an airline catering business. After that, his competition was existing caterers, who knew more about catering than he did.

Grounded research tells us to start with a wide search of all kinds of data. Then comes insight. It tells you when to narrow your search and how, and where to look next. Competitive analysis is one method among many that can be used for the wide and narrow search. Use that plus others, until you see what to do.

Five Sources

Let's use the methods of grounded research to combine expert intuition and Porter's industry analysis.

We look at Porter's five forces: suppliers, buyers, competitors, potential entrants, and substitutes. But we ask a different question: Is anyone doing something with unusual success that we should think about trying ourselves? We can look outside our industry, too, but the first place to look is within it, as Porter advises.

Our question does not replace any of Porter's. It just adds one more. And the one it adds is a big one, because it makes Porter's five forces become five sources as well, in the ceaseless search for what works.

In this new light, let's take another look at the five.

With suppliers and buyers, we might want to outsource or take over more of our own value chain if we see something that works in supply or distribution. Or we might want to reward the successful suppliers and buyers with more of our business or advise our other suppliers and buyers to do what their successful competitors do, and so drive our costs down across the board.

With potential entrants and substitutes, you're looking for elements to imitate directly. Sometimes such elements are hard to see. At first a new entrant has a tiny share of the market, so you might overlook it. And substitutes have no clear boundaries. For example, Southwest Airlines became the fourth largest U.S. airline by competing with the automobile on trips of under 500 miles. Yet a recent study by Icon Group "benchmarked" Southwest's practices only against those of other airlines. That's not Southwest's biggest competitor.[16]

Current competitors are easier to study to find what works. But even here, the way is not always clear. We find a poignant case in the accounting scandals of 2002.

After WorldCom joined the list of wrongdoers, the *New York Times* reported that 3 years before, in 1999, "AT&T replaced the chief of its huge business services division, Michael G. Keith, after barely nine months on the job." At the time, it seemed like a routine case of underperformance. But now, 3 years later, the *Times* reported that Keith had lost his job "because his division could not match the reported profit margins of its biggest competitor, WorldCom."[17]

AT&T broke into three companies in 2000 at least partly because it could not compete with WorldCom. AT&T studied WorldCom's public data to figure out the secret of its success, to no avail. By the art of five sources, AT&T did the right thing: It looked for the secret of WorldCom's success. When it did not find that secret, Wall Street punished it with a lower stock price.

When the secret came out—false accounting—it was too late for Michael Keith. His expert intuition had told him that something was wrong, but at the time no one would listen. An AT&T "insider" recalled that Keith had been judged not on the basis of AT&T margins, but on the basis of WorldCom margins. Keith argued that achieving those margins wasn't possible, but that didn't solve the problem as AT&T saw it, and he was moved out.

Competitive Insight

Competitive strategy dates from the 1980s. In the 1990s, Porter made one more major statement about it, in a 1996 article, "What Is Strategy?" Let's see what he says a decade later about his own ideas.

First, he tells us that "today's dynamic markets and changing technologies" are making businesses question his advice. The "new dogma" says that "rivals can quickly copy any market position," so any position is "at best, temporary." Porter calls these views "dangerous half-truths." Yes, firms copy one another. But they don't copy strategy. They copy "operational effectiveness," which gives you "productivity, quality, and speed," but not a competitive strategy.

The more firms adopt "total quality management, benchmarking, time-based competition, outsourcing, partnering, reengineering, change management," or other operational tools, the more they "look alike." So they lose their competitive advantage.

Porter argues that "competitive strategy is about being different. It means deliberately choosing a different set of activities to deliver a unique mix of value."

So even though everything is changing fast, you have to choose a unique strategy that sets you apart, and stick to it. That's Porter's advice in the fast-paced 1990s. But once again we ask, where does that strategy come from?

For the first time, Porter favors insight over analysis:[18]

> Strategic competition can be thought of as the process of perceiving new positions that woo customers from established positions or draw new customers into the market. . . . Strategic positionings are often not obvious, and finding them requires creativity and insight.

Here Porter responds to the likes of Schumpeter, Hamel and Prahalad, Christensen, and Foster and Kaplan, who cite innovation as the source of business success. Porter seems to agree. Successful strategy comes from perceiving something new, not just from analyzing the five forces of your industry. Porter even notes an "entrepreneurial edge," by which new entrants "discover unique positions" that are not new but have been "simply overlooked" by previous firms in the sector.

Bit by bit, we find ourselves wandering away from analysis and closing in on coup d'oeil.

Porter's "entrepreneurial edge" seems to favor new entrants, who "can be more flexible because they face no trade-offs with their existing activities." Thus, they can respond faster to new "customer groups," new "distribution channels," new "technologies" or "information systems." On the other hand, "incumbents" have a hidden advantage: what's already working.

Here Porter directly endorses the art of what works. He tells us that "most companies owe their initial success to a unique strategic position." Everything they do fits together. But thanks to the "passage of time" and the "pressures of growth," they stray. A "succession of incremental changes" makes them lose their focus. Worse, they come to look more and more like their rivals. So they lose their competitive difference. But all is not lost:

> A number of approaches can help a company reconnect with strategy. The first is a careful look at what it already does.

So to find your focus again, you don't do more industry analysis; rather, you study your own activities. What worked before might work again.

But how exactly do you do this? Well, "most well-established companies" have "a core of uniqueness." To find that core, Porter asks which of your products or services is the most "distinctive" or "profitable"; which of your customers are most "satisfied"; which "customers, channels or purchase occasions are the most profitable"; and which of your value-chain activities are most "different" and "effective."

In these questions, we get "uniqueness" twice, as "distinctive" and "different." That comes from Porter's original idea of competitive strategy. But we get something else as well. In these questions, we find "profitable" twice, and we also find "satisfied" and "effective." In other words: what worked.

There's more.

Porter tells us to study a company's history, too. Go back to the "vision of the founder" and the "products and customers that made the company." Maybe you can implement the "historical positioning" in a "modern way" that is "consistent with today's technologies and practices":

> This sort of thinking may lead to a commitment to renew the strategy and may challenge the organization to recover its distinctiveness. Such a challenge can be galvanizing and can instill the confidence to make the needed trade-offs.

This sounds exactly like coup d'oeil and resolution. You see what worked in the past, and you see a way to draw on it into the future. That has a "galvanizing" effect, giving you the "commitment" and "confidence" to do what needs to be done.

So in the end, after all these years, competitive strategy and the art of what works are not so far apart.[19]

Expert Analysis

This chapter has looked at Porter's work because competitive strategy continues to reign as the leading method of economic analysis for business strategy. Yet expert intuition applies to other methods of strategic analysis as well. Whatever your assessment of your firm's environment, of the future it faces, or of the trends in your industry and among your competitors, you need expert intuition to give you a strategy. Analysis can thin the fog of business, but only coup d'oeil cuts through it.

Porter's work is a fitting end to our review of different schools of strategy and what expert intuition adds to them. Porter offers tools and techniques for competitive analysis, and in the next chapters we offer tools and techniques for the art of what works. Many of these methods include analysis, but they always involve asking our key question first: what works? That's what experts do. And that's what makes success.

PART III

The Application of Expert Intuition

CHAPTER
7

Arrows in the Quiver
Tools and Techniques

THE PREVIOUS CHAPTERS looked at three leading schools of strategy and what expert intuition adds to them. In this chapter, we take a closer look at some of the key tools and techniques from those schools, so that we can add expert intuition to them in practice. We also study some tools and techniques that spring directly from the art of what works.

These methods can be seen as a toolbox, a menu to choose from, or a quiver of arrows that you carry on your back. You never know which ones you will need until the situation arises. A traditional step-by-step approach, where you do first this, then that, then a third thing, doesn't work. In strategy, everyone starts from a different position, in a different situation. You can't predict the steps you need to take, in what order, or over what period of time.

Or you can think of these tools and techniques as being like the elements of the 83 campaigns of the 7 great captains that Napoleon studied. He could not predict which ones he would need to draw on, in what combination, in what situation. So, like Napoleon, you gather as many tools and techniques as possible.

When the moment comes, coup d'oeil gives you the signal. You reach back into your quiver, pull out the arrow you need, and let it fly.

Brainstorming

In recent decades, strategic planning has spread down through the Saqqara pyramid, and now all departments have to do it.

But how?

That's easy. The department gets together and brainstorms.

In emergent strategy, you do the same thing, except that you do it over and over again, whenever your strategy changes.

In the learning organization, you brainstorm spontaneously, in small or large groups that cut across departments.

Even in competitive strategy you find a common technique in which a team does all the research it needs, then goes into a room and brainstorms. That's how you arrive at a strategy.

So now we ask, what is "brainstorming"?

The dictionary defines it as "a group problem-solving technique that involves the spontaneous contribution of ideas from all members of the group." The word entered the English language in 1953 thanks to the first book on brainstorming, *Applied Imagination,* by Alex Osborn.[1]

Osborn was a founder of the great advertising firm BBDO (his name gave it the O). In 1938, BBDO almost went out of business, thanks to the Great Depression. Osborn came up with brainstorming as a way to get more ideas, fast. He won a major account, B. F. Goodrich. That saved BBDO and gave brainstorming its first official success. Thanks to Osborn's book, brainstorming spread beyond advertising to organizations of all kinds.[2]

Osborn tells us that science supports his method. The University of Buffalo taught a course in brainstorming, and two professors there studied 330 students over 14 months. Osborn reports that this "scientific test" showed that subjects who took the course produced 94 percent more "good ideas" than subjects who did not take the course.[3]

But again we ask: What is a good idea?

Osborn tells us: "The ideas which the researchers scored as 'good' were those which were potentially useful and relatively unique."

If we go back to the study Osborn cites, we find that it asked the students to "list all possible uses for a wire coat hanger." A "good" score had two dimensions:

1. *uniqueness*—degree to which the response departed from the hanger's conventional use
2. *value*—the degree to which the response was judged to have social, economic, aesthetic, or other usefulness.

We can see right away that the value score depends on who is judging. Nobody tried to implement the ideas that came up during the study, so we have no empirical test of whether they worked or not. Instead, you use your judgment and I use mine to decide what we think is "useful." Most likely, the scorers use expert intuition: They think an idea is useful because it resembles something else that's useful. But from the study, we just don't know whether the judges were right. So the value score is not very scientific.

That leaves us with uniqueness, and here Osborn shines. The results are "beyond question":[4]

> One group produced 45 suggestions for a home-appliance promotion, 56 ideas for a money-raising campaign, 124 ideas on how to sell more blankets. In another case, groups brainstormed one and the same problem and produced over 800 ideas.

This is what Osborn was really after: lots of different ideas. Nothing less and nothing more, as Osborn himself insists:

> In the early 1950s, brainstorming became too popular too fast, with the result that it was frequently misused. Too many people jumped at it as a panacea, then turned against it when no miracles resulted.

The mistake that people made was to believe that group brainstorming was "a complete problem-solving process." Instead, for Osborn, it's "only one of several phases of idea-finding," which in turn "is only one of the several phases of creative problem-solving."

So Osborn thinks that finding good ideas is only one step in solving a problem. First, you come up with as many ideas as possible. Second, "to record the ideas a secretary should be appointed. No idea is identified by the name of its suggestor." Third, the same group or a different group screens the ideas and selects the most promising ones.

This third step separates brainstorming from the art of what works. In brainstorming, an idea wins out because a group of people like it better than other ideas. In the art of what works, an idea wins out because it combines elements of past achievements in similar situations.

And we saw earlier that insights arise at unpredictable moments. You can't force them in group settings, around a table in a conference room. At times, Osborn seems to agree. He cites two scientists who found their solutions somewhere else:

> Said Darwin in his autobiography, "I can remember the very spot in the road, whilst in my carriage, when to my joy the solution occurred to me." Hamilton, describing his discovery of quarternions, reported that his basic solution came to him as he "was walking with Lady Hamilton to Dublin, and came up to Brougham Bridge."

So what good is brainstorming in a group? If it's not the best way to spark good ideas, and it doesn't select them on solid grounds, why do it at all?

There's one clear benefit to brainstorming: deferment of judgment.[5] Osborn tells the group to come up with a maximum number of ideas before starting to sort the good ones from the bad. Instead of judging, Osborn advises each person in the group to "suggest how ideas of others can be turned into better ideas" or how to join "two or more ideas" into "still another idea." He especially likes joining ideas, because "most new ideas are combinations of old ideas."

Yet in the end, Osborn stops short of endorsing the art of what works. He does not define a good idea as one that is based on something that worked before. You can build on and combine ideas from many sources, but that's still not the same as developing new combinations of past achievements.

Yet brainstorming and the art of what works can go very well together. Tossing ideas back and forth without judgment is a worthy source of coup d'oeil. It can spark your expert intuition. You hear something and say, "You know, that reminds me . . . ." Instead of trying to make the idea better or judging it later, the other members of the group should draw you out. They should ask: Where did the idea come from? What made you think of it? Does it come from something that worked in the past?

Still, you can't expect coup d'oeil to happen in a group. It's more likely that the brainstorming stimulates your mind. It helps you to see the problem from the different angles of everyone else in the group. Then later, as you work on the problem—as you study the numbers, talk to other people, or walk with Lady Hamilton up to Brougham Bridge—the answer strikes.

To brainstorm what works:

- Discuss a problem from all angles with one or more other people.
- Defer judgment—take the time to draw one another out.
- Ask one another what past achievement might have provoked the idea.
- Have several sessions with the same group spread out over time.
- Between sessions, research the problem, discuss it with others, and engage in lone musing on it.
- If possible, include in the group whoever has to approve the result.

Is It SMART?

In many settings, brainstorming has evolved into participatory strategic planning. Using the technique Osborn describes, the group throws out and selects ideas for a mission, goals, and activities. But we still have the same problem: How do we decide what's a good mission, or goal, or activity? Just because the group likes it doesn't mean that it can work.

But often we find a way to check on the goals that the group selects. You ask if they are "SMART," meaning specific, measurable, achievable, realistic, and time-bound. A search of sources reveals no origin for SMART—it seems to be a popular tool that has evolved in recent decades without a single author.

For the art of what works, "achievable" and "realistic" stand out within SMART. In a coup d'oeil, you see a battle that you can win and a course of action that you can follow to win it. Therefore, that course of action is achievable and realistic.

In most cases, however, the group asks the question in the wrong place. In participatory strategic planning, the mission comes first, then the goals, and only then do you check whether the goals are SMART. To do that, you need to know the activities. If the activities needed to reach the goal can succeed, then the goal is achievable and realistic. But usually the question of whether the goals are SMART comes before the determination of the activities.

And how do we know whether goals are attainable and realistic? In the art of what works, we see whether anyone has achieved anything similar in similar situations. In strategic planning, we get no guidance at all.

To use SMART goals in the art of what works:

- Start with activities: What course of action would lead to success?
- What makes you think so? (Are the activities based on past achievement?)
- Are the activities possible? Do you see a way to carry them out?
- What specific goals would the activities reach, over what time period?
- How will you know when you reach the goals? What measures will you track?

SWOT

SWOT is another popular tool from participatory strategic planning: internal strengths and weaknesses, plus external opportunities and threats. You lead the group through this exercise before you move on to your mission and goals.

We recognize in strengths and opportunities a chance to look for what works. However, we have to alter the questions a bit. Instead of asking, "What are our strengths?" you ask, "Are we doing anything well that we can build on for greater success?" And instead of asking, "What opportunities does the environment offer us?" you ask, "Is anyone else doing something well that we can adapt for our own success?"

For the most part, SWOT results seldom carry over into strategic planning. That is, your goals and activities don't come out of SWOT—they come out of your mission. In the art of what works, SWOT results lead straight to your course of action. From that come your goals and your mission.

To use SWOT in the art of what works:

- For strengths, ask what you're doing right that you can do more of.
- For opportunities, ask what others are doing that you might adapt.
- Carry the SWOT results into planning, as the course of action you start with.

Creative Stimulation

Some companies try to foster strategic innovation by using a variety of methods aimed at stimulating creativity among employees. These methods include a special room with beanbag chairs, toys, and balloons; training sessions where you solve puzzles with ropes, juggle numbers, or mix words at random; or group exercises where you put on a play, compose songs, or invent dances.

Do these methods work?

For the most part, we don't know. It's very hard to measure the results, and seldom does anyone try. These methods come from the belief that creativity is something novel, rather than a combination of things that worked in the past. You can measure novelty, and researchers do. But measuring success is something else.

Perhaps the leading scholar of creative stimulation in business is Teresa Amabile. In her research, Amabile reports on a study of 13 similar tests given to a total of 772 subjects of all ages. Everyone made collages. The researchers told some of the subjects, but not others, that judges would evaluate their work for how creative it is.[6]

Amabile reports the result: "Evaluation expectation" has a "negative effect" on creativity. That is, you dampen creativity just by telling the subjects that someone will judge their work. That means that even if you give people a high mark in the end, you "may undermine future creative performance" before you even start.

So the lesson is: Don't judge creative work. It reduces creativity.

Amabile followed up her collage tests with a study of 129 scientists engaged in research and development at several different companies. Interviewers asked the scientists "to describe in detail two significant events from their work experience: one that exemplified high creativity, and one that exemplified low creativity." In their answers, the scientists emphasized "the work environments . . . regardless of whether the story described high or low creativity."

This led Amabile to study the work environment in more detail. She developed a "78-item questionnaire" to assess the "Climate for Creativity." It "asks employees to rate their perceptions of their current work environment," scored "according to 10 scales" based on the collage and interview studies. Then Amabile used the questionnaire along with "independent assessments of project creativity." Sure enough, creative environments produced creative projects.

Amabile concludes: "Much can be done to enhance and maintain creativity by establishing stimulating, supportive, and positively challenging environments."

What does this have to do with what works?

On the one hand, Amabile's 78 items serve as a good checklist for managers. For example: "People are encouraged to solve problems creatively in this organization," and "There is free and open communication within my work group." If your environment scores low on these items, you should fix it.

On the other hand, we still don't know whether creative environments and creative projects lead to successful strategy. Imagination, von Clausewitz's erratic goddess, gives you what's new, not what works. The closest we come to achievement in Amabile's checklist is 6 items on "Productivity," such as: "My area of this organization is effective." But this is hardly a measure of success. And the 72 other items on Amabile's checklist don't deal with effectiveness at all.

This does not diminish the value of Amabile's work. She successfully measured how environments affect creativity. She did not set out to measure how environments affect success. But no one else has done so either. At this point, no one knows the answer. Perhaps in the future, someone will figure it out.

As for specific techniques to stimulate creativity, Edward de Bono stands out. We have no evidence that de Bono's techniques lead to success, but he has made them very popular.

In *Lateral Thinking, Six Thinking Hats*, and *Serious Creativity*, de Bono offers "lateral" thinking as an alternative to "linear" logic.[7] His favorite stimulus for lateral thinking is the method of "six thinking hats." Alone or in a group, you pretend to put on different hats in order to see the same problem from six different angles. You can use the hats in any order, but de Bono gives a suggestion.[8]

First comes the white hat. That's your "information base." It asks, "What do we know?"

The green hat comes second. That gives you "alternatives, suggestions, and ideas."

Third, the yellow hat judges the "feasibility, benefits, and values of the ideas."

Fourth, the black hat points out the "difficulties, dangers, problems, and points for caution."

Fifth, the red hat gives you "intuition and feelings about the ideas."

Sixth, the blue hat draws conclusions for action.

In these six hats, we find intuition in the red one. De Bono describes intuition as "a composite judgment based on years of experience in the field." It can be "very valuable," even if you can't spell out "consciously" the "reasons behind the intuition."

So on the one hand, de Bono believes in expert intuition. On the other hand, it comes in the wrong place.

Let's go through the hats again.

The white hat of information comes first. That's fine.

De Bono puts the green hat second, to provide "creative thinking" and "new ideas." Then the third (yellow) and fourth (black) hats evaluate those ideas. The red hat of intuition comes fifth, to react to those ideas, after their evaluation by the yellow and black hats. That's far too late for the red hat to matter.

However, all the elements are there. We can just reorder de Bono's hats to yield the art of what works. Here's how: The red hat of intuition comes second, after the white hat of information. Then come the others.

The same is true for most methods of creative thinking: You can usually find a way to adjust them to allow for expert intuition.

Let's take another example, from *Creative Problem Solving* by Arthur VanGundy.[9]

Here we find the group technique of "successive integration of problem elements." You take a problem and ask each member of the group to write down in silence ideas to solve it. Then you read the ideas aloud, but in a special sequence.

First, two members of the group each pick one idea that they wrote down and read it aloud. Second, the whole group chimes in to combine the two ideas into one idea. Third, someone else reads out one idea. Fourth, the whole group chimes in again, to combine its combined idea with this new one. Fifth, someone else reads out one idea.

And so on through the whole group. The result is one idea, based on the ideas of everyone in the group. If at the end you're not satisfied with the final idea, you use it to start again. That is, everyone writes down one idea to add to that idea. Repeat as needed. You keep going "until a workable solution is found or time expires."

So that is "successive integration of problem elements." How can we add expert intuition?

At each step, you ask what past experience the idea or combination of ideas might come from. A successful strategy is a course of action, not a single decision, so this sequential method might offer a way to put several activities together. In a series of coups d'oeil, you assemble a strategy.

To use creative stimulation in the art of what works:

- Researchers know what environments stimulate creativity.
- Researchers don't know what environments stimulate success.
- You can add expert intuition to methods of creative thinking.

Bootstrapping

Expert intuition is not the opposite of analysis. It uses a certain kind of analysis, based on the rapid recognition of familiar patterns. In his study of chess masters, Herbert Simon converted their moves into complex computer programs that captured their expert intuition. More recently, IBM developed a computer program that beat Garry Kasparov, the reigning world champion, in 1997, after losing in 1989 and 1996.

But chess is easy. You know all the rules and all the possible moves. In business, every important decision has unforeseen angles and implications. How well do computers do in business intuition?

In a 1993 article, "A Pyramid of Decision Approaches," Paul Schoemaker and J. Edward Russo present methods of capturing expert intuition on a computer.[10] Sure enough, they begin with a quote by our own expert strategist, Napoleon:

> Nothing is more difficult, and therefore more precious, than to be able to decide.

Schoemaker and Russo note that "most managers still make decisions based on intuition." They may use computers to gather and display information and to automate "routine decisions" like "credit applications and credit ordering," but most managers don't use technology or even any formal method for most of their decisions. The answer is not to replace intuition with computer programs—you can't. Instead, Schoemaker and Russo suggest basing computer programs on the modern science of expert intuition.

They highlight three methods for doing this: rules, bootstrapping, and value analysis.

For rules, you just ask managers what the rules are. For example, they might say that they grant a loan if the borrower "has no record of payment defaults," has debt less than "50% of current income," has not moved or changed jobs in "at least a year," and has a job as "at least a skilled laborer." Given these rules, it's easy for a computer program to accept or reject applications.

But this method has a key weakness: It reflects what managers say they do, not what they actually do. Typically, good managers make exceptions all the time. They accept loans that violate these rules, and they reject loans that fit the rules but fail some other rule of thumb that they use without really knowing that they use it.

Bootstrapping tries to capture what good managers really do. You study the decisions they make, write a computer program to do the same thing, and then hand it back to the managers. Research shows that managers do better with such a program than without it. They pulled themselves up by their own "bootstraps."[11]

Schoemaker and Russo offer a real-live case. A "gifted claims handler" had "an excellent nose for sniffing out fraudulent cases." It was a clear case of expert intuition: "She had that rare ability to make good intuitive decisions—decisions based on 'automated expertise.'" Before she retired, her company wanted to find out how she did it, so that others could learn it too. But, of course, she didn't know:

> All she could say was that she looked at such factors as lack of adequate support data, valuable property that did not fit the insured's income level, evasiveness in the police report, financial difficulty such as loss of a job, personal problems like divorce, and frequent or suspicious past claims.

But how did she weigh all these factors and combine them with the more ordinary data on debt, employment, and income? To find out, the company turned to bootstrapping. They took "a wide cross section of applications" and asked the expert to rate them for "fraud potential." Then they took her results and plotted them out across the various factors she listed. That gave the weights she used. For example, the data might show that she counted an evasive police report twice as much as divorce. It was not something she knew she did. She just did it.

Bootstrapping is quite a compliment to experts: It enshrines what they do. But very often, experts don't like it.

On this score, Schoemaker and Russo give the example of Harris Investment Management. It used a bootstrapping program for investment strategy that gave analysts and portfolio experts the power to override it. The program "improved the company's bottom-line results." Even so, "several intuitive experts left the bank because they perceived their role as having been 'diminished' by the new process."

Schoemaker and Russo's third method of computerizing expertise is value analysis. It applies complex rules to complex decisions by asking what decision makers want, or "value," and what characteristics they think they should look at.

For example, "a large oil and gas multinational" used value analysis to make "an important strategic investment decision": Where should it build "a $500 million pilot plant"? The company considered more than 10 countries, each of which had "dozens of advantages and disadvantages." Senior executives and technical experts first laid out the criteria they thought were important, then rated each country on how well it met those criteria. Thanks to a "complete, careful, and generally honest" analysis, the company agreed on the rankings quickly and picked the country that "came out on top."

As we see from this example, value analysis does not draw on the actual results of experts; instead, it draws on their judgments. For this reason, it is weaker than bootstrapping. But value analysis has the added advantage of drawing in some way on all the experts involved through a method that seems fair to all. It is no small achievement that the company came to a quick decision on such a complex question. We imagine everyone pitching in after the decision in order to make it work, rather than second-guessing a decision made by someone else.

Among the three methods, Schoemaker and Russo note that rules get weak results, while value analysis costs a lot in time and money. So bootstrapping wins. They expect it to "become more common" in future years.

We find a recent example far afield, in a business that is famous for its high-paid experts: major league baseball. Everyone knows that money buys the best players, who win more games. But in a *New Yorker* article, "The Buffett of Baseball," James Surowiecki tells about Billy Beane, the general manager of the Oakland A's.[12] Over the past few years, the A's have rivaled the New York Yankees as baseball's best team. But Beane does it on a third of the Yankees' payroll. He just doesn't have the money.

How does Beane do it?

Bootstrapping.

Surowiecki tells us that most baseball managers pick players on the basis of "talent, character, and the chemistry of winning teams." Beane uses numbers. In recent decades, "scientific research" on baseball statistics has shown what kinds of players, in what kind of mix, win the most games. The "Copernicus of this revolution" was Earnshaw Cook, a mechanical engineer who loved baseball. In the 1960s, Cook wrote *Percentage Baseball* to explain what accounts for winning games.[13] Since then, some baseball managers have used some of Cook's methods, but Beane is the first one "to build his organization around it."

For example, data show that walks and home runs both win games. So, "Beane has stocked his team with sluggers who take walks." Other sluggers on other teams might hit more home runs (and so get higher salaries), but they also strike out more, and so take fewer walks. Therefore, Beane saves money and still wins more games. On the other hand, sacrifice bunts and stolen bases are very exciting, but they don't win games. So the A's have fewer of each than any other team in baseball.

Beane shows that bootstrapping helps wherever data can show you what works. You then trace backward to come up with guidelines to help you decide what to do. It's a form of grounded theory in action, and a direct application of expert intuition.

To use bootstrapping for the art of what works:

- List what experts think makes for successful decisions.
- Study the data on successful decisions.
- Analyze the data, using the experts' list, to see which elements matter most, in what combination.
- Write a computer program that applies the winning combinations.
- Use the program to help you make decisions, not to make decisions itself—sometimes you must override it.
- Integrate the program into your operations as much as possible, rather than treating it as a separate operation.
- Keep track of results to improve the program.

Normal Science

In recent decades, there have appeared a number of "problem-solving" models to help groups make decisions. Figure 7.1 presents one of the most popular. Xerox used variations on this model to help revive its fortunes in the 1980s.[14] Since then, various versions have spread to many other companies as well.

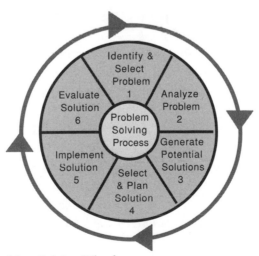

Figure 7.1 Problem-Solving Wheel

This model has two key advantages. First, it includes evaluation, so you are checking to see how well your solution worked. Second, when the evaluation turns up more problems, you start the cycle again. Thus, the model promotes continuous improvement.

For the art of what works, the model has one key weakness. Step 3 is "Generate Potential Solutions"—but how do you do that? The model doesn't say.

Step 2, "Analyze Problem," can't help. Analysis breaks down a problem. It doesn't give a solution. We can add expert intuition and propose solutions based on what worked in similar situations elsewhere. But Step 3 is too late in the process: In the two steps we've already been through, we've identified, selected, and analyzed the problem. But we can't know whether we've picked a problem that we have a chance to solve. So expert intuition should come at the start, in Step 1.

Rather than changing the model, let's look for another. But where? In *The Structure of Scientific Revolutions*, Kuhn showed how scientists solve problems first of all by building on the achievements of the scientists who came before them.[15] That's the essence of "normal science." Does it offer a model for problem solving in general?

We see a picture of normal science in a recent article in *Technology Review* about gene research and development at Maxygen, a biotechnology company.[16] Here's how the research starts: "Pick several versions of the gene of interest." That means that either you or some other scientists isolated and identified the gene in the past. Whoever did so thought the gene was enough "of interest" for this to be worth doing. Now you think it has enough interest to work on it further.

That interest comes from expert intuition. You see something in the gene that might make a useful product. A lab and a research budget give you the opportunity to try it. Next, you "recombine" the genes. The new combinations use different proteins. Now you use your expert intuition again: "Selected genes go on for commercial development or back into the cycle for further refinement."

Figure 7.2 shows a more general version of the process used at Maxygen. Note that there are four main arrows, just as in the

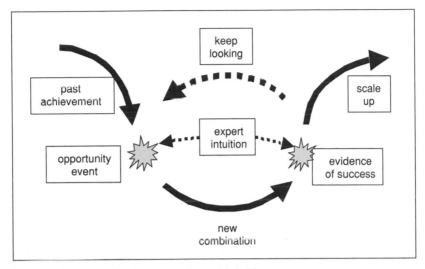

Figure 7.2 Normal Science and Expert Intuition

problem-solving wheel. But here the arrows show forward motion, not a wheel spinning in place. And expert intuition has a central role in identifying the problem and finding a solution.

To use normal science in the art of what works:

- Scan past achievements for problems that you might be able to solve.
- Try out what seems to be the best combination of past achievements.
- See if it works.
- If it doesn't work, try a new combination.
- If it works, take it to scale.

What-Works Scan

Scientists can scan the past achievements of other scientists through hundreds of printed journals that report those achievements. There is no such system for business.[17] The stock market and other public measures track company performance, but you can't trace the results to any particular action that the company took. Achievement equals action plus positive result. If you know the positive result, but you don't know what action led to it, you can't pin down the achievement.

In earlier chapters we saw examples of companies, such as Chevron and General Electric, that set out to document their achievements in order to draw on them later. To use the Trotter matrix, you scan for what works, both inside and outside your own company. We saw how DuPont and General Electric scanned competitors and other industries for models of what works. A scan for what works is a clear case of grounded research, where what you find shapes what you search for.

Yet we lack a model for conducting a strategy scan for what works. You can set up a Trotter matrix to capture the answers, but how do you search in the first place?

Benchmarking can help, but it's not the same thing as a strategy scan. For example, you might benchmark how long other airlines take to turn planes around at the terminal, and then imitate what the fastest do. But how did you decide in the first place that turnaround speed was part of your strategy? If you benchmark all possible courses of action before deciding on your strategy, your entire budget will go to benchmarking instead of to making and selling your product. Note that GE did not benchmark during the Trotter exercise: It has the advantage of having prior best practices assessments before it turns to strategy. But you're not GE, so what do you do?

Instead of inventing a method from scratch, let's borrow from other schools of strategy. Among these schools, only competitive strategy offers a method of industry research. Can we adapt that method to scan for what works?

In Porter's *Competitive Strategy*, we find an appendix, "How to Conduct an Industry Analysis."[18] We learn that there are two types of data to collect: published reports and field interviews. Industry analysis is a "massive task" that takes months. You have to narrow your search, or it will take even longer. Porter tells you to concentrate on three elements: "the key structural features of industries, the important forces causing them to change, and the strategic information necessary about competitors."

These three elements give a good overview of your industry. But they do not lead directly to past achievements to imitate, which you need for the art of what works. We come a little closer in the details in Porter's "strategic information about competitors." There we find four "diagnostic components": the competitor's future goals, current strategy, assumptions, and capabilities. For goals and assumptions, Porter directs us to history.

We want to know how the competitor's current "financial performance and market share" compare to those in the "relatively recent past." Over time, where has the competitor "failed or been beaten" in the marketplace? Where has it "starred or succeeded"? How has it "reacted" to what has happened in its industry?

When Porter asks where a company has "starred or succeeded," he wants to know what worked. But for him, you do not want to know this so that you can imitate it. Instead, it helps you predict what the company might do in the future. When a competitor succeeds, it "may feel confident to initiate a move again or to do battle in the event of a provocation." But for our scan, we can ask the same question about success as part of our search for achievements to copy and adapt.

Porter also gives us a checklist for "Areas of Competitor Strengths and Weaknesses," with 40 items in 11 categories. Again, Porter's purpose is to help predict what the competitor will do next. But we can use the same checklist to search for elements that are worth emulating. For example, "training and skills of the sales force" might reveal a successful method that could help you greatly in key ways that you could not predict. And so on through Porter's whole checklist.

Armed with our checklist, we go to published sources first. In his appendix, Porter gives us an inventory, including "book-length studies of the industry," mostly by economists; "shorter, more focused studies conducted by securities or consulting firms," which you find out about "through industry observers or participants"; "trade association data," "trade magazines," and the business press like the *Wall Street Journal*; published company documents, including speeches; and government reports.

Then we use our checklist for interviews with industry "participants" and "observers." Porter's appendix gives plenty of tips for interview research too.

But remember, Porter is showing you how to analyze your own industry. Yet both activities to emulate and your own future strategy can fall wide of your current industry. Ray Kroc was in the restaurant equipment industry; when he discovered McDonalds, he leapt into restaurant operation. Wilbur Marriott was in restaurant operation. When he discovered restaurant number 8's airport trade, he leapt into airline catering. When DuPont looked at other companies that it might imitate, the first industry it studied was publishing.

And a what-works scan need not be the "massive task" that Porter charts out for competitive research. A lighter touch saves time and money, and also gives top executives a more direct view of the scene. With a comprehensive industry study, top executives probably will not have time to read more than the conclusions and recommendations. With a what-works scan, they can go through the whole thing and pick out what strikes their eye.

In *Strategic Leadership*, Finkelstein and Hambrick once again tell us what top executives actually do in this regard.[19] Some "expend great effort reading formal reports from external consultants and research organizations," but most just scan these reports as best they can. Research shows that executives don't have time to read everything, and they don't absorb everything equally. They filter information, consciously or unconsciously, in order to save time: "Strategists only see a portion of what they are watching, and they hear only a portion of what they are listening to."

Steven Jobs is a very busy man. Do you give him a thick report analyzing the computing industry, or do you tell him that Xerox has a graphical user interface that he might want to look at?

To do a what-works scan:

- Read published reports and conduct interviews in search of striking achievements in your industry.
- Include competitors, suppliers, major customers, new entrants, and substitutes in your scan.

- Look also at other industries that have any features similar to yours or that your expertise might lead you into.
- Make your report short and vivid—just describe what you did, what you found to be of value, and why what you found deserves a closer look.

Wei Wu Wei

Stephen Mitchell is a modern translator of the *Tao Te Ching*, the founding text of philosophical Taoism. Mitchell says that many people mistakenly think that its author, Lao Tzu, was a "hermit" or a "dropout from society." He thinks that this "misperception" might come from Lao Tzu's "insistence on *wei wu wei*," which means "doing-not-doing." You might think that's passivity. But to Mitchell, "Nothing could be further from the truth."[20]

To explain, Mitchell cites this verse from the *Tao Te Ching*:

Less and less do you need to force things
Until finally you arrive at non-action
When nothing is done
Nothing is left undone

Mitchell points to t'ai chi and aikido as "powerful" examples of *wei wu wei* in action. T'ai chi is an exercise routine, whereas aikido is a martial art—a weapon. In *On War*, von Clausewitz describes the same thing for the military strategist: "There is only one cause which can suspend the action . . . which is, that he waits for a more favorable moment for action."

So when you wait for the right moment, the right action, you are doing everything, not nothing. *Wei wu wei* is another angle on von Clausewitz's presence of mind, where you expect the unexpected. Yet *wei wu wei* feels even more active. Instead of waiting, you're doing. And von Clausewitz offered no help in developing your presence of mind, whereas Tao and its younger cousin, Zen, offer a world of theory, practice, and expert advisers for *wei wu wei*.

Some guides apply Tao and Zen directly to business, like *The Tao at Work*, by Stanley Herman, and *Zen at Work*, by Les Kaye.[21]

Such guides are especially helpful in dealing with the emotional ills of modern business life: stress, conflict, frustration, and disappointment. When you succumb to these ills, you waste effort on the wrong action instead of waiting for the right one. And they cloud your eyes, so that you miss the right action when it comes along.

Stress might spring from impossible deadlines. Mean or incompetent bosses and coworkers may spark conflict or frustrate your worthy ideas or activities. Or you may meet disappointment instead of just rewards, as when you don't advance the way you should or you even lose your job. These are all daily fare in many companies around the world.

Wei wu wei can help. It keeps you from battles you cannot win. You are the one who decides when something becomes a battle. Everything else is just circumstance, beyond your control. By cutting out stress, conflict, frustration, and disappointment, you concentrate on your expertise, your strategy, the content of your profession. You get better at what you do. So even when you have setbacks, you know that you are still better off.

In addition to martial arts, sports offer a good example. Mitchell explains:

> A good athlete can enter a state of body-awareness in which the right stroke or the right movement happens by itself, effortlessly, without any interference of the conscious will. This is a paradigm of non-action: the purest and most effective form of action.

Even when they lose, good athletes stay calm and study what they did. That makes them better, even in defeat. So there is no loss. There is only more and more expertise.

To practice *wei wu wei* at work:

- Choose one or more guides—book, video, or person—to teach you the basics of Tao or Zen.
- Practice what you learn at work.
- Explain what you're doing as you go along to at least one person—it helps to think aloud.
- Look for battles that you can win.
- Accept the rest calmly as circumstance.

Quality

In our review of strategic planning, we met W. Edwards Deming as a leading foe of management by objectives, in which you receive goals from the pharaoh above and convert them into your own sub-pharaoh goals. Instead, Deming wants you to find out what's working and what's not as the key to setting your goals. He learned statistical methods for doing that from Walter Shewhart and taught those methods to the Japanese, who added teamwork to improve them even more.

In its great coup d'oeil of the 1980s, American business rushed to imitate the Japanese methods. They learned them from the Japanese directly, from Deming, and from J. M. Juran, a contemporary of Deming's who sang the same song. Juran's *Quality Control Handbook* came out in 1951 and has gone through numerous updates and revisions through the decades.[22]

Big companies in particular made major investments in quality control, starting with Motorola, which won the first Baldrige Award for quality in 1988. Motorola called its quality control system "Six Sigma." In 1990, it set up a Six Sigma Research Institute that welcomed other companies too, including IBM, Kodak, and ABB. Over the next decade, dozens more companies adopted Six Sigma, including Allied Signal and GE.

Today, you can learn Six Sigma at various training centers, including the Six Sigma Academy in Scottsdale, Arizona. There are several published guides, including *Six Sigma*, by Mikel Harry and Richard Schroeder; *The Six Sigma Revolution*, by George Eckes; *The Six Sigma Way*, by Peter Pande, Robert Neuman, and Roland Cavanagh; and *Six Sigma for Managers*, by Greg Brue.[23] Harry deserves special note, as he was one of the founders of Six Sigma at Motorola.

Sigma is a statistical measure of deviation from a mean. In quality control, you want everything to be close to a mean. A ball bearing that is too large is just as bad as a ball bearing that is too small. So sigma is a measure of errors. A process with one sigma has many errors. A process with six sigma has only 34 errors in 10 million. That's almost no errors at all. As products grow more complex and expensive to make, companies find that preventing errors in the first place saves loads of money. Above all, customers have less to complain about. Guides to Six Sigma report major increases in capacity and profits and major decreases in capital and employees for companies that make the switch.

For big companies, Six Sigma works. It built on what works from Deming and Japan, and took it to greater heights. At its core remains the study of what works and what does not. So Six Sigma is clearly a tool for the art of what works.

But what about small companies? A big company can hire Six Sigma experts as consultants, send staff members to training sessions, set up a full-time team, and otherwise allocate a big budget to a Six Sigma program. *The Six Sigma Way* cites the example of GE Capital, which spent $53 million on its first Six Sigma program in 1996. The company earned that back in savings in just the first year. By 1998, the annual cost was $98 million versus annual savings of $310 million. That cost/benefit ratio looks good for any company, but the initial investment might be far beyond your reach.

So for smaller firms, is there a way to do it yourself?

Yes.

Start with Deming's simple charts and equations from *Out of the Crisis*. Read all the Six Sigma guides. If you can afford it, go to a training session. Call around to find a company close to you that uses Six Sigma. You can usually find at least one person with the knowledge and interest to talk to you about it. Go visit, as many times as you can. Spend as much money as you can on Six Sigma experts to come in and help you. But if your budget is tight, there's plenty that you can do yourself. It will just take you longer, maybe years instead of months.

Just the introduction to Six Sigma will heighten your expert intuition. It's no accident that Six Sigma borrows "belts" from Japanese martial arts. You need presence of mind—*wei wu wei*—to see improvements that are within your grasp from the data that Six Sigma yields. Finding errors is one thing. Preventing them is something else. At the end of the day, someone has to propose a change that removes the error. Where does that come from?

Coup d'oeil.

Six Sigma gives a picture of how the belts work. Green belts work day to day on the product or service you want to improve, so they need some training in Six Sigma methods. You need 1 green belt per 20 employees. Black belts work full-time on Six Sigma, so they need to know the methods well. You need 1 black belt for every 5 green belts. A master black belt is a qualified expert in Six Sigma. You need 1 master for every 30 black belts.

That makes 1 master black belt for every 3000 employees. That seems to be the threshold for a major Six Sigma initiative. That is, you have a large enough volume of products and services to merit the investment, and enough people to spare for the work. You can send everyone off for training all at once and get started right away. If you have fewer than 3000 employees, your master black belt might take a few months or even years to become fully expert. You might start out with a low-key initiative while everyone gets up to speed.

You will also discover along the way the sigma that's right for you. Six is a very high standard. Some products have to go even higher. Aircraft engines, for example, need seven sigma, because a single error can be fatal. But many companies stop at four or five. You might stop at three. Once you get started, sigma will take on great meaning for you. You will want to move higher, if only by small degrees. You will see that every bit counts.

Even the belt colors have meaning. Green is the color of a growing plant. That means that you're learning and growing too. Black is the color of darkness. You can perform your craft with your eyes closed or in total darkness, without fear, because you are confident of your skill. The fog of war is so thick that you can't see anything, but your coup d'oeil still works. The opposite of black is white, the novice's color, a blank slate with no knowledge yet of the craft.

To use Six Sigma in the art of what works:

- Read as much as you can about it.
- Visit anyone you can who's doing it.
- Get as much training and expert advice as you can afford.
- Make a major initiative if you can.
- Start small and slow if you must.

Dialogue

In *The Fifth Discipline*, Peter Senge tells us that the fundamental "learning unit" in modern organizations is the team, not the individual, so "unless teams can learn, the organization cannot learn." Team learning starts with "dialogue," in which team members "suspend assumptions" and enter into a genuine "thinking together." Thus, dialogue stands out as a key tool of the learning organization.

In *The Fifth Discipline Fieldbook*, compiled by Senge and several colleagues, William Isaacs and Bryan Smith describe the basic components of a dialogue session.[24] First comes the "invitation," which gives people the choice of participating and lets them know "that their resistance and fears are safely answered." By "generative listening," you "slow your mind's hearing" to "hear beneath the words to their meaning." Next, "observing the observer" means that the environment is quiet enough "so people can observe their thoughts, and the team's thoughts." You "suspend assumptions" by bringing them forward, so that the "entire team can understand them collectively."

You need at least 2 hours for every session. Agendas and elaborate preparations "inhibit the free flow of conversation." You should agree to hold three meetings. After that, you can decide whether to continue.

The fieldbook tells us how some teams used dialogue to great advantage. For example, management and labor at GS Technologies, a faltering steel company, held two meetings a month of 3 hours each for a year. The two sides learned to stop blaming each other and work together. Workers' compensation costs fell by more than half. The grievance backlog fell from 485 to none. The company was still struggling, so its parent corporation sold it. But thanks to good labor relations, it was able to find a buyer. So dialogue helped the company survive.

As *The Fifth Discipline Fieldbook* presents it, dialogue seems far removed from the art of what works. Success comes from mutual understanding, not from past achievements in new combinations. There is nothing in dialogue that lets expert intuition steer the mutual understanding. In fact, nothing steers it at all.

Yet dialogue tries to solve a very real problem. In many companies, people who need to work together often don't. Many people lack basic communication skills for working with other people. Real conflicts may arise, as when management reduces the budget of one department in favor of another. We're only human. Hurt and resentment build. It takes a thousand words to make a friendship and only one to lose it.

Over time, everyone you work with will probably say or do something that you find unforgivable at least once. When you bring people together, all those past and current conflicts either come out or lurk beneath the surface. And when you add the pyramid problem that you can't disagree with a pharaoh above you, it's a wonder that anyone works together at all.

Dialogue gets beyond all that, and that's good. But it just doesn't seem very businesslike. Isaacs says explicitly, "Dialogue will backfire if channeled to the intent of making a decision." Instead, "It is best to approach dialogue with no result in mind, but with the intention of developing deeper inquiry, wherever it leads you." For Isaacs, the aim of dialogue is "to create a setting where conscious *collective mindfulness* could be maintained."

We admire the endurance of GS Technologies, but how many companies will spend a year in 3-hour meetings that mostly go nowhere, on purpose?

Yet Isaacs gives clues for bringing dialogue into the art of what works. His "no result in mind" comes close to von Clausewitz's presence of mind. And "mindfulness" comes right out of Zen, as another term for *wei wu wei*.

So what you need to do is put dialogue in motion. Don't tell people to slow their mind's hearing, or to observe the team's thoughts. Tell everyone that you're meeting to throw your expert intuition together. All of you report what you think is the problem and any solutions that you have in mind. You try to understand one another's views, not to arrive at a common one. You're looking for a problem that almost everyone can see how to solve. Don't say, "You're wrong. Here's the right way to look at it." Say instead, "I see what you mean. Here's another way to look at it."

Spend an hour at most. Then let everyone chew on what you heard. Next week, do it again. You'll find that the search goes faster. You cut to the chase, because you already know where everyone stands.

How is this different from brainstorming? Osborn tells you to pick the problem beforehand. Dialogue applies instead to the more common situation where no one agrees on what the problem is. In the learning organization, dialogue aims for a common view of the problem. In the art of what works, dialogue searches through different problems to find one that the group can see how to solve. For that, you have to treat your own view as just one of many, like the rooms off a corridor that James describes for Pragmatism. You pick which room to enter not because it's yours, but because the group sees a solution inside it.

And keep the group small. To involve a larger number of people, change some members from week to week or meet in subgroups. But in any one session, don't go over 10. Think of the numbers. In 1 hour, if 10 people talk for an equal amount of time, each one will be listening for 54 minutes and speaking for only 6. If there are 30 people in the room, each one will be listening for 58 minutes and speaking for only 2. That's a terrible bore. Five people at a time is even better, so that everyone listens for 48 minutes and speaks for 12.

At least one person must attend all sessions. That person should write up the highlights of each session in less than a page and send it out to the wider group. That same person also can start each session with a reminder about presence of mind, past achievement, coup d'oeil, and resolution. From week to week, you'll find that a solution and problem emerge that everyone sees how to work on.

To use dialogue in the art of what works:

- Keep each meeting small and short.
- Remind the group how expert intuition works.
- Welcome all problems and all solutions.
- Change the group week by week, but update everyone.
- Include as many people as possible until you hit on the answer.

Reengineering

In the 1980s, advances in computer technology made it possible to eliminate assembly lines for paperwork. Instead of flowing from person to person, a document could stay in a central computer file, where many people work on it from their own desks. So administration for all kinds of business, and the core product of service companies, saved vast amounts of time.

But to reap those savings, you had to reorganize who does what. The more complex the business, the greater the gain, but that meant more reorganization too. In *Reengineering the Corporation*, Michael Hammer and James Champy show you how to do it.[25] When this book was written, American business was still feeling the crisis of competition with Japan, so the book carries a subtitle typical for the times: "A Manifesto for Business Revolution." Today, reengineering is standard business practice. Everyone wants to take full advantage of computers for streamlining work.

At first glance, reengineering seems counter to the art of what works. Hammer and Champy tell us that

> Reengineering a company means tossing aside old systems and starting over. It involves going back to the beginning and inventing a better way of doing work.

Out with the old. In with the new. Yet their methods of doing so follow the art of what works. After all, expert intuition is the leading source of successful innovation. It's the best way to find the new.

We see this right in their first example. IBM Credit needed 6 days on average, and sometimes 2 weeks, for a credit request to go through five steps and be returned to the sales representative as a quote letter. To find out how long it should take, two IBM managers walked a request from office to office, asking each person to handle the request right away instead of placing it in an in-box. Lo and behold, the whole chain took 90 minutes.

So what did IBM do? It taught a single generalist everything it was necessary to know in order to perform the five steps in 90 minutes. Exceptions took longer and went to specialists for treatment. But most cases proved routine. Each customer now knew exactly whom to talk to, someone who always knew the status of the account.

IBM Credit did not solve its problem with analysis, design, or a plan. Walking a document from office to office is an age-old emergency method. IBM used that method to see what worked: the 90-minute run. Then it turned that into a formal system. You don't reengineer from a drawing board. You put together what works on the ground, and then scale it up.

The IBM reorganization seems minor, but it completely changed what everyone did. Five specialists who used to see everything now see only exceptions. A new job, generalist, handles most of the cases.

For more complex systems, where more jobs must change, a 90-minute walk-through is not enough to find what works. For example, Bell Atlantic found that its customer service orders involved 13 steps that drew from 27 different data systems. Its walk-through cut the time required from 15 days down to 10 hours. Then the company set up a pilot team to work out the details in practice in one location. In a year, the team saved $1 million in just that one location. Then the company spread what was done there to all locations.

As core jobs change, so do support jobs like human resources and finance. Everything changes to some degree. In another case, Hallmark used a mission statement to reassure its staff that its values and core business would not change, although reengineering would change everything else. This is a striking use of a mission statement as a tool for innovation: to give a picture of the past, not of the future. Hallmark stated what already worked so that staff members would not feel that they had been doing everything wrong.

Hammer and Champy give many different examples of reengineering as a practical search for what works in using computers to streamline business. Your own company will probably fit one of their cases to some degree. But all the examples follow the same basic shift from an assembly line to a generalist supported by specialists. Exactly how it works in each situation needs pilots and tests, like any new product or service.

To reengineer in the art of what works:

- Do a walk-through of your product or service to see what a generalist might handle.

- Imitate what other companies in your industry have done to reengineer.
- Try out the new systems as pilots, to work out all the details.
- Scale up what works.

Game Theory

As economists followed Porter into business strategy in the 1980s, some of them turned to game theory instead of industry analysis. They harked back to a classic work from the 1940s by John von Neumann and Oskar Morgenstern, *Theory of Games and Economic Behavior*. Three game theorists—Nash, Harsanyi, and Selten— won the Nobel Prize in economics in 1994. For business, we have *Co-opetition*, a 1996 book by Adam Brandenburger and Barry Nalebuff. Here we learn that game theory shows you "in strategic terms what is the best thing to do."

At the center of *Co-opetition* we find a diagram similar to Porter's five forces, but with five "players" instead: customers, suppliers, competitors, complementors, and your own company. You compete with competitors and cooperate with complementors; hence the term *co-opetition*. For example, Intel and Compaq cooperate (chips complement computers), whereas Coke and Pepsi compete. Game theory tells you whether to compete or cooperate with the other players in your game, and how to do so.

To some degree, you have to guess:[26]

> Games in business are played in a fog—not von Clausewitz's fog
> of war, perhaps, but a fog nonetheless.

So game theorists accept the fact of uncertain information, like our Nobel Prize winners of 2001. The best you can do is to understand the many "interdependent factors," where "anything that changes one is likely to affect many others." They respond to complexity by breaking down the game into "key components," so that you "see what's going on and what to do about it."

Yet as we look more closely, we find that game theory takes us only as far as Porter's competitive strategy. It's a method of analysis, not of decision making.

For example, *Co-opetition* presents the case of rebate programs, like GM's partnership with Household Bank and MasterCard, which lets customers build up a rebate through ordinary credit card purchases. The GM Card was the most successful rollout ever in the credit card business. Other car companies copied it right away, with positive and negative effects for GM. So *Co-opetition* gives this lesson for rebates:

PROs:
1. Allows you to charge your own customers low prices without threatening your rival's customer base.
2. Encourages customers—even price shoppers—to become loyal.
3. Creates synergies with credit card partners.

CONs:
1. Rewarding loyalty in cash rather than kind, doesn't raise your added value.
2. Is ineffective on small-ticket items.

These are good lessons, and the GM Card story gives you plenty of details to copy or avoid in your own case. Yet if you're considering a rebate program, game theory cannot tell you whether or how to do it. It can only show you the various options and the trade-offs involved in each one. The final decision is up to you. So how do you decide?

By coup d'oeil.

Like Porter's work, *Co-opetition* gives many detailed cases to feed your expert intuition. For example, we watch the complex bidding for LIN Broadcasting, in which surprising players win and lose. And we find the pros and cons of many other cooperative tactics in addition to rebates, such as most-favored-customer and meet-the-competition clauses and take-or-pay contracts.

We even find that "win-win" strategies deserve direct imitation, whereas competitive strategy rules them out because it deals only with "win-lose" situations. A win-win example is frequent-flyer programs. American Airlines started the first such program, and its competitors quickly copied it. Overall, the programs made customers more loyal, so all the airlines were able to raise their prices. Under competitive strategy, in contrast, a frequent-flyer program gives American no unique advantage because others can easily imitate it, and so it is not a wise move.

Co-opetition provides a good balance to competitive strategy, but both are still cut from the same cloth: analysis rather than decision making. Both still need coup d'oeil in order to make decisions.

To use game theory in the art of what works:

- Identify your current and potential customers, competitors, suppliers, and complementors.
- For each player, identify the options for cooperating or competing.
- For each option, study cases of how it turned out in similar situations.
- When you see a case of success in a situation similar to yours, study it further for possible emulation.

Trotter Matrix

In Chapter 5, we saw how the Trotter matrix at GE provided a group method of using expert intuition to develop strategy. Let's study an example in greater detail.

Figure 7.3 is based on an actual case from GE's Crotonville Institute in the late 1990s.[27] The strategic question was how to move to on-line retail sales of appliances. GE had no retail sales of appliances at the time. It sold wholesale to big retailers like Sears. The Internet offers great advantages for reaching customers directly. But Sears might see on-line sales as direct competition. So what should GE do?

The procedure is this: Your team starts a Trotter matrix. You write the problem up at the top. It will probably change as you go along. The team determines the rows by asking the question, "What do we have to do well for successful on-line sales?" Again, this list will change. The columns of the matrix cover wherever

Problem: wholesale to e-commerce in appliances

Solution?	Appliances	NBC	GE Equity	Comm. Fin.	Fin. Assur.	Real Estate	Empl. Insur.	Equip. Fin.	Plastics	Struc. Fin.	Consumer Fin.	Cap. Services	Etc.
Customer identification	1					5			3			4	
Customer retention													
Consumer credit								5					
Inventory management					2								
Shipping												5	
Wholesaler retention		4											
Customer service						1							
Sales force incentives													

Figure 7.3 Trotter Matrix

you think it's worth looking. In this case, the columns are GE's 20 businesses. They too can change as you proceed. But a first draft of rows and columns is enough to get started.

Your team looks through the updates of best practices that Crotonville collects each year. As you proceed, you record what you find on the matrix. A 1 means that there is nothing going on there. A 2 means that there is activity but no results yet. A 3 means that the business is doing well enough. A 4 means that it thinks it has a best practice. A 5 means that Crotonville agrees.

You keep filling in the matrix until you see the solution. In Figure 7.3, two 5s and two 4s did it. The team then described these practices briefly and identified where to find them. In the actual case, the team found a GE division that offered an on-line service to GE staff and family as an employee benefit. Since GE has 300,000 employees, that's quite a large customer base. The Crotonville team recommended that GE sell appliances on-line the same way. Its big retail customers could not complain about that. So the strategic question changed to "how to get started in on-line retail for appliances."

The result of a Trotter matrix is a statement of the strategic question, the rows that make it up, the best practices to study further, and where those best practices can be found. The next step after a Trotter matrix is further study of exactly how those best practices were done. You might find they are too complicated, or too expensive, to adopt yourself. Or you might see a way to do them too.

Outside GE, you don't have such a file of best-practice records to sort through, so it's harder to know what worked. You will find more 4s than 5s—that is, self-reported success without verification from someone else. That's fine. Study the evidence and decide for yourself.

To use the Trotter matrix:

- Take a strategic question and break it down into a list of activities.
- Identify where you'll look for what works on each activity.
- Start searching.
- Record what you find on the matrix.
- When you find a combination that seems to solve your problem, study it further to see exactly what your source did in order to succeed.
- Do this alone or as a group.
- Make sure to include or at least get the support of whoever will have to implement what you find.

S-Curve

In the study of innovation, you often encounter the S-curve. It's a warning about imitation. As soon as you succeed, you have only so long before others start copying you. They overtake you, and it's all downhill from there. Everyone suffers from excess competition. So before that happens, you need to switch to something else.

This picture of the S-curve gives a gloomy cast to imitation. It shows it as a great destroyer. The moment you succeed, look over your shoulder. The shadow of doom is approaching. The only answer seems to be an innovation that is so complex or so secret that others find it hard to imitate. But that only postpones your fate. In the end, it's still switch or die.

But we ask: Is that how the S-curve really works?

It was Gabriel Tarde, a French judge, who discovered the S-curve a century ago. Tarde first noticed imitation among criminals. When one of them made an innovation, others quickly picked it up. If a method succeeded especially well, copycat crimes were sure to follow. Then Tarde noticed the same thing among all successful social phenomena. In *Laws of Imitation*, he describes the pattern these phenomena follow:[28]

> A slow advance in the beginning, followed by rapid and uniformly accelerated progress, followed again by progress that continues to slacken until it finally stops: these, then, are the three ages of those real social beings which I call inventions or discoveries.

Figure 7.4 shows the path of Tarde's S-curve. Note that the curve levels off at the end. It does not curve down. Tarde saw that

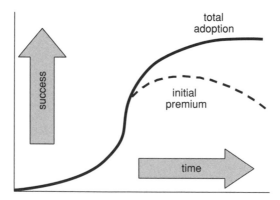

Figure 7.4 The S-Curve (adapted from Tarde, *Laws of Imitation*)

the progress just stops. There is no regression. The invention or discovery becomes a normal part of life.

Yet the first innovator has a different story to tell. When you have the market all to yourself, you can charge a premium. As others enter the field, your initial premium declines. Yet the product itself remains successful. You can still make money, but from volume rather than from a big initial premium.

Tarde's normal S-curve brightens the sky of imitation. In most cases, markets don't decline. They level off. It's true that we find many cases of one technology replacing another, the way records gave way to cassettes, which gave way to CDs. But in many other cases, markets stay healthy and even keep growing. We still have telephones, and televisions, and automobiles, and Coca Cola, and radios, and Disney movies, and mortgages, and clocks, and credit cards, and computers, and oil rigs, and vacuum cleaners, and thousands of other innovations where adoption leveled off but shows no sign of declining.

Business thrives on variations on successful themes. Each variation carries a smaller premium than the initial one, but much greater volume makes up part of the difference. As Tarde noted, what worked in the past is still the best guide to what will work in the future. The S-curve is a ladder to success, not a ball and chain to drag you down.

To use the S-curve in the art of what works:

- Know where you are on the curve at all times.
- Use your initial premium to prepare for volume.
- Make new variations at smaller premiums to keep up with your market.
- Imitate successful imitators—what are they doing right?

After-Action Review

If Napoleon was an artist of what works, and von Clausewitz applied Napoleon's method to military strategy in general, what is the state of what works in the military today?

Methods of quality control from Deming and Japan spread to the American army in the 1970s. That was a decade before they swept through American business. One of the main results was the "after-action review," or AAR. Today, all the American armed forces and more and more armies around the world use AARs to study and build on what works.

We find a full description of the method in a 1993 U.S. Army training circular, "A Leader's Guide to After-Action Reviews."[29] In business, you make a product or deliver a service, and you want to improve its quality. In the army, you produce "events." An event is an action that a unit takes in order to engage the enemy. In an AAR, the participants study an event after the fact to learn how they can improve what they do next time in a similar situation. Afterwards, the army compiles the AARs and circulates them to other units, much as scientists publish the results of their work for use by other labs, or as General Electric compiled best practices for use in the Trotter matrix.

An AAR takes place as soon after an event as possible. Everyone who took part in the event should take part in an AAR. In a large event involving several units, each unit conducts its own AAR, and then the commanders of the units bring their results together for a joint AAR, and so on up the chain of command. In training exercises, a specialist in AARs might lead the review, to show everyone how to do it well. In real action, the unit does it itself, on the spot.

A recent round of live-action AARs for the American military took place during and after the Afghan war of late 2001 and early 2002. A few months later, in September 2002, the *New York Times* reported on interviews with the chiefs of the American armed forces about the Afghan AARs.[30] In the results of these AARs, we see the method for finding what works in action, but we also see what worked in the past brought forward in new combinations to suit the new situation.

The Afghan war began with an air campaign that repeated the success of the Kosovo war 5 years before. Kosovo was the first time that laser-guided bombs outnumbered ordinary bombs. The Afghan war built on that success, with even more laser-guided bombs for ever-swifter success. As for the ground war, General James Jones of the Marines gave this assessment:

The battlefield of the future will be defined, if we do this right, by smaller units doing what larger units used to do in the 20th century. The rifle company of the 21st century will be doing what the rifle battalion of the 20th century used to do.

The *Times* article tells us that a company has 160 troops, while a battalion has 1000. That's a ratio of more than 6 to 1. It reminds us again of Musashi's *The Book of Five Rings*, where "The strategist makes small things into big things, like building a great Buddha from a one-foot model." The Afghan war used new technology to great advantage, like the laser bombs and satellite hook-ups that give you a bird's-eye view of your battlefield. But the technology did not overturn the past. It took elements from the past, like a rifle company, and made their effect even bigger. The army built on what worked.

AARs in general, and this AAR in particular, seem to emphasize tactics over strategy. For example, in Afghanistan, the standard-issue rifle did not have enough power. You had to fire three times to have an effect, although you had time to fire only once. So the army will now issue a heavier rifle. But what does that have to do with strategy?

Well, with a heavier rifle, one soldier can do the job that two or three did before. That lets you do more with the same number of soldiers. As you estimate the strength of the enemy and where they are, you deploy troops based on how much effect you think they can have. Napoleon, for example, would take a battle where the numbers were even, because of his greater skill with mobile artillery. Handling artillery is tactics, not strategy, but your knowledge of tactics makes all the difference for figuring out which strategy will work.

The AAR tells you what arrows you have in your quiver and how they work, so that you know better how to combine them. We see this in a portrait of the most successful American battlefield strategist of the twentieth century, General George Patton. The army still quotes Patton in training manuals; for example, "A good plan violently executed now is better than a perfect plan executed next week."[31] Patton fought by the "snap judgments" and "sixth sense" of expert intuition. But his coup d'oeil was backed up by solid knowledge of all the technical details of war.

In *The Patton Papers*, Martin Blumenson cites a 1945 radio broadcast by Vincent Sheean, a war reporter who spent 6 weeks with Patton's army in action in the last months of World War II. Sheean tried to pin down the secret of Patton's success:[32]

> A general, whether great or merely good, had first to be master of the technical or professional matters of warfare. Beyond that, he had to be right in his critical decisions. . . . Everyone knew of Patton's familiarity with military history, theory, and literature, with Napoleon, Clausewitz, and others, with the command of units at every level of the Army. The combination of practical experience and theoretical preparation gave Patton the solid base, the stage, on which he played his role as a spectacular, yet sound leader.

So the secret of Patton's success was that he knew his stuff. He was an expert, in both the past and the present. That was the source of his "right" decisions in action.

Patton died right after the war, but he left behind his own AAR, "Reflections and Suggestions." His wife, Beatrice, published it as a chapter of his memoirs, *War as I Knew It*.[33] Patton gives a detailed picture of a modern version of Napoleon's mobile war, right down to how you cross rivers and when you rely on your own eye instead of on maps.

As Sheean notes, not only did Patton know his stuff, but everyone knew he knew it. That's what made him a great leader. So maybe we find here a secret of leadership too.

To use AARs in business:

- Do an AAR after every big event, such as a product launch, a key presentation, or the clinching of a big deal.
- Bring together everyone who had a key role, including administrative staff.
- Explain to the group how an AAR works, and let them know that everyone can speak the truth without fear of reprisal.
- Remind everyone of what was supposed to happen.

- Ask each person in turn to tell her or his experience of what actually happened, what worked well, what worked poorly, and how to make things work better next time.
- As the leader, show a good example by being self-critical.
- Make sure everyone speaks.
- Write it down!
- Circulate the results to whoever might be in a same situation in the future.
- Cite your sources, especially AARs, as the roots of your future strategic decisions.

CHAPTER 8

The Art of Synthesis

Expert Intuition
in Strategy Consulting

I N THE PREVIOUS CHAPTER, we studied methods of expert intuition that can be applied in all kinds of unforeseen situations. In this chapter, we look at a more predictable case: strategy consulting, where you have more control over your starting point and what the situation calls for.[1]

On the other hand, in strategy consulting you have to deal with existing methods from other traditions. You can't just waltz in with the art of what works. The music comes from the other schools of strategy. You have to dance to it, at least to some degree. Thus, you don't push the other methods aside. Instead, you add expert intuition.

Let's take an example from the world's leading strategy consulting firm, McKinsey. The "McKinsey way" uses analysis to "think" a new strategy, whereas coup d'oeil lets you "see" a strategy based on what worked in the past. Yet once again, there is a "way of what works" that combines expert intuition with McKinsey's method to yield the best of both worlds.

Whose Strategy Is It?

Sometimes consultants provide a direct product or service. This is a form of outsourcing: The consultant designs a Web site, or does a market survey, or manages employee benefits. In this case, you as the consultant touch on strategy indirectly, by asking the company how what you're doing fits in with its other activities. Other times, consultants deal with strategy directly, by helping a company figure out what to do. Instead of a Web site, you give them an IT strategy. Or you work out a strategy for marketing, investment, training, staff retention, product distribution, or anything else the company asks for.

At some time in your career, you will probably find yourself on one end or the other of a consulting contract that has some element of strategy in it. As consultant or consultee, you will meet up with the methods of strategy that are common to most consulting firms.[2] These methods apply most directly to situations involving direct strategy, but they also apply to a lesser degree to indirect strategy in outsourcing.

We single out McKinsey because it is the oldest and most prestigious of the major consulting firms. It was founded in Chicago in 1926 by James O. McKinsey, a former accounting professor and logistics officer in World War I, where strategic planning à la Jomini prevailed. Marvin Bower, a Harvard MBA, took over in the 1930s and changed the emphasis from "management engineering" to "management consulting." As of 1967, when Bower stepped down as managing director, annual revenue was $20 million. Today McKinsey has 84 offices in 44 countries, and annual revenue of $2.5 billion.[3]

To see what a McKinsey consultant does, go to its Web site and click on "Careers." There you are invited to "Solve a Case" and asked to try your hand at a "case study" to get a glimpse of "the kind of work we do."

As you keep clicking, you find case material and questions, just like in a business school classroom.

The Web site of Mercer Management, a close rival of McKinsey, is similar. Under "Join Us: Interview Prep," its Web site gives two cases. The interview is a case discussion, and "the vast majority of cases that Mercer interviewers give are strategy cases." And at the Boston Consulting Group Web site, "Careers at BCG: Interview Prep" leads to four practice cases.

We see that management consulting has embraced the case method as taught in most business schools today. McKinsey and the other big firms see consulting assignments as cases, where the consultants do in real life what MBA students do in the classroom: Analyze a company's situation and recommend a strategy.

But is that how strategy really works?

There is a key difference between a classroom assignment and a consulting assignment. In the classroom, the company is nowhere to be found. In consulting, you enter the company by the front door. There you find the company staff. As any consultant will tell you, the staff members are not all happy to see you. Someone high up has brought you in—not them. And when you leave, the staff are the ones who must implement your strategy.

Rumor has it that most consulting reports die on a shelf. In fact, many consulting assignments begin in the office of a top executive, who pulls the last report off the shelf, thumbs through it, and tells you: "There was a lot of good stuff in here. Pity we never used it. This time we're hoping for something we can really use."

More likely, the company started to implement the last report and ran into problems that made it stop. So it is trying again, with you.

In *Execution: The Discipline of Getting Things Done*, Larry Bossidy and Ram Charan begin with the story of a CEO whose "great strategic initiative had failed."[4] The CEO thought he had done everything right: He had held two off-site meetings, used benchmarking and metrics, involved "people from all the divisions," and brought McKinsey in to help. It was "the brightest team in the industry," and "everybody agreed with the plan." The CEO explains how it all turned out:

> Yet the year has come to an end, and we missed the goals. They let me down; they didn't deliver the results. . . . We've lost our credibility with the Street. . . . I don't know what to do, and I don't know where the bottom is. Frankly, I think the board may fire me.

Bossidy and Charan add, "Several weeks later the board did indeed fire him."

Most likely, the next CEO will "go back to the drawing board" and create a new strategy. But Bossidy and Charan think the problem lies elsewhere. For them, "the strategy itself is not often the cause. Strategies most often fail because they aren't executed well."

So which is it, strategy or execution?

There is a third possibility, too: the method of creating strategy. Meetings, benchmarking, metrics, and McKinsey may not be enough to come up with a strategy in the first place.

In the art of what works, resolution comes out of coup d'oeil. That is, the company's staff executes well precisely because people see what they need to do and why it can work. The conventional method of strategy consulting divorces coup d'oeil from resolution. The consultants have the coup d'oeil, but the staff must have the resolution. That's not how strategy succeeds.

Like a classroom case, the conventional model of strategy consulting mostly leaves out the company's staff. The doomed CEO discussed by Bossidy and Charan brought in "people from all the divisions," but how you include them makes all the difference. Does the strategy come from McKinsey or from the staff members themselves? And in that question—whose strategy is it?—lies a secret of success.

The McKinsey Way

Let's take a closer look at McKinsey.

For that we have an excellent guide, Ethan Rasiel, author of *The McKinsey Way* and coauthor with Paul Friga of *The McKinsey Mind*.[5] Rasiel is a former McKinsey consultant. His first book mostly describes McKinsey's methods, and the second book gives tips on how to use them yourself.

In *The McKinsey Way*, we learn the three major steps of strategy consulting: thinking about business problems, working to solve business problems, and selling solutions. Thus, the first thing you do is think. That's fine, if we remember that Finkelstein and Hambrick's research in *Strategic Leadership* showed that "Strategists" combined "thinking" and "intuition." Does the McKinsey method do the same?

Not quite. The McKinsey "problem-solving process" combines "very careful, high-quality analysis of the components of the problem" with "an aggressive attitude toward fact-gathering." Analysis plus facts: that's the formula. So, "any McKinseyite will tell you that no business problem is immune to the power of fact-based analysis."

Do McKinsey's facts and analysis leave room for intuition?

Rasiel tells us that facts "compensate for lack of gut instinct." It seems that most McKinsey consultants are generalists who know less than the specialists in the companies they assist. "The folks who have been running the distribution operations of Stop & Shop for the last 10 years" know more about "inventory management practices for perishable foodstuffs" than any McKinsey-ite can. "Gut instinct" will let those Stop & Shoppers solve "an inventory management problem in 10 seconds," whereas "McKinsey will go to the facts first."

Curious.

"Gut instinct" seems to be better than "facts," but facts win because that's what McKinsey consultants can master. And note that McKinsey seems to be competing with the gut instinct of the Stop & Shop experts. Why not work together instead?

Because not all company staff members are so expert. It's true that with years of experience, as you "see and solve" more problems, you get "a fair idea of what works in your industry and what doesn't." However, Rasiel quotes a former McKinsey consultant, now a merchant banker:[6]

> A sharp manager with a lot of business experience can often reach the same conclusions as McKinsey—and in a much shorter time—by gut instinct, but most executives aren't that good.

The consultants at McKinsey can take the time that even "the best executive" cannot, and so can produce "a more robust solution." Rasiel concludes, "So even though your initial instinct may be—and probably is—right, take enough time to verify your gut with facts."

Good. Here we have facts and gut instinct working together. But wait: It's the gut instinct of the McKinsey consultant, not that of the Stop & Shop experts. The company's staff is still out of the picture.

That's all we hear directly about intuition in *The McKinsey Way*. But can we find it indirectly? Let's follow McKinsey's fact-based analysis through the cycle of a consulting assignment and see.

Rasiel presents two major tools of fact-based analysis. The first is MECE, or "mutually exclusive, collectively exhaustive." MECE uses an "issue tree" that starts with an "initial hypothesis" and breaks it down into sub- and sub-sub- and sub-sub-subissues, as far as you can go. Figure 8.1 gives an example.

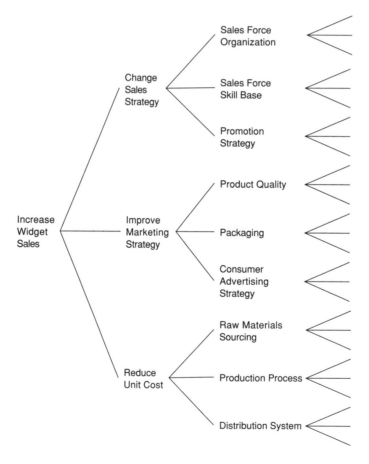

Figure 8.1 Issue Tree for Acme Widgets (from *The McKinsey Way* by Ethan Rasiel © 1999 The McGraw Hill Companies)

Rasiel identifies the three major items of change sales strategy. Improve marketing strategy, and reduce unit cost as the initial hypothesis. But where did that initial hypothesis come from? It "emerges from the combination of facts and structure." The structure is the issue tree. But to make the issue tree, you start with the initial hypothesis.

That's circular reasoning. It doesn't make sense—or does it?

Rasiel admits that of the various parts of McKinsey's problem-solving process, the initial hypothesis is "the most difficult to explain":

> The essence of the initial hypothesis is "Figuring out the solution to the problem before you start." This seems counterintuitive, yet you do it all the time.

Rasiel gives the example of driving to a restaurant. It's in a part of town that you don't know. However, you have instructions: Take the third left off Smith Street, then the first right, just after that corner. Since you know where Smith Street is, "you'll just follow your directions from there. Congratulations, you have an initial hypothesis." So the initial hypothesis is "a road map, albeit hastily sketched, to take you from problem to solution."

At first glance, this example makes no sense at all. To get to the restaurant, someone gave you sketchy directions to start with: third left off Smith Street, first right after that corner. But with a business problem, no one gives you the solution, sketchy or otherwise. So where does it come from?

Rasiel calls this process "counterintuitive," but really, it's intuitive. He's struggling to describe coup d'oeil. He calls it "figuring out the solution to the problem before you start," but that's not quite right. You see the solution first, and that tells you the problem you can solve.

Rasiel knows that the issue tree cannot give you a solution. Yet he puts the initial hypothesis far too early: "After you've brainstormed using your knowledge of the widget business, but before you've spent a lot of time gathering and analyzing the facts." You can change your hypothesis later: "If it turns out to be wrong, then, by proving it wrong, you will have enough information to move toward the right answer."

By the art of what works, this is a serious mistake. It means that you are stepping onto the battlefield with a theory already in hand. Von Clausewitz tells you to leave your theories behind. Instead, you should enter the battle with presence of mind, where you expect the unexpected and leave yourself open to coup d'oeil.

The McKinsey Way tells you to make your initial hypothesis before you even talk to the company's staff. It is wholly your solution—not theirs. It completely ignores the expert intuition of our Stop & Shop old hands.

Let's look at McKinsey's second tool of fact-based analysis:

> We made frequent use of an analytical framework called Forces at Work. . . . The technique involves identifying the client's suppliers, customers, competitors, and possible substitute products.

We recognize this tool as Porter's five forces of competitive analysis. Rasiel lists only four, but the missing "new entrants" can easily fall under "competitors." As we learned earlier, the five forces can become five sources of past achievement to draw on. Does Rasiel see that too?

Yes.

He describes "PDNet," an "electronic database of all practice development (PD) work done by the Firm." Rasiel used it in his very first assignment as a McKinsey consultant, to help a client expand internationally:

> The client especially wanted to understand how major foreign conglomerates maintained financial and managerial control of their offshore subsidiaries and what the pros and cons of their various methods were.

So Rasiel went to PDNet. There he found a profile on Daimler-Benz that fit the bill, including the names of the McKinsey team that had done the work. Rasiel called the team members for follow-up questions. In one afternoon he saved "a week's concentrated research."

In this case, it was the client who wanted to know how other companies solved a problem. Rasiel used an internal tool that resembles the Trotter matrix at GE, where you find who has a best practice and follow up with that organization directly.

And yet McKinsey's PDNet does not filter for what works. A 2002 headline in the *Wall Street Journal* tells us: "Growth at McKinsey Hindered Use of Data."[7] The article quotes an internal McKinsey report from June 2001:

> The ability of our consultants to tap into and effectively leverage our knowledge is poor. . . . It takes much too long to find the right knowledge, and in many cases, the best existing knowledge is not identified to the client.

The article goes on to cite the same problems that we saw with knowledge management in our chapter on the learning organization. At McKinsey, the "databases frequently turn into information dumps, teeming with poorly classified or outdated information." And "the knowledge floating around in an individual employee's head" does not reach others because "employees are often reluctant or too busy to share information."

In contrast, General Electric used the Trotter matrix to drastically reduce the amount of information in circulation by singling out what works. Will McKinsey now do the same? From the article, no. Instead, McKinsey will invest ten times as much money as before in knowledge management systems and technology.

So at McKinsey, past achievement is mixed up with all kinds of other information. It isn't singled out for special treatment. That makes us wonder about past achievement among the client's own staff. Does McKinsey ever ask them what works?

Yes and no.

Under "Specific Research Tips," Rasiel tells us to "look for best practice." He sounds like Jack Welch or Steve Kerr at GE: "There's an old saying that no matter how good you are at something, there's always someone better." So you should look for "what the best performers in the industry are doing and imitate them." Or "find best practice within your company," where "someone, some team, or some division is outperforming the rest of the company." You "find out why," and then "figure out how to implement the top performer's secrets throughout your organization." That will yield "a huge payoff for your business."

Otherwise known as the art of what works.

And yet, we don't seem to carry this insight into the interviews with the company's staff. There we just gather "facts," we don't look for best practices or insights for future strategy.

In addition to the interviews, you meet with the company's staff "to get them on your side. Make sure they want to help you." In the section "Engage the Client in the Process," we find that you must keep your client "engaged in the problem-solving process." That means that the client supports "your efforts," provides resources "as needed," and "cares about the outcome."

Here it's clearly the staff helping you, not you helping them. It's your show, not theirs. You want their support, resources, and interest in the outcome. You don't want their insights or expertise.

Why not?

Because if they could solve the problem, you wouldn't be there in the first place. They've failed. Now it's your turn:

> Let's face it. Most large, modern corporations are chock full of intelligent, knowledgeable managers who are darned good at day-to-day problem solving. McKinsey offers a new mindset, an outsider's view that is not locked into the "company way" of doing things. That's what clients need when problems cannot be solved within the organization.

That's why you keep the most important work for the McKinsey team. You get the assignment, assemble the team, do the preliminary research, and now begin "the real work." You get the team in a room and brainstorm a strategy:

> Brainstorming is the sine qua non of strategic consulting. It's what the clients really buy. . . . The most important ingredient for successful brainstorming is a clean slate. . . . The point of brainstorming is the generation of new ideas.

These "new ideas" come from the McKinsey team and no one else. Perhaps the team carries past achievement or a coup d'oeil from one of the company staff members into the room, but *The McKinsey Way* offers no guidance for doing so.

But when it comes time to implement the strategy, we return to the company staff. To "create real change" with "lasting impact," everyone that "your solution" touches has to accept it. So once the board approves your strategy, you go to the "middle-level managers" and "people on the line" who will have to implement it. You do this "to let them know what's going on," not to get the benefit of their strategic insight. You give them an "implementation plan" with specific instructions on "what will happen and when—at the lowest possible level of detail."

No wonder implementation is the Achilles heel of strategy consulting. In *The McKinsey Mind*, Rasiel reports that "for a long time" McKinsey was known for "outstanding idea generation but poor implementation." That translated into a lot of reports full of insight just gathering dust on corporate bookshelves.

Rasiel tells us how to "avoid the same fate for your ideas": You "focus on the ability of the client to implement your solution" through "a clear implementation plan that includes exactly what should be done, by whom, and when." Only then do you "head off to the next problem."

In the end, the company staff implement "your solution," according to "your implementation plan." It's your strategy, not theirs. But they're the ones who have to do it, while you move onto something else.

No wonder consultants' reports gather dust.

We single out implementation for special note because of its role in the resolution that follows coup d'oeil. If you don't understand and commit to your part of the strategy, you won't do it well, or even at all. You have to have your own coup d'oeil that gives you resolution. In making strategy, the McKinsey method bypasses the company staff. No wonder implementation fails.

In *The McKinsey Mind*, we do find a bit more on intuition and client involvement than in *The McKinsey Way*. Our eyes even light up at this heading: "See Through Your Client's Eyes." But Rasiel means something else: "your view of what the five or six priorities of the organization ought to be." That's "the first step toward seeing through your client's eyes because it forces you to concentrate on the client's foremost needs."

Too bad. Instead of asking the clients what they see, you see for them.

But then we find this heading: "Share and then Transfer Responsibility." Here you "identify areas where the client can safely become involved in the efforts designed to meet the particular client's needs." Then, once you're rolling, "you can broaden the effort throughout the organization." It's worth the "risk of some inefficiency" to "involve the client in a greater role."

We're happy to see the company staff involved here, but we're still not sure whether they play a role in making strategy. We get a clearer view from two McKinsey alumni who are now at other organizations.

The first, Bob Garda, tells you to take your preliminary analysis to "the person who gave you the data." When you "let them help you interpret it," it builds friends and allies.

Well, that's a start. You involve the client in analysis. But you still don't let the client come up with a solution. That you do yourself.

The second alumnus, Jeff Sakaguchi, tells you to complement the usual "steering committee at the top" with a "team that involves the client at all levels." After all, clients are "much more capable than many people believe." With "accountability and exposure," they will be "just as committed to achieving success." Sakaguchi concludes:

> They will take ownership, and it is our job to help them get the job done.

This is the only time, in either *The McKinsey Way* or *The McKinsey Mind*, when someone suggests including the client in the process of coming up with a strategy. It's the only time when "it is our job to help them get the job done," instead of its being their job to help us do it. And for Sakaguchi, it's not just a question of "buy-in." He thinks you get quality, too. The client is actually "capable."

The main reason McKinsey keeps the client out of making strategy comes back to fact-based analysis. Whoever does the analysis makes the strategy, and only McKinsey has the time. The company staff is busy with the day-to-day work.

And yet, in *The McKinsey Mind*, we note a retreat from complete faith in fact-based analysis. We read that "sooner or later every executive has to make a major decision based on gut instinct." Especially outside McKinsey:

> In many organizations executives make major strategic decisions based as much on gut instinct as on fact-based analysis. Almost all the McKinsey alumni we interviewed found this a radical change from their time at the Firm.

Note the source of this nod to gut instinct. When you leave McKinsey to join another company, you find "a radical change" from fact-based analysis to intuition. So McKinsey's method is very different from the way most companies operate.

As a result, *The McKinsey Mind* works intuition into its basic consulting model. As Figure 8.2 shows, intuition joins data at the center of the "Problem-Solving Process."[8] The central triangle shows the "tension between *intuition* and *data*." Although Rasiel favors "McKinsey-style fact-based problem-solving," you can't gather "all the relevant facts before reaching a decision." Let's call it the fog of consulting. Since "most executives make business decisions based partly on intuition—gut instinct tempered by experience," your own decisions need "a balance of both."

So in theory, Rasiel gives equal billing to fact-based analysis and expert intuition. In practice, however, McKinsey seems to do one and not the other. Its fact-based analysis replaces expert intuition instead of striking a "balance."

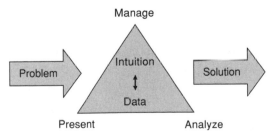

Figure 8.2   McKinsey Problem-Solving Process (Rasiel and Friga, *The McKinsey Mind*)

Strategic Synthesis

Most strategy consulting uses some form of McKinsey's method—with one major exception. In participatory strategic planning, a mixed group of consultants and staff agree on every step of the way. Examples include Interaction Associates, which offers a popular course in Essential Facilitation for participatory planning workshops, and Objexis, an on-line version that lets a large number of staff members participate right from their desktops.[9]

This method is agreement-based rather than fact-based like McKinsey's method. It has the same virtues and vices as the learning organization: Everyone rows together, but how do we know we're going in the right direction? Group consensus does not increase your chances of hitting on a successful strategy. Only coup d'oeil does that.

We can also combine the McKinsey method and participatory planning. Team members gather and analyze facts, and group workshops hash out agreement. Sakaguchi's advice in *The McKinsey Mind* resembles this combination. But that still does not guarantee the proper role for expert intuition. Again, fact-based analysis plus group consensus does not equal coup d'oeil and resolution.

Surely there are many cases of strategy consulting, at McKinsey and elsewhere, in which expert intuition does prevail. We just don't know about them, because other explanations get in the way. Coup d'oeil remains invisible, a mysterious force behind the scenes.

At every stage—whether your method involves gathering data or holding group sessions—you can give equal time to what works. You do not have to give up your current methods. Just add expert intuition. Best of all, add the Trotter matrix and use it the way Kerr used it at GE's Crotonville Institute.

Let's go back to the problem-solving triangle in *The McKinsey Mind*. Of the three key elements—manage, present, and analyze—analyze stands out as the most important. That's what gives you the answer. But to add what works, the triangle must become a square (see Figure 8.3). There's a fourth element, but what shall we call it?

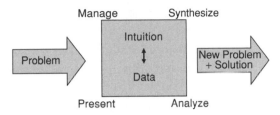

Figure 8.3   McKinsey Problem-Solving Process + Expert Intuition

How about: synthesize?

It's the mirror image of analyze, as the *Oxford English Dictionary* tells us:[10]

> *Analysis*: The resolution or breaking up of anything complex into its various simple elements, the opposite process to synthesis.

> *Synthesis*: The putting together of parts or elements so as to make up a complex whole (opposed to analysis).

You break down a problem by analysis, and you build up a solution by synthesis. The first coup d'oeil starts off the solution by combining the first key elements. Other coups d'oeil follow, to make a complete strategy.

So the leader of a consulting team is above all a synthesist. Others can do the analysis, but one person must take the responsibility for building up the solution. The original coup d'oeil might come from anyone. However, the team leader must pick it up and put together the rest of the solution. It's best when each key person on the client's staff comes up with her or his own coup d'oeil as to what that department should do. That way, the ability to implement the solution gets built right into the solution itself.

The result will cover the same terrain as the "issue tree" in Figure 8.1, but with some adaptations. You leave gaps where nobody sees a solution. The headings change to show the actions that each part of the company must take, with a single heading announcing the overall strategy. Thus, the shapes of the "issue tree" and the "solution tree" may match, but the content will not—just as the Trotter matrix keeps its shape while the content changes throughout the search for what works.

Wherever the first and follow-up coups d'oeil come from, it's always the job of the team leader to weave all the strands together. It must be done by one person, just as Napoleon always insisted on "unity of command." Someone has to use expert intuition to see that the whole course of action can work.

Figure 8.4 shows a "strategic synthesis" that mirrors Figure 8.1. Our team leader, Keri S., sees a solution, through her own insight or someone else's.[11] In this case, Acme Widgets, the solution comes from past experience. In recent decades, a host of companies—most famously in computers and telephones—have combined products and service as an integrated whole.

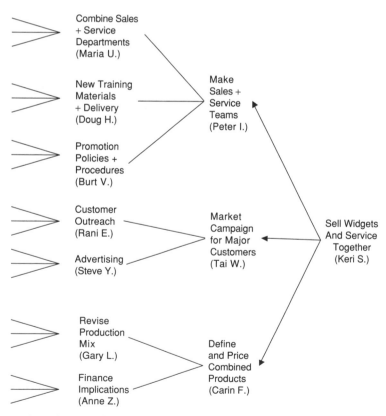

Figure 8.4 Strategic Synthesis for Acme Widgets (see Figure 8.1)

Keri sees what she should do: Take the strategy from person to person throughout Acme to help others see what they should do. As a result, various department heads have their own coups d'oeil—or maybe it was one of their coups d'oeil that sparked Keri's in the first place.

At this point, the outline is far from comprehensive. It is filled in not through analysis and planning, but as each key person sees what he or she should do. So Keri fills in the outline bit by bit as she succeeds in her synthesis. Her expert intuition tells her when the outline is complete enough to write up the strategy as a formal proposal. When she does that, the strategy is already understood and agreed to by the key people who will need to make it work.

This portrait of Keri S. simply makes explicit the unspoken, unconscious art of what many successful consultants do, at McKinsey and elsewhere. Strategic synthesis based on coup d'oeil is the key to strategy consulting. It's the greatest of all consulting skills—and it's another name for the art of what works.

CHAPTER 9

The Way of What Works
Your Hero's Journey

The so-called Industrial Revolution, then already well in progress, owed little or nothing to scientific discovery. Ingenious though they may be, such inventions as Richard Arkwright's power loom or Eli Whitney's cotton gin are works of mechanics, not of scientists. William Murdock, who produced the first gas light in London in 1803, merely exploited commercially what the Persians had known since the time of Zoroaster.
—J. C. Herold, *The Age of Napoleon*[1]

THE INDUSTRIAL REVOLUTION and the Age of Napoleon: industry and strategy born at the same time, of the same elements. Both drew on past achievements in new combinations to suit a new situation—otherwise known as the art of what works.

The heroes of the age were not great thinkers but pragmatic inventors, both in the factory and on the battlefield. The word *invent* comes from the Latin *invenire*, "to come upon, find, discover." Its original meaning in English was "to find out or discover by search or endeavor."[2] You don't dream something up. You see what's there. It's an act of the eye: coup d'oeil.

Today, tomorrow, or whenever you finish this book, you will face yet another era, one that is more important to you than the Industrial Revolution or the Age of Napoleon: the rest of your life.

History may never record it, but for you, it's the greatest era of all. And like all great ages, it awaits its heroes: you plus whomever you draw from the most. Remember the Trotter matrix. To start your search, you ask, "Who has made progress in solving a similar problem?" And remember Isaac Newton. He stood on the shoulders of giants.

So can you.

And the rest of your life includes far more than your work for your company. As I wrote this book, I discussed it with many people along the way. They saw the main point: how to give up what you want in order to get what you want for your company. Then they said, "Great. Thanks. Now what about me?"

I found that they wanted much, much more on the inner struggle that they would have to go through in order to follow the path that I showed them. And they saw their professional and personal lives as two sides of the same coin. You work hard to make a good life for your loved ones and yourself, but no matter how much you work, it seldom makes life better. Working less does not help, either.

According to a recent Conference Board report, most Americans are unhappy in their jobs.[3] You bring that unhappiness home. The stock market slumps, you lose money, or even your job, as a result of forces that are completely beyond your control—your work life, your love life, and your family life all suffer together.

When you are in your twenties or thirties, you may look ahead to a brighter future. But in later years, you find out that's not going to happen. The future never comes. All you ever have is now.

So what should you do now?

Here we move from company strategy to personal strategy. And we find more than just a literature to learn from. A whole industry precedes us. Americans buy more books on self-improvement than in any other category. Companies spend enormous sums on motivational seminars and workshops, "success coaches" and "personal strategists" for their staff. Day and night, television shows bring dozens of self-help experts right into your home.

First we ask if it works.

The experts base their methods on cases from their own workshops or private practice, or on conversations with successful people that they pass on to their audience. We find very little empirical evidence that any of their methods work. On the other hand, scientific research yields few conclusive results, as we see from reviews of the literature: *Persuasion*, by Daniel O'Keefe; *Motivation*, by Robert Beck; *Intrinsic and Extrinsic Motivation*, by Carol Sansone and Judith Harackiewicz; *Motivation*, by Douglas Moock; and *Motivational Science*, by Tory Higgins and Arie Kruglanski.[4] In hundreds of studies, scientists find myriad factors that persuade or motivate someone to take a particular action. But they don't know what matters most.

Yet as we scan these reviews, we seldom find the key question for the art of what works: Is there more motivation when an action has past success to back it up? Instead, scientists ask who proposes the action, what emotions the message provokes in the subject, the character traits or cultural values of the subject, or the brain functions involved. However, Beck, Moock, and Higgins and Kruglanski cite one major exception: the work of John Atkinson at the University of Michigan.

In *An Introduction to Motivation*, Atkinson tells us that an individual carries a motive to achieve success (M) from one situation to another. Each situation has an expected probability of success (P) and an incentive value of success (I). Thus, the strength of motivation or the tendency to approach success (T) for certain actions works out to

$$T = M \times P \times I$$

In other words, you try to do something if you have a drive for success (M), you think you can succeed (P), and the result is something you want (I).

In the art of what works, M has no place. You never assume that some people don't want success. Perhaps they just lack the right opportunity, which might appear at any moment. I is fine: You try for something only if you want it. As for P, that's the key: the chance of success. That's what makes opportunity. That's what coup d'oeil sees.

Sure enough, Atkinson tells us that the chance of success is a big motivator. He cites the work of Norman Feather as the "most instructive application of the theory of achievement motivation." The results of Feather's research show that "the expectancy" that an activity will succeed has a "motivational effect."[5]

So the chance of success P motivates you to do something. But what determines P? What makes you think that something can succeed?

Atkinson replies: That's a good question. He tells us that it is the "most critical problem in contemporary research on achievement-related motivation." Atkinson doesn't know the answer, but he cites an experiment as a possible clue.

If you mix professional golfers with novices for the task of "putting golf balls in a cup from various distances," the pros will try to do it from much longer distances. If you did not know that those subjects were pros, you would think that they were "setting their aspirations unrealistically high." But no. The pros had the same realistic expectancy of success at 10 feet as the others had at 5 feet.

The difference?

Expertise.

If we just take the task of "tries from 10 feet," the pros see a way to succeed. The others do not. The pros set a higher goal than the others not because they have a greater desire to succeed at the task or a greater drive to succeed in general, but because they see a chance of success. That's why success seems mysterious from the outside, but obvious from the inside. The novices had no idea how the pros did it. For the pros, it was simple.

In the art of what works, expertise is not just a sporting skill, but everything you know and see that comes from past achievement. When you see a way to draw on that expertise—as in coup d'oeil—it shows you the path to success. That chance of success gives you the motivation to try, like Atkinson's pro golfers.

So much for research on motivation. Overall it's inconclusive, but it hints at expert intuition as a motivating factor.

Let's turn now to the popular experts. They draw their authority not from science but from their success in reaching millions. And what do the experts say to those millions?

In Search of Success

Let's start with Dr. Chérie Carter-Scott, whose Motivation Management Service Institute has worked with many Fortune 500 companies. Carter-Scott has written three popular books: *If Life Is a Game, These Are the Rules*; *If Love Is a Game, These Are the Rules*; and *If Success Is a Game, These Are the Rules*.[6] Let's study the last one, because of its subject: success.

Some of Carter-Scott's rules are strictly motivational. They tell you to make your own definition of success, to trust yourself, and to learn from setbacks. The rules that apply directly to strategy start with "wanting success." Then come "goals" as "the stepping stones on your path." Then come "actions," which you plan, and unforeseen "opportunities" to advance your goals.

We recognize Carter-Scott's school of strategy: strategic planning. You set goals, plan actions to reach those goals, and then implement your plan, just as Jomini says. We find some strategic flexibility, too, as unforeseen opportunities can change your path to your goal.

Carter-Scott gives more detail on how to turn goals into actions. She reports: "The question I am asked most frequently when it comes to getting from where you are to where you want to go is: 'I want to, but *how* do I do it?'"

In reply, she tells you to "make lists of all the possible things you can do to take your wish forward." You must "be brave and write down everything you can imagine." Then you start with "the one action step that jumps off the page at you." If nothing jumps, "choose the one that's easiest to get done." Then you do the next one. And so on through your list.

We wonder whether it is expert intuition that makes an action "jump off the page." We just don't know. Otherwise, here's how you decide what action to take: You do what it's "possible" to do, what you can "imagine," and what's "easiest to get done." That's not much guidance. But no matter. In strategic planning, for life or for work, the key is not what action you choose, but how much concentration and persistence you bring to it. That's where motivation comes in, to keep you plugging away.

Not so in the art of what works. What action you choose makes all the difference. You combine elements of past achievement. That's what makes for success.

Carter-Scott accepts without question the value of strategic planning:[7]

> "Goal-setting" has become a rather overused term in the field of career and life guidance, but there's no way around it: It is still the most effective way to get you from where you are now to where you want to go. Conventional wisdom may seem ordinary, but the power of its effectiveness lies in its universality.

In contrast, the art of what works gets you from where you are now to where you can go, which is not necessarily where you want to go most. And Mintzberg's book *The Rise and Fall of Strategic Planning* showed us that a "universal" method is not the same as an "effective" one.

Yet Carter-Scott correctly notes that goal setting dominates the field of personal strategy. It has done so for a long time, starting in 1937 with the first modern best-seller on the subject: *Think and Grow Rich*, by Napoleon Hill.

Hill offers "proven steps to riches" that he discovered from interviews with Andrew Carnegie and 500 other "wealthy men." Like Carter-Scott, he offers some motivational steps, such as "faith" and "auto-suggestion." His steps follow the classic sequence of strategic planning: "desire," then "organized planning," then "persistence." That adds up to Hill's core advice: "definitiveness of purpose." Again, the key is not what action you choose, but whether you do it with concentration and persistence.

Yet Hill hints at expert intuition too. There's a step for "specialized knowledge," where you learn "the service, merchandise or profession which you intend to offer in return for a fortune." So expertise counts, but only to help you reach your goal. It does not help you set the goal in the first place, as in the art of what works.

There's also a step for "imagination," but Hill dismisses "synthetic" imagination that combines existing elements. He favors instead "creative" imagination that comes from "direct communication with Infinite Intelligence." It's the old definition of intuition as magic. The same is true of three other steps: "the mystery of sex transmutation," which means that animal urges fuel the drive to achieve; "the subconscious mind"; and "the sixth sense":[8]

> The sixth sense is that portion of the subconscious mind which has been referred to as the Creative Imagination. . . . The result of sex transmutation is the increase in the rate of vibration of thoughts to such a pitch that the Creative Imagination becomes highly receptive to ideas, which it picks up from the ether.

Magic again.

But let's remember that Hill wrote his book before modern science revealed the secrets of expert intuition. Perhaps if he had lived much later, he would have seen expertise, not magic, as the source of sudden insight.

And by the way, Hill refers to Andrew Carnegie throughout. Meanwhile, Carnegie himself offered this wisdom on strategy:

> Do not be fastidious; take what the gods offer.[9]

It's a version of Leonardo da Vinci's advice: "As you cannot do what you want, want what you can do." In contrast, Hill urges you to do what you want, through planning and persistence.

Almost 50 years later, the first popular experts to follow in Hill's footsteps studied corporations, not people, for their secrets of success. *In Search of Excellence,* by Thomas Peters and Robert Waterman, became the most popular business book of the 1980s.[10] While others looked to Japan, Peters and Waterman searched for excellence right in the United States:

> We did not have to look all the way to Japan for models with which to attack the corporate malaise that has us in its vicelike grip. We have a host of big American companies that are doing it right.

Peters and Waterman studied 36 "highly regarded companies" that stayed in the top half of their industries on at least four out of six performance measures from 1961 to 1980. Since America's "corporate malaise" came from bureaucracy and overplanning, it's no surprise that *In Search of Excellence* does not cite strategic planning as a key to success. Instead, it tells us that the "rational model" does not work:

> People reason intuitively. . . . It probably is only the intuitive leap that will let us solve problems in this complex world.

We learn more about the "intuitive leap" in a section entitled "Autonomy and Entrepreneurship." Here we meet the innovation "champion." Not a "blue-sky dreamer, or an intellectual giant," the champion "might even be an idea thief":

> But, above all, he's the pragmatic one who grabs onto someone else's theoretical construct if necessary and bullheadedly pushes it to fruition.

We recognize the "champion" as a strategic synthesizer: an artist of what works. Sure enough, Peters and Waterman cite Jack Welch as an example. At GE Plastics, Welch championed Lexan, from Robert Fox's research on electric wiring, and made it into "GE's fastest growing business."

As we saw before, American industry did regain its prominence in the 1980s and 1990s. *In Search of Excellence* was one of the books that helped this happen. Yet it fell out of favor in the 1990s after an investment firm, Sanford Bernstein, studied the same companies from 1980 to 1994 and found that nearly two-thirds of them showed below-market returns over that period.[11] So excellence did not last—which led Collins and Porras to their longer-term study of successful companies for *Built to Last*.

Despite its virtues, a "search for excellence" is not the same as a search for what works. Excellence attributes do not produce success; only excellent activities do, meaning a course of action based on past achievements. Excellence helps you prepare; it does not show you the path to success. Without a winning strategy, you won't succeed, no matter how excellent you are. And no winning strategy lasts forever: You must look for others all the time. So it's no surprise that excellent companies fall behind. Excellence matters, but not as much as coup d'oeil.

Yet the search for excellence goes on. In the mid-1980s, Anthony Robbins wrote *Unlimited Power*, based on his study of "enormously successful people." Robbins notes the "mental trap" of thinking that those people "have some special gift." But their real gift is "their ability to get themselves to take action."

We're back to motivation: The key to human excellence is getting yourself to do something, anything. Just get moving.

But how? I can think of a million things that I could do. How do I choose among them?

Robbins says that "there are no limits" to what you can do through the key power of "modeling":[12]

> Excellence can be duplicated. If other people can do something, all you need to do is model them with precision and you can do exactly the same thing, whether it is walking on fire, making a million dollars, or developing a perfect relationship . . .

Here Robbins moves from modeling excellence to imitating successful action: You can "do exactly the same thing."

That's the art of what works. Good. But then, in his "ultimate success formula," Robbins reverts to classic strategic planning.

First you make "an inventory of your dreams," what you "want to have, do, be, and share." Then you make a schedule for when you will achieve each of these dreams. Then you pick out "the four most important goals" for this year. For each goal, you create "a step-by-step plan on how to achieve it." Then you "come up with some models." Then you "create your ideal day" and design "your perfect environment" to keep you on track toward your goals.

So in the end, Robbins's formula is very much like Carter-Scott's and Napoleon Hill's: Your dreams lead to goals, and then to a plan. We get a dose of what works in "models," but too late. They don't affect your goals, or even your plans. For Robbins, Carter-Scott, and Hill, your goals and plans come from your desires, not from an opportunity to achieve success that coup d'oeil reveals.

We find yet another search for excellence in *The Seven Habits of Highly Effective People*, by Stephen Covey.[13] Four of Covey's seven habits touch on the learning organization, where you work in harmony with everyone else instead of against them or just on your own, and you keep on learning and growing throughout your life. The other habits combine motivation and strategic planning. Once again, goals come from desires and lead to plans. Covey's method of planning, where you "Put First Things First," shows in great detail how you plan by year, by month, and by day for all the different parts of your life: work, family, self, and anything else you wish. Covey also publishes a range of calendars and planners to help you do this.

That's fine. But without coup d'oeil, planning won't lead to success. So to Covey's habits, we must add the art of what works.

Let Go

Another school of self-improvement draws from Tao, Buddhism, and Zen. Instead of relying on persistence to reach your dream, you let go and take what comes. That's a form of presence of mind. But can it lead to success alone, without the other elements of expert intuition?

We find a version of Buddhism in *A Spiritual Solution to Every Problem*, by Wayne Dyer.[14] When you give up "intellectual reasoning" and accept the world as it is, "divine guidance" propels you "in the direction of a solution to anything that might be troublesome." The problem may not go away, but it will no longer be "troublesome" to you. For you, it's solved.

There is great power in such a "spiritual solution." Although it's central to Buddhism, you can find traces of it in most other religious traditions as well. But that's not the same as the art of what works. In pure Buddhism, success comes from acceptance, whereas Tao and Zen add successful action.

We come closer in *The Seven Spiritual Laws of Success*, by Deepak Chopra. Here we find a play on words with "responsibility," which Chopra breaks into "response" plus "ability." You accept responsibility for problems as simply circumstances in which you have the ability to make a creative response:[15]

All problems contain this seed of opportunity, and this awareness allows you to take the moment and transform it into a better moment or thing.

Chopra goes on to describe the Tao concept of *wei wu wei*, the patience to wait until the right action arises by itself. If you "force solutions on problems," that only creates "new problems":

But when you put attention on uncertainty, and you witness the uncertainty while you expectantly wait for the solution to emerge out of the chaos and the confusion, then what emerges is something very fabulous and exciting.

Yet in the end, even Chopra lapses into goal setting:

In order to acquire anything in the physical universe, you have to relinquish your attachment to it. You still have the intention of going in a certain direction, you still have a goal. However, between point A and point B there are infinite possibilities.

We recognize here strategic flexibility—the path may change—as a variant of strategic planning. But still the goals come first. And where do these goals come from? Chopra subtitles his book, "A Practical Guide to the Fulfillment of Your Dreams." So again, goals come from desires. In the art of what works, they come from coup d'oeil. That changes your dream, as you see what exactly you are able to reach.

We find another version of "letting go" in *Practical Intuition*, by Laura Day.[16] You give up your preconceptions, rational thoughts, and old ways of solving problems. Instead, you open yourself up to your inner intuition. Day tells us that "you already know everything." Intuition gives you "the ability—right now—to get useful information instantly on any topic at any time, whether intellectually you know anything about it or not." So Day's practical intuition harks back to Napoleon Hill's "sixth sense"—it just comes to you from the universe, not from expertise.

In *Practical Intuition for Success*, Day comes closer to the art of what works. She tells you to get "clear on your goal and your priorities," and then "your intuition will reveal the most direct route to your goal." If the original goal is general enough, this fits expert intuition. Napoleon had the general goal of defeating the enemy army, and then coup d'oeil showed him the battles to do it—specific goals arose from that. So Day sides with von Clausewitz over Jomini, except that she does not credit expertise as the source of her intuition.

We find one more version of letting go, but this time what you're letting go of is not your attachment to the world or to rational thinking; it's denial of what you're doing wrong. Denial gives comfort. But to reach success, you have to let it go.

So says Phillip McGraw in *Life Strategies*. As a regular on Oprah Winfrey's television show, McGraw became perhaps the leading popular expert on personal strategy today. McGraw talks about "what works," but he means something different from the art of what works. In his version, you ask yourself what is wrong, why you keep doing the things you do—especially when you hate what you do. Why do you do it? Why do you keep doing it?

McGraw knows the answer: We do the things we do because they work at some level. Somehow, on some level, even apparently unwanted behaviors serve a purpose.

So "doing what works" is something to overcome. You have to let go of your attachment to "unwanted behaviors" that you secretly enjoy.

Most of McGraw's book is a wake-up call to get back on track with your life. Toward the end, we find a "Seven-Step Strategy" that once again combines motivation with strategic planning. McGraw tells you to "express your goal" as "specific events or behaviors" and "in terms that can be measured." Then you make a "timeline" for your goal and "plan and program a strategy that will get you to your goal."

Your big problem is "downtimes," when you meet "temptations and opportunities to fail" and lose "emotional energy." So you have to "design a solid strategic plan" to keep you on the right track. Like Covey, McGraw publishes extra planning tools to help you do this. But again: Without coup d'oeil, planning won't lead to success.

McGraw illustrates his points with anecdotes from his counseling practice, plus one big example. In 1988, he helped Oprah

Winfrey win a big lawsuit. McGraw tells us: "Without Oprah, there would be no *Life Strategies*." It was the turning point of his career.

The lawsuit followed an outbreak of mad cow disease in Britain. On her show, Oprah hosted a debate between experts on the possibility that the disease might break out in the United States too. Beef prices fell. Five Texas cattle companies sued her. The trial took place in Amarillo, Texas, on the cattlemen's home ground.

McGraw reports that Oprah refused to take the lawsuit seriously. On her show and in public appearances, she laughed it off. Meanwhile, two top lawyers, Gary Dobbs and Chip Babcock, helped McGraw develop "a plan, a well-thought out, well-researched strategy" for the case. Babcock especially knew from experience that "nationally, 80 percent of these cases are lost at the trial level." To carry out their strategy, they needed Oprah's complete cooperation. But instead, "our star witness was struggling with the 'insanity' of it all, stuck in denial."

At the last minute, McGraw took action:[17]

> Finally, I just took her hand and said, "Oprah, look at me, right now. You'd better wake up, girl, and wake up *now*. It is really happening. You'd better *get over it* and get in the game, or these good ol' boys are going to hand you your ass on a platter."

It worked.

Oprah woke up. She cooperated.

They won the case.

For McGraw, Oprah succeeded because his straight talk cut through her denial. And she lacked a plan:

> Without a strategic plan that included clearly defined objectives, she probably would have sent a very bad message to the jury.

So that's what McGraw's book is about: letting go of denial and making a plan. But the lawsuit shows that there's something else: The plan must come from past achievement.

Dobbs and Babcock were expert lawyers. The law especially works on precedent. You have to show that previous rulings support your case. You can be very creative in the range of previous rulings that you use, but you must rely on what worked in the past. And Babcock knew the odds of winning, again from expertise. McGraw offered Oprah more than a hard look at herself and clear objectives. He offered a winning strategy, based on past achievement.

At first, Oprah ignored their expert strategy. She had her own strategy, based on her own past success. She would charm the judge and jury, just as she charmed her audiences. McGraw looked for the right moment, the right words, to make her accept a better strategy. For that, he used his expertise from years of counseling. But the most important element was the strategy itself, based on expertise, that Oprah was to adopt instead of her own. It showed her the winning path.

After McGraw's harsh words woke her up, Oprah did not start McGraw's seven-step strategy: "Express your goal in terms of specific events or behaviors," and so on. But in this case, they already had a general goal: win the lawsuit. Then came a strategy that had been worked out by McGraw and her lawyers. Oprah traded in her own expert strategy of charming the public not for a goal setting exercise, but for an existing legal strategy that was even more expert than her own.

In the end, this leading example from McGraw's book is a case of expert intuition in action. And McGraw's own part in winning the lawsuit led him to write his book and appear on Oprah's show. Most recently, McGraw has turned his weekly Oprah segment into a successful television show of his own, *Dr. Phil*, starting in September 2002, produced by Oprah's company. So instead of laying out a plan with goals and objectives, he built on success through a series of coups d'oeil.

McGraw is an artist of what works.

The Hero's Journey

We have seen that most motivational speakers, writers, and coaches favor Jomini over von Clausewitz. That is, they propose some form of strategic planning rather than the art of what works.

Yet their great success must tell us something about personal strategy. Their methods must fill some need, as so many people buy their books, attend their seminars, and watch them on T.V. It's true that motivation and goal setting are essential to human achievement. But our popular experts misplace them.

Motivation and goal setting don't come first. They come second, after coup d'oeil.

As it turns out, coup d'oeil is the greatest motivator of all, the surest route to a winning goal. You say to yourself, "That's it! Now I see what to do!" Or you say it to someone else or silently to yourself, or you speak it aloud to the night sky or the rain outside your window. In the blink of an eye, you're on your way. It's coup d'oeil—not a pep talk or a kick in the pants—that starts your journey on the road to success.

And remember, the journey to success is not the same as your life's journey. We know when your life's journey begins and ends: at birth and at death. The journey to success is something else. You can't predict when it begins, and it ends when your strategy either succeeds or fails. Another journey can start at any moment.

James Champy and Nitin Nohria take us part of the way down this road in *The Arc of Ambition*. Sure enough, they point to past achievement.

We learn that some dreams are "truly original," like Einstein's theory of relativity. But most "ambitious creators" use "existing ideas in some brand new combination." William Shakespeare is a perfect example. He was a genius at recycling plots time and time again into new forms that were made timeless by his extraordinary use of language.

Artists, writers, and "imaginative entrepreneurs" all "transform the familiar," because "to accomplish the impossible, you must first begin with the possible."

We are very close here to the art of what works. But wait: Where does the journey start? In *Arc of Ambition*, as the title suggests, ambition comes first. It is "the root of all achievement." Then you "see what others don't" and "follow a steadfast path." Opportunities arise, and you "seize the moment."

For example, we learn that Andrew Carnegie was a 17-year-old telegraph clerk in 1852 when "he began formulating the huge aspirations that eventually made him the country's top steel tycoon."[18] Yet at the time, Carnegie had no idea that steel was in his future. Henry Bessemer invented modern steelmaking 4 years later, in 1856. Carnegie first entered the steel business in 1866, and he made it his principal business after 1872. But according to *Arc of Ambition*, his arc began way back in 1852.

In the art of what works, the journey to success begins not with aspirations and ambition, but the moment you see a way to succeed, based on past achievement. That's what gives you a specific ambition, aspiration, dream, desire, or goal. There were plenty of ambitious young men in 1852; that's not what made Carnegie so successful. It was his big move to steel 20 years later, in 1872.

The Carnegie story makes us reorder the steps of Champy and Nohria's arc: First you "see what others don't," then you "seize the moment," then comes a "steadfast path," and that gives you your "ambition." So ambition comes fourth, not first.

By putting ambition first, *Arc of Ambition* conforms to the motivation and goal setting of our popular experts in personal strategy. Yet we also read that "the arc begins with a fresh insight, or discovery," as "some perception unseen by others." There are "millions of such original thoughts" all the time, but they die on the vine:[19]

> What saves the few that propel human progress is the spell of ambition—the urging of a dream transformed by the mind's eye into a belief that something is possible, and from there into a conviction that hard work must and will make it actually happen.

Here we see ambition playing a different role. It comes second, after the "insight" or "discovery." That sounds like von Clausewitz's resolution. By this account, Carnegie's journey started not in 1852, before modern steelmaking existed, but in 1866 or 1872, when he saw how to make a successful steel business. His ambition then made him work hard to achieve it. We are closer here to the art of what works, although we still find "original thoughts" and "a dream transformed," which take us farther away.

At the end of the journey, *Arc of Ambition* again comes close to the art of what works. We read that the arc can't "last forever":

The external environment becomes less favorable, you become more complacent, others emulate you and whittle away your unique claim to fame. Unexpected rivals—just as ambitious as you once were—find ways to change the rules and creatively destroy things you built to last. To stay on the arc, one must change or die.

We see again Schumpeter's "creative destruction." A successful strategy fits a particular situation; when the situation changes, the strategy no longer works. So either you alter the strategy to "stay on the arc" or you start a new arc, like your "unexpected rivals."

But *Arc of Ambition* points to other causes too: You become "complacent," you're no longer "unique," and you're not as "ambitious as you once were." In the art of what works, successful strategists are seldom complacent, are seldom unique, and seldom decline in ambition. Circumstances change. Sometimes there's nothing you can do. If your strategy stops succeeding, often it's not your fault. Maybe it's time to look for another strategy.

In the end, *Arc of Ambition* shifts back and forth between a popular notion of motivation and goal setting on the one hand, and the art of what works on the other. As in *Built to Last* and some of our other key sources, we find expert intuition mixed in with other schools of strategy. But half is still a lot. It provides an encouraging sign that maybe we're on the right track.

Champy and Nohria don't say so, but a journey's "arc" is an ancient model for myth, legend, and stories of every kind. In *The Hero with a Thousand Faces*, Joseph Campbell shows how myths around the world all follow the same dramatic arc. And in *Story*, Robert McKee traces the same arc in successful Hollywood movies and Aristotle's three-act structure of drama.[20] An event "throws a character's life out of balance" in Act I. That launches him on a "Quest for his Object of Desire" in Act II. In Act III, "he may or may not achieve it."

Figure 9.1 combines Campbell's picture of the "hero's journey" with Aristotle's three acts. We see how similar it is to Figure 7.1, the course of normal science. And we see the same thing again in Figure 9.2, the ancient Tao symbol of yin-yang. Note how the small circles in the yin-yang match the color of the large shapes opposite. The future comes out of the past to make a new past, and so on through the ages.

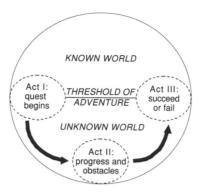

Figure 9.1 The Hero's Journey (adapted from Joseph Campbell, *The Hero With a Thousand Faces.* © 1999 by Bollingen Foundation, Inc. Reprinted by permission of Princeton University Press.)

An event—not a goal, a desire, or an ambition—starts the hero's journey. It comes from the known world, but it leads you into the unknown. The hero is not someone who performs super-human feats. The hero is simply the main character. So you are the hero of your own hero's journey.

The event that starts you on your journey to success is a coup d'oeil. It shows you the path to take. It gives you your goal, your desire, your ambition. A happy life is a series of hero's journeys. Sometimes you win. Sometimes you lose. But you're always ready for the next time. There is joy in the readiness, too.

Here is the essence of popular self-help: If you really decide to do something, you can find a way to do it. The "something" must come from your deepest desire. That's why you decide to do it. Motivation, planning, persistence—in that order.

Figure 9.2 Yin-Yang of Tao

Here is the essence of the art of what works: When you see a way to do something, that's when you decide to do it. The "something" is unpredictable. It comes not from your deepest desires, but from its chance of success. Motivation, planning, and persistence follow.

Above all, our popular experts tell you to look inside yourself to overcome whatever it is that prevents you from achieving success. Their message is: Where there's a will, there's a way. In the art of what works, you look outward, to see what you can seize on to start your quest for success. Where there's a way, there's a will.

If you start with goals instead, you work harder and harder to reach them, yet after a while it feels like you're swimming against a current that's sweeping you out to sea. That drains your motivation, so you turn to experts in motivation to perk you up for a while.

But what's really missing is not motivation, it's how. The "how" comes first, before the goal. First you see the path, then you see the destination. And that destination is not ideal. Go where you can, not where you want to. And when you get there, you'll find: surprise—it's where you want to be.

This is the way of what works.

It's a state of mind. A basic philosophy. A view of life. Once you master it, nothing can stop you. Nothing can throw you. It's not a guarantee of success; it guarantees a fair fight, where even if you lose a round, you live and learn to fight again.

Happily.

Because all along, you take up what works and drop what doesn't. You get better. Your work gets better. Your life gets better. Your love gets better. The pursuit of happiness loses its drudgery. It turns into a happy pursuit: the ancient path of the hero.

Creative Strategy

Strategic planning and flexibility, the learning organization, competitive strategy, the motivation and goal setting of popular experts—all of these are good, but they are incomplete.

No amount of planning can tell you what activity to choose in order to reach your goal. No amount of flexibility can tell you when or whether to change course. Only coup d'oeil can do that.

No amount of teamwork or systems thinking can tell you when to join with others, or what action to take when you do. Only coup d'oeil can do that.

No amount of competitive analysis can tell you what alternatives to consider, or what options to choose from among those alternatives. Only coup d'oeil can do that.

No amount of motivation can tell you what goal to set, or what are the best activities to take up in order to reach your goal. Only coup d'oeil can do that.

Yet in the end, despite the science of expert intuition, a mystery lies at the heart of what works. The elements come from the past, but what exactly makes you combine them—right then, just so—in a strategy for the future? Science marches on, but this is something that we will never know.

Schumpeter chose his words well: a "creative" response to opportunity. Creative success comes from combining what worked in the past, yet the combination itself is new. So the art of what works amounts to a school of "creative strategy" alongside all the others.

Wherever you are in the Saqqara pyramid—high or low or stuck at the bottom—or whether you're out on your own, try creative strategy. It reaches for tools from Chapter 7, like arrows from a quiver. It helps you think outside the box, inside the box, wherever there's something worth taking up and building on to make success. It's an old method, tried and true, the equal of strategic planning and flexibility, the learning organization, competitive strategy, and the motivation and goal setting of personal strategy. Or use them all together.

But always remember, coup d'oeil comes first. It's the key to creative strategy, and the start of your hero's journey.

Between campaigns, in his Council Room in Paris, Napoleon put up an army tent to keep up his feeling of motion as he ran the French government. On that front too, he fought battles only when he saw a chance to win them, based on what worked in the past.

So put up a tent yourself, if only in your mind. Creative strategy puts you in motion, with your eye out for the right moment, the right action, the right opportunity to start your quest.

So if you find you're not succeeding, you now know the reason. Chances are that it's not lack of ambition, lack of motivation, lack of planning, lack of analysis, lack of flexibility, lack of persistence, lack of teamwork, or lack of systems thinking. More likely, you haven't yet seen a way to succeed.

After reading this book, maybe now you'll see it. Perhaps not tomorrow, or even next year. Whenever it comes, you'll be ready. Starting now, you're a synthesist, a creative strategist. You know the art of winning strategy, how success really happens, from the ancient past, right now in the present, and forever into the future:

Successful strategy starts with what works.

Right versus Might
What Works in the
Social Sector

AROUND THE WORLD, business leaders are social leaders too. They advise local, state, and national governments and international bodies. They start and serve on the boards of foundations and other nonprofit organizations. They move into key jobs in all these sectors. They both "do good and do well" through for-profit social ventures and business partnerships with governments and nonprofits. And sometimes they run for office: The current mayor of New York and president of the United States are just two of many examples.

The social sector borrows more than people from business. It borrows methods, too. Business school courses and dozens of published guides tell you how to run your government agency or nonprofit organization on sound business principles. Accounting, finance, management, marketing—every field of business applies.[1]

For strategy, the social sector mostly looks to the three leading schools: strategic planning, the learning organization, and competitive strategy. And there is a further twist to strategy in the social sector: a moral commitment to do the right thing.

On the one hand, that's the whole point. On the other hand, it can blind you to coup d'oeil. If you look only for what's right to succeed, you can miss what might succeed. We recall Kuhn's comment in *Structure of Scientific Revolutions*: The natural scientist aims "to concentrate his attention on problems that he has good reason to believe he will be able to solve." But social scientists "defend their choice of a research problem—e.g., the effects of racial discrimination or the causes of the business cycle—chiefly in terms of the social importance of achieving a solution." That's why natural scientists solve problems faster than social scientists.

Around the world, major social and economic problems remain unsolved. That includes the United States, the richest country of all.

Perhaps the art of what works can help.

Schools of Social Strategy

Just as with business strategy, strategic planning is the oldest and most popular school of social strategy. Mintzberg's *Rise and Fall of Strategic Planning* shows how "big government" after World War II thrived on "big planning," especially in the United States. In the late 1960s, America's War on Poverty gave government money to nonprofit organizations for social programs, so the nonprofits adopted planning too.

Often they did so backwards, through evaluation. In *Evaluation Research*, Carol Weiss tells how government evaluators arrived at the nonprofits to check their progress toward their goals. Many nonprofits admitted, "We don't have any goals." The evaluators replied, "Then get some." Weiss and other social scientists showed them how to do so.[2]

Weiss makes a direct application of classic strategic planning. You start with goals, then you move on to "planned activity (or several activities) aimed at achieving those goals," and then you measure "the extent to which the goals are achieved." Thanks to Weiss and many others, strategic planning spread through the social sector from the 1970s on.

Today we find a large literature on strategic planning tailored to the social sector—for example, Bryan Barry, *Strategic Planning Workbook*; John Bryson, "Strategic Planning and Action Planning for Non-profit Organizations," in Robert Herman, *Handbook of Non-Profit Leadership and Management*; Harry Hatry, *Performance Measurement*; and Paul Joyce, *Strategy in the Public Sector*.[3]

As for the learning organization, it spread from business to the social sector in the 1990s, thanks to Senge's *Fifth Discipline*.[4] Foundations especially encouraged their grantees to work together in "partnership initiatives," where different organizations form a single team. In a recent example, from the Annie E. Casey Foundation Web site, we learn that "Making Connections" aims to "help transform tough neighborhoods into family-supportive environments" by bringing together "residents, civic groups, political leaders, grassroots groups, public and private sector leadership, and faith-based organizations."

Senge himself entered the social sector in 2000 with *Schools that Learn*.[5] He declares:

> Schools can be recreated, made vital, and sustainably renewed not by fiat or command, and not by regulation, but by taking a *learning orientation*. This means involving everyone in the system in expressing their aspirations, building their awareness, and developing their capabilities together.

For competitive strategy, we have *Strategic Management for Non-Profit Organizations*, by Sharon Oster.[6] Here we learn that nonprofits "earn more than $100 billion in revenue in the United States each year, in more than 1 million organizations." To earn this revenue, they face competitive pressures, both from one another and from "for-profit corporations and public agencies." To help them compete, Oster adapts Porter's five forces. We find "customers" changed to "users" and "funders," to make a "Six Forces" model for the social sector.

Porter himself addressed the social sector with a 1998 essay, "Competitive Solutions to Societal Problems," and a 1999 article with Mark Kramer, "Philanthropy's New Agenda." Porter and Kramer also have founded two organizations—the Center for

Effective Philanthropy and the Foundation Strategy Group—to help bring competitive strategy to the social sector.[7]

Last but not least, we find all three schools of strategy in *Private Sector Strategies for Social Sector Success*, by Kevin Kearns.[8] The "visioning approach" starts with a goal set by the organization's leader, as in classic strategic planning. The "incremental approach" follows Mintzberg's emergent strategy and Senge's learning organization. And the "analytical approach" starts with an environmental scan based on Porter's competitive strategy.

Just as in the business sector, we can add the art of what works to these three schools of strategy in the social sector. Yet in business, we also found direct examples of expert intuition: from Ohmae, Bhidé, Chandler, General Electric, Collins and Porras, and many other sources. Can we find the same thing in the social sector?

As it turns out, we can. Once again, few authors name it directly. Expert intuition remains elusive and hard to describe. But it's there, as the key to success for social strategy too.

In Search of What Works

We find what works front and center in *Common Purpose* by Lisbeth Schor.[9] She tells us:

> All over this country, right now, some program or some institution is succeeding in combating such serious problems as high rates of single parenthood, child abuse, youth violence, school failure, and intergenerational poverty.

These successes, however, are "small and scarce." In her study, Schor set out to find what stops these "exceptions" from becoming "the rule," and "what could be done about it."

Among the successes to learn from, Schor highlights the Youth-Build program. Its founder, Dorothy Stoneman, "set out to organize East Harlem teenagers, asking what changes they wanted to make in their community." When one group of teenagers "expressed an interest in renovating housing," Stoneman started a program to help them do it. Over 10 years, the program succeeded and grew. When others tried to replicate it, Stoneman created "a national intermediary organization that could support the spread of the YouthBuild idea." Replication followed in "five and then fifteen cities." As of 1997, YouthBuild had become a federal program that "awarded more than $100 million to grantees in thirty-four states."

In another success story, Schor tells of Robert Slavin, Nancy Madden, and other scholars from Johns Hopkins University, who developed Success for All in Baltimore schools. They reviewed the literature and talked with the staff of the school district in order to design a program "based on two essential principles":

> First, that major learning problems must be prevented by providing children with the best available classroom programs and by engaging parents to support school success; second, that when learning difficulties do appear, corrective interventions must be immediate and intensive.

In their literature review, Slavin and his colleagues found what works. They put the elements together and then made sure that they kept checking what works through in-class testing to trigger "corrective interventions."

After a successful pilot at Abbottston Elementary in Baltimore, Success for All went into "five other schools in Baltimore and one in Philadelphia." Four years later, there were "fifteen schools in seven states" where "Success for All achieved higher reading levels throughout the elementary grades." Three years later, in 1996, Success for All was in "more than 450 schools" in "thirty-one states."

In YouthBuild, Success for All, and Schor's many other examples, we see the key elements of the art of what works. Yet Schor contends that replicating success is not enough. The failures still outnumber the successes by a wide margin. We need a big push to solve the problem of poverty once and for all:

> Virtually all the elements that are part of the solution can be identified and described; they are a reality today, somewhere in this country. Taken to scale, these elements could be combined into a powerful Public Purpose Sector.

Schor cites seven "place-based neighborhood transformation initiatives" that make such a combination:

> All have created synergy by putting together a wealth of knowledge and experience from many different domains. They show how extraordinary, but still underestimated, neighborhood transformation efforts could combine into a major national strategy to combat poverty, rebuild the inner city, and reverse the growth of an American underclass.

For Schor, these seven "comprehensive community initiatives" represent a "new synthesis." Since "no single strand of intervention can be counted on to produce significant results," we have been forced to address "poverty, welfare, employment, education, child development, housing, and crime one at a time." That will take forever to work. But in the new synthesis, "the multiple and interrelated problems of poor neighborhoods require multiple and interrelated solutions."

So in the end, Schor departs from what works.

Instead, we find a new idea: Solve everything at once. Then come seven examples of the new idea in action. It's too early to tell whether they work, but Schor calls them "successful" anyway. That means that the initiatives fit her definition of a good program, in that they try to solve everything at once. That's a different standard from the one used in the earlier parts of her book, where "successful" meant having positive results.

We can understand Schor's impatience. Given the scale of the problems, replicating "single strands" of interventions seems like a futile task. But must we jump to the other extreme, from single strands to comprehensive initiatives? Isn't there anything in between? To make something larger, might we try instead to combine a few strands of what we know already works?

Let's turn to a case that does exactly that.

GRAD

In the 1980s, many corporations "adopted" schools in cities where they had offices. In Houston, Tenneco started providing mentors, tutors, and special courses for Davis High School, the worst in the city, in 1981. In 1983, Tenneco added college scholarships for students who graduated with average grades or above, plus Communities in Schools (CIS), a national program that counsels students with family and personal problems that distract them from schoolwork. In 1989, the Houston Endowment joined in, as a sponsor of summer classes that help scholarship hopefuls prepare for college.

From 1983, when the scholarships began, to 1992, college enrollment by Davis graduates rose from 20 to 81. On the one hand, a fourfold increase can be seen as good results. On the other hand, 600 students started at Davis in grade 9, so 81 still meant that fewer than 15 percent made it to college. And 425 of the students—70 percent dropped out before graduation from grade 12. They dropped out because they arrived at high school so far behind that they could never catch up. It was just too late. The problem started way back in elementary and middle school.

In 1992, James Ketelsen retired as CEO of Tenneco. Instead of leaving Davis behind, he and his wife, Kathryn, set up shop in their garage. At this point, there was still nothing remarkable about Davis—many other "adopt-a-school" programs had had similar results. But then Ketelsen did a remarkable thing: He looked upstream from Davis to the six elementary and middle schools that fed into it, and asked the question, "What works?" That is, were there existing programs elsewhere that showed success in turning around failing elementary and middle schools?

Ketelsen set out on a treasure hunt for programs to add to the scholarships, summer classes, and CIS. Over the next year, he found three that showed convincing success: Success for All (SFA), Consistency Management and Cooperative Discipline (CMCD), and Move it Math (MIM).

SFA we've already met, as one of the "single strands" of proven success in Schor's book. Ketelsen picked it up, to weave in with other strands. For CMCD, evaluations showed good results in solving the discipline problem in schools. MIM was riskier: There were no evaluations yet. But nationwide, there was no successful math program that Ketelsen could use. So he observed MIM in action and saw good results in the classrooms he studied. Thus, MIM joined the list.

Each program came with an existing support system of professionals who already knew what to do. Like SFA, CIS had a national organization that was ready to go. For CMCD, there was a small group at the University of Houston. For MIM, there was the husband-wife team who had developed it. In August 1993, Ketelsen brought the leaders of the four programs together at a working lunch in downtown Houston. He asked them in detail whether and how the different programs might mesh. All four gave thumbs up. And so was born Project GRAD, for "Graduation Really Achieves Dreams."

The Ketelsens served as coordinators and problem solvers for bringing the three programs to the Davis "feeder"—that is, the high school plus the six lower schools that fed into it. SFA and CMCD asked teachers to vote on whether they wanted to bring the program to their school, so Ketelsen adopted the same practice for all the GRAD components. Six of the seven schools voted yes in the first year. The seventh school came on board in the second year.

By year three, the early results convinced Ketelsen to establish a nonprofit organization to run the program. He raised funds and hired an executive director, who in turn hired a coordinating staff. In 1997, a professor at the University of Houston, Dr. K. A. Opuni, evaluated GRAD. The results were outstanding: Both math and reading scores and high school graduation rates had increased on average by more than half. And the costs were moderate: about 5 percent of the total school budget.[10]

At that point, GRAD stood out as perhaps America's most successful model for turning around failing public schools. Other programs had had good results in a single school, or had had good results in many schools, but at high cost. GRAD had scale, moderate cost, and, above all, strong results.

Since 1997, GRAD has spread to four more feeders in Houston and to eight other cities across the country. In 2001, GRAD set up a separate national organization, GRAD-USA, to help new cities bring GRAD to their schools. The federal budget in 2001 and 2002 included funding for GRAD. Today there are more than 100,000 students in GRAD schools. And the way is clear to bring GRAD to the million students who need it.

Ketelsen himself is an artist of what works. And GRAD has attracted others like him, including the staffs of GRAD-Houston, GRAD-USA, and the GRADs in other cities. Almost everyone joins up for the same reason that Ketelsen has stayed with GRAD through his retirement: It works.

We can catch a glimpse of GRAD's growth in a documentary film. *Scaling Up Successful Work*, by Junko Chano, features an interview with Steven Zwerling of the Ford Foundation.

Zwerling tells us that his job was to "think about how community colleges" might "provide more opportunity for people from low-income backgrounds." He "developed a hypothesis" that you had to form "very broad kinds of partnerships within cities that could then develop a plan of action," with community colleges playing a central role. So that's what he did.

And the results?[11]

> They were developing plans—they had a little special project over here, a little special project over there. . . . Not a lot was occurring on the ground in a substantial way, at scale, of a sort that was going to really contribute to closing the achievement gap in these places.

And then Zwerling found out about GRAD. His first reaction was negative:

> It was pretty obvious no community college was in sight. It didn't have a partnership. It did not fit our theory of change.

Zwerling's comments hark back to Schor's original question: "What stopped us from turning the exceptions into the rule" by scaling up what works? The answer in this case: Zwerling already had his "hypothesis," his "plans," his "theory of change." To scale up what works, he would have to give them up.

He finally went to Houston, but he was "very skeptical." He visited the schools and studied the data. Zwerling found "real evidence that the program could make a difference in the lives of kids." It marked a turning point in his work:

> I began to become a different kind of program officer. I began to figure out that my job was not to figure out the solutions to problems but, more profoundly, to have my eyes open wide enough and my understanding sufficiently available to help identify things that contribute to the solution of problems. Then I had to try to figure out what I could do to be helpful to them.

Zwerling gave up his theories in favor of presence of mind: "to have my eyes open wide enough." He expected the unexpected. Sure enough, a coup d'oeil showed him what to do.

Zwerling made grants to enable GRAD to go into a second feeder in Houston, which was what Ketelsen wanted most, and also to "expand beyond Houston." What it took for GRAD to spread to other cities was for Zwerling's whole outlook on strategy to change. Thanks to Ketelsen, Zwerling learned the art of what works.

Globe-Trotter

Let's turn now to the social sector in poor countries.

In those countries, a host of international development agencies are leading the fight against poverty. They have not fared well: In the past few decades, poverty has increased in most developing countries. But despite the overall picture, can we find any successes within it? If so, that might show the way to build up more, to carry success to scale.

So we search the globe for what works, as if we were casting the Trotter matrix across it. Latitude and longitude become the matrix grid. Our "globe-Trotter" covers the earth. What do we catch in its net?

First, we must choose among the many organizations to study. Let's start with two: the World Bank and the International Monetary Fund (IMF). Both date from the 1940s, when Europe began to rebuild after World War II. In later decades, the same agencies moved on to developing countries. The World Bank makes loans for economic development projects, while the IMF makes loans to tide countries over when their whole economy slumps. Today, these two institutions dominate aid to developing countries. Other agencies toil in their shadow, like it or not.

For the World Bank, we have a recent report by a former Bank economist: *The Elusive Quest for Growth*, by William Easterly. He notes the economic theory that rules World Bank lending: External aid leads to internal investment leads to economic growth. Then he tests this theory against actual results in 138 developing countries. He finds that the theory holds for just one country:[12]

> Tunisia. Before Tunisians throw a national celebration, I should point out that 1 success out of 138 is likely to have occurred by chance.

So investment is not the answer, even when you include a hefty investment in education:

> What has been the response of economic growth to the educational explosion? Alas, the answer is: little or none.

Education is of little value without economic opportunities that put that education to use. That means that education can accelerate growth, but it can't start it.

So what is the answer?

Policy.

It's not how much you invest, but how you invest. With the wrong policies, the investment is wasted. With the right policies, the investment pays off. But even here, the World Bank and other agencies have erred: "To try to create the right incentives, international institutions started making loans conditional on policy reforms."

So what happened? The countries promised to introduce reforms and took the loans. Then either they failed to implement the reforms or the reforms themselves failed. Easterly has a solution: to "tie aid to past country performance, not promises, giving the country's government an incentive to pursue growth-creating policies."

On the one hand, this has a "what works" appeal: If a country's policies have worked, we lend it the money to keep going. On the other hand, what policies should a country try in the first place? We can't just punish the poor performers by cutting off their loans. We also have to offer them policies that will help them succeed in the future.

So we ask: What policies help create growth?

To answer this question, Easterly looks for positive examples. He tells one story in detail, that of the textile industry in Bangladesh.

As of 1979, there were only 40 workers in the whole textile sector. In that year, a former government official named Quader allied his textile company, Desh Garments, with Daewoo Corporation of South Korea. Daewoo brought 130 Desh workers to its plant in Pusan to learn the trade, in return for a share of Desh's future revenue. But something happened:

> Of the 130 Desh workers trained by Daewoo, 115 of them left Desh during the 1980s to set up their own garment export firms. . . . The explosion of garment companies started by ex-Desh workers brought Bangladesh its $2 billion in garment sales today.

Here we have a clear case of expert intuition in action. The Desh workers learned how Daewoo made textiles, practiced those methods at Desh, and then saw how to strike out on their own.

Easterly draws this policy lesson: "conscious government intervention in knowledge creation." That is, Quader had special knowledge of Daewoo's interest in Bangladesh, and his workers gained special knowledge in Korea. It was "sheer luck" that everything worked out so well. In other countries, the government should make this special knowledge available from the start. Easterly concludes: "Markets will often need an injection of government subsidies to start the knowledge ball rolling."

But wait: In the art of what works, you can't predict what knowledge you'll need. Next time it won't be knowledge of textiles that's key, it will be knowledge of something else. A government can't subsidize knowledge about everything, all the time, to everyone. You have to choose, but how?

For this, we return to Schumpeter. Easterly gives us a chapter entitled "Creative Destruction: The Power of Technology," with a subsection, "Imitation among the Poor." The Bangladesh example shows that "poor countries can leap right to the technological frontier by imitating technologies from industrialized nations":

> Bangladeshi garment workers imitated Korean garment workers during their apprenticeship in Korea, and Bangladeshi managers imitated Korean managers. The result was a multibillion dollar garment industry in Bangladesh.

So, Easterly concludes,

> The government should subsidize technological imitation because it brings benefits to other firms in the economy besides the imitator. And of course, the business climate has to favor foreign direct investment and imports of machines, not to mention entrepreneurs in general.

We come very close here to the art of what works. Still, we ask of Easterly: which technology? Should the government subsidize the visit of Quader's 130 workers to Korea before we have any evidence that the textile industry might work in Bangladesh? If so, we have the impossible task of subsidizing visits of everyone to everywhere, for all kinds of technology, in the hope that something will click. For, as Easterly notes, we can't know beforehand which technology will work out the best:

> In general, it's hard to predict success when there are intangible factors behind success.

Yet Easterly fails to offer specific policies on how to "subsidize technological imitation" before it starts to happen. That's because it's an impossible task. You can't know what's worth imitating until it has started to succeed. You can't predict coup d'oeil. But you can subsidize resolution after the imitation starts. So your policies must be able to react quickly to what works, rather than trying to predict it.

Easterly does not quite solve the puzzle of "elusive growth," but he comes close. And we're just glad to find a World Bank economist who favors the art of what works.

Let's turn now to the IMF.

Here we meet the familiar face of Joseph Stiglitz, our 2001 Nobel Prize winner in economics. He led off our first chapter with a quote on "imperfect information"—the fog of strategy that expert intuition cuts through. In the 1990s, Stiglitz served on the president's Council of Economic Advisers for 4 years and then spent 3 years as chief economist and senior vice president of the World Bank.

In *Globalization and its Discontents*, Stiglitz reports especially on his dealings with the IMF. He endorses the original mandate of the IMF, in the tradition of Lord Keynes, the great economist who helped found it. But over the decades, Stiglitz believes, the IMF has strayed:[13]

> Founded on the belief that markets often work badly, it now champions market supremacy with ideological fervor. . . . Keynes would be rolling over in his grave if he were to see what has happened to his child.

For Stiglitz, the IMF "has failed in its mission" to provide funds "for countries facing an economic downturn, to enable the country to restore itself to close to full employment." Instead, the IMF imposes free-market policies on countries as a condition for receiving its funds.

Stiglitz hates that. He notes that "most of the advanced industrial countries" departed from free markets early on, "by wisely and selectively protecting some of their industries until they were strong enough to compete with foreign companies." His examples include the United States and Japan. And even more recently, "European countries banned the free flow of capital until the seventies."

In making his argument, Stiglitz invokes "examples from history," just as von Clausewitz did. He looks to what worked in the past. But instead of heeding these precedents, the IMF applies "mistaken economic theories" that have led to poverty for many people, and "for many countries social and political chaos."

Stiglitz calls on the IMF to study what works instead. A single free-market model has won the day in policy debates, but economists know that "there is not just *one* market model." He cites Japan, Germany, Sweden, the United States, Malaysia, Korea,

China, and Taiwan as successful examples of different market models:

> Over the past fifty years, economic science has explained why, and the conditions under which, markets work well and when they do not.

So what's the problem? The IMF "presents as received doctrine propositions and policy recommendations for which there is not widespread agreement":

> For the believers in free and unfettered markets, capital market liberalization was obviously desirable; one didn't need evidence that it promoted growth.

So the IMF enters battle with a single theory, instead of expecting the unexpected and drawing on whatever theories and methods suit the situation at hand. And Stiglitz sounds like Kuhn when he adds:

> One of the important distinctions between ideology and science is that science recognizes the limitations of what one knows. There is always uncertainty.

Above all, the "believers" think that "free and unfettered markets" are morally right and good for mankind. Pure markets are right to succeed: but might they succeed? According to Stiglitz, no. Their record of success is dismal.

Stiglitz gives the experience of Russia compared to that of China as a major illustration of his point. In the 1990s, Russia obeyed the IMF. China did not. The result? Russia collapsed while China boomed.

> Russia's transition has entailed one of the largest increases in poverty in history in such a short span of time (outside of war or famine). . . . In the meanwhile, China unleashed a process of creative destruction: of eliminating the old economy by creating a new one.

Our old friend Schumpeter again.

A key to China's success was a new form of ownership, based on the old:

> Township and village public enterprises were central in the early years of transition. IMF ideology said that because these were public enterprises, they could not have succeeded.

Stiglitz notes that building on what works sounds slow, but it ends up being faster in the end. In an "ultimate irony," gradual policies "succeeded in making deeper reforms more rapidly." In Russia the reforms went fast, whereas in China they went slowly. And yet

> China's stock market is larger than Russia's. Much of Russia's agriculture today is managed little differently than it was a decade ago, while China managed the transition to the "individual responsibility system" in less than four years.

Stiglitz goes on to cite other successful examples of building on the past that depart from IMF orthodoxy, in the Czech Republic and Poland.

To save the situation, Stiglitz would start by "forcing the IMF to return to its original mission." To do that, you would have to change its governing board. Right now, industrial countries dominate. Stiglitz wants more seats for countries that are on the receiving end of IMF policies. And he wants transparency in all decisions, so that economists and others from all over the world can voice their opinion before it's too late. He also wants an independent think tank, free from IMF influence, to give the receiving nations advice.

These suggestions are fine. But will greater democracy and transparency lead to the right decisions? The march of science says yes: Truth wins out in the end. Yet the art of what works eludes committees. The more voices there are, the less there is "unity of command." Everything Stiglitz wants will help, but still there comes the moment when Desh's workers strike out on their own, or China's village industries succeed. No one predicted it. A worldwide committee can't react in time to make a difference. Only a strategist can, armed with expert intuition.

Easterly and Stiglitz bring what works to high-level policy. That's grand strategy; to win battles, you also need strategists on the ground. Thousands of professionals make up the army of international development assistance. Right now they operate according to one or more of the leading schools of strategy. They need instead the art of what works, so that wherever they are, whatever happens, they can seek out and build on success.[14]

Like Zwerling and GRAD. Like Keri S., our synthesist in strategy consulting. Like the multitude of successful examples we saw in our business cases. You need artists of what works in the poor countries themselves—like Quader of Desh—but you also need them in the international development agencies.

Easterly opens his book with a comment on the elusive "quest" for growth that his entire profession pursues:

> The theme of the quest is ancient. In many versions, it is the search for a precious object with magical properties: the Golden Fleece, the Holy Grail, the Elixir of Life. . . . Like the ancient questors, we economists have tried to find the precious object, the key that would enable the poor tropics to become rich. We thought we had found the elixir many different times. . . . None has delivered as promised.

But don't give up. There is no one precious object, one magic formula. There are many, one for each situation. You find them by coup d'oeil.

Notes

Preface

1. Quoted in José Ortega y Gasset, *Man and Crisis* (New York: Norton, 1958), cited in Joseph Campbell, *Creative Mythology* (Baltimore: Penguin, 1968). The original Italian is, *Che non puo quel che vuol, quel che puo voglia.*
2. Quotation from *Jack Welch and the GE Way* by Robert Slater, © 1998 The McGraw-Hill Companies.
3. Quotation from Joseph Campbell, *The Hero with a Thousand Faces.* © 1999 by Bollingen Foundation, Inc. Reprinted by permission of Princeton University Press.

Chapter 1: Introduction

1. Joseph Stiglitz, "The Contributions of the Economics of Information to Twentieth Century Economics," *Quarterly Journal of Economics,* November 2000.
2. Quotations from *On War* by Carl von Clausewitz (1982). Reprinted by permission of Taylor & Francis.
3. The *Oxford English Dictionary* gives us this original definition of *strategy* in English: "The art of a commander-in-chief; the art of projecting and directing the larger military movements and operations of a campaign." And it cites the first appearance in English—by way of C. James, *Military Dictionary* (1810): "Strategy differs materially from tactic; the latter belonging only to the mechanical movement of bodies, set in motion by the former."
4. See Herbert Simon, *Models of Thoughts,* vol. II (New Haven, CT.: Yale University Press, 1989); Gary Klein, *Sources of Power* (Boston: MIT Press, 1998); Thomas Kuhn, *The Structure of Scientific Revolutions* (Chicago: University of Chicago Press, 1969); and Louis Menand, *The Metaphysical Club* (New York: Farrar, Strauss & Giroux, 2001). Kuhn writes most about expert intuition in a postscript to the 1969 edition of *Structure of Scientific Revolutions,* in reply to comments he received about the original 1962 edition.

5. Lao Tzu, *Tao Te Ching* translated by Stephen Mitchell (New York: Harper Perennial, 1992); Sun Tzu, *The Art of War* (Oxford University Press, 1984); Miyamoto Musashi, *The Book of Five Rings* (translated by Victor Harris, New York: Overlook, 1992).
6. The Napoleon quote comes from J. C. Herold, *The Mind of Napoleon* (New York: Columbia University Press, 1955). Reprinted with permission of the publisher.
7. Joseph Schumpeter, "The Creative Response in Economic History," *Journal of Economic History*, November 1947.
8. Kenichi Ohmae, *The Mind of the Strategist* (New York: McGraw-Hill, 1982).
9. Ryuei Shimizu, *The Growth of Firms in Japan* (Tokyo: Keio Tsushin, 1980).
10. Amar Bhidé, *The Origin and Evolution of New Businesses* (New York: Oxford University Press, 2000).
11. James Collins and Jerry Porras, *Built to Last* (New York: HarperBusiness, 1994).
12. Alfred Chandler, *Strategy and Structure* (Boston: MIT Press, 1962).
13. Henry Mintzberg, *The Rise and Fall of Strategic Planning* (New York: Free Press, 1994).
14. James Quinn, *Strategies for Change: Logical Incrementalism* (Chicago: Irwin, 1980).
15. Peter Senge, *The Fifth Discipline: The Art and Practice of the Learning Organization* (New York: Doubleday, 1990).
16. Warren Bennis, *Organizing Genius* (Cambridge, MA: Perseus, 1998).
17. Michael Porter, *Competitive Strategy* (New York: Free Press, 1980).
18. For bootstrapping, see Paul Schoemaker and J. Edward Russo, "A Pyramid of Decision Approaches," *California Management Review* 36 (1993). For the Trotter matrix, see Robert Slater, *The GE Way Fieldbook* (New York: McGraw-Hill, 1999). For grounded theory, see Barney Glaser and Anselm Strauss, *The Discovery of Grounded Theory* (Chicago: Aldine, 1967). For normal science, see "The Nature of Normal Science" in Kuhn, *Structure of Scientific Revolutions*.

Chapter 2: An Eye for What Works

1. Carl von Clausewitz, *On War*. (1832; reprint, translated by J. J. Graham, London, England: Penguin Books, 1968). For a concise scholarly essay on coup d'oeil, see Katherine Herbig, "Chance and Uncertainty in *On War*," in Michael Handel, *Clausewitz and Modern Strategy* (London: Cass, 1986)
2. Ray Kroc, *Grinding It Out* (Chicago: Regnery, 1977).
3. Quotation from "The Next Insanely Great Thing," *Wired* (February 1996) by Gary Wolf. Reprinted by permission of the author.
4. Quotation from *Triumph of the Nerds* (video, 1996) by Robert X. Cringely. Reprinted by permission of the author.

5. Shira White, *New Ideas about New Ideas: Insights and Creativity from the World's Leading Innovators* (Cambridge, MA: Perseus, 2002).
6. The web site of Harvard Business School Publications lists 20 Apple cases and 4 McDonald's cases. A case by W. E. Sasser and David Rikert, "McDonald's Corp.," comes closest to expert intuition by describing the features that make for the success of McDonald's. It is telling as well that this is not a classic case that asks you to recommend a strategy, but rather provides contrast for a Burger King case.
7. Antoine Jomini, *Summary of the Art of War* (1838; reprint, translated by G. H. Mendell and W. P. Craighill, Washington, DC: Military Service Publishing, 1947).
8. The Hittle quote comes from his Introduction to Jomini, *Summary of the Art of War*.
9. The military debate between Jomini and von Clausewitz continues in the modern era: Both are still on the reading list at American military academies. And in *On Strategy* (Presidio, 1995), Harry Summers applies the insights of von Clausewitz to the Vietnam War. Most recently, Colin Gray compares the advantages of following Jomini and von Clausewitz for fighting international terrorism in "Defining and Achieving Total Victory" (U.S. Army War College, 2002). In *Grant Wins the War: Decision at Vicksburg* (Wiley, 1999), James Arnold makes an explicit comparison between Grant at Vicksburg and Napoleon's great victory at Jena in 1806, where the French took von Clausewitz prisoner. See also John Keegan, "Grant and Unheroic Leadership," in *The Mask of Command* (New York: Viking, 1987). For mobile war in general, see Basil Liddell Hart, *Strategy* (New York: Meridian, 1991); and Martin van Crefeld, *The Art of War* (London: Cassell, 2000).
10. Quotations from *The Mind of Napoleon* by J. C. Herold © 1961, Columbia University Press. Reprinted with permission of the publisher. In Napoleon Bonaparte, *l'Art de la guerre* (Paris: Club de l'honnéte homme, 1965), we find this quote too: "Success in war owes so much to *coup d'oeil*." But Napoleon used the term in its more traditional sense of an eye for the terrain. For a detailed look at Napoleon's methods, see David Chandler, *The Campaigns of Napoleon* (New York: Macmillan, 1973).
11. Quotations from *On War* by Carl von Clausewitz (1982). Reprinted by permission of Taylor & Francis.
12. A recent book helps in applying von Clausewitz to business strategy: Tiha von Ghyczy, Christopher Bassford, and Bolko von Oetinger, *Clausewitz on Strategy* (New York: Wiley, 2001). The book presents the excerpts from *On War* that the authors judge most relevant to business strategy. They title the first section of excerpts "Coup d'Oeil," yet they do not mention coup d'oeil in their introduction. For decades, the most common citation from von Clausewitz has had little to do with coup d'oeil: "War is the mere continuation of policy by other means." Some scholars interpret this

quote to mean that von Clausewitz was pro-war—that is, that he thought war was morally equivalent to politics. But a strategist might read this quote a different way: Von Clausewitz is saying that politicians will decide when to go to war and against whom, and will hand that decision to the general. That freed von Clausewitz to use most of *On War* to deal not with politics, but with strategy, that is, with how the general wins the war. More modern military authorities use the term *grand strategy* for what von Clausewitz calls *policy*. For grand strategy, see for example, "The Theory of Strategy," in Hart, *Strategy*.

13. For Frederick's essay, see "Article 6: Of the Coup d'Oeil," in Frederick II, King of Prussia, *Military Instruction from the Late King of Prussia to his Generals* (London: Egerton, 1797).

14. For early studies on intuition, see Norman Maier, "Reasoning in Humans," in *Journal of Comparative Psychology* 12 (1931); Frederic Bartlett, *Remembering: A Study in Experimental and Social Psychology* (New York: Macmillan, 1932); Eric Berne, "The Nature of Intuition," in *Psychiatric Quarterly* 23 (1949); Kenneth Hammond, "Probabilistic Functioning and the Clinical Method," in *Psychological Review* 62 (1955); and Egon Brunswik, *Perception and the Representative Design of Psychological Experiments* (Berkeley: University of California Press, 1956). For recent updates on brain research, see Antonio Damasio, *The Feeling of What Happens* (New York: Harcourt Brace, 1999), and Lise Eliot, *What's Going On in There?* (New York: Bantam, 1999). Science tells us that there are indeed two sides to the brain: an intuitive right side and an analytic left side. Eliot writes: "Babies appear to be born with a slight right-hemisphere advantage. The left hemisphere apparently catches up by the second year. Later still—around four years of age—communication *between* the two hemispheres improves dramatically, integrating a child's analytical and intuitive sides." On two modes of thought, see Shelly Chaiken and Yaacov Trope, *Dual Process Theories in Social Psychology* (New York: Guilford, 1999); S. Epstein, A. Lipson, C. Holstein, and E. Huh, "Irrational Reactions to Negative Outcomes: Evidence for Two Conceptual Systems," in *Journal of Personality and Social Psychology* 62 (1992); and Steven Sloman, "The Empirical Case for Two Systems of Reasoning," *Psychological Bulletin* 119 (1996).

15. Quotation from *Models of Thought*, vol. 2, by Herbert Simon (1989). Reprinted by permission of Yale University Press. For Simon's earlier work, see *Administrative Behavior* (New York: Macmillan, 1947), and "A Behavior Model of Rational Choice," *Quarterly Journal of Economics* 69 (1965). For an early influence on Simon, see Chester Barnard, *The Functions of the Executive* (Cambridge, MA: Harvard University Press, 1938).

16. Quotations from *Sources of Power* by Gary Klein (1998). Reprinted by permission of MIT Press.

17. Robin Hogarth, *Educating Intuition* (Chicago: University of Chicago Press, 2001).

18. Quotations from *Handbook of Creativity* by Robert Sternberg (1999). Reprinted with the permission of Cambridge University Press. Sternberg's definition of *creativity* comes from the introductory chapter by Sternberg and Todd Lubart. Weisberg's key book is *Creativity: Beyond the Myth of Genius* (New York: Freeman, 1993).

19. In his concluding chapter to *Handbook on Creativity*, Mayer notes further: "Creativity was at the heart of the cognitive psychology proposed by Gestalt psychologists in the 1930s and 1940s. . . . The motivating question for those researchers involved understanding the nature of insight, that is, where creative ideas come from. . . . The focus on insight, however, was lost when cognitive psychology opted for the precision of the information-processing approach in the 1960s." Mayer's "insight" points toward coup d'oeil. Many other writers have noted similarities between Gestalt and Zen philosophy, which we encounter later in this chapter. See, for example, Frederic Perls, *Gestalt Therapy Verbatim* (Lafayette, CA: Real People Press, 1969).

20. Henri Poincaré, *Science et méthode* (Flammarion, 1908); Henri Bergson, *L'Évolution créatrice* (Paris: Presses Universitaires de Paris, 1907); and Mario Bunge, *Intuition and Science* (Englewood Cliffs, NJ: Prentice-Hall, 1962). See K. W. Wild, *Intuition* (Cambridge: Cambridge University Press, 1938), for a review of the "intuitionist" school of science. In a chapter entitled "The Scientist's Intuitions," Bunge cites experimental evidence from Charles Osgood, *Method and Theory in Experimental Psychology* (Oxford: Oxford University Press, 1953), and from Bartlett, *Remembering*.

21. Quotations from *The Structure of Scientific Revolutions* by Thomas S. Kuhn © 1962, 1970 by University of Chicago Press. Reprinted by permission of University of Chicago Press.

22. Peter Medawar, *Advice to a Young Scientist* (New York: Basic Books, 1979).

23. The Bacon quote comes from his *Opus Maius*, ed. J. H. Bridges (Oxford: Clarendon Press, 1897–1900), cited in Joseph Campbell, *The Hero with a Thousand Faces* (Princeton, NJ: Princeton University Press, 1968), via Lynn Thorndike, *A History of Magic and Experimental Science* (New York: Columbia University Press, 1958).

24. On the difference between mathematics and other sciences, see especially Karl Popper, *The Logic of Scientific Discovery* (London: Hutchinson, 1959). But even in mathematics, a proof is simply a test of consistency with axioms, which are consistent among themselves but remain unprovable.

25. William James, *Pragmatism* (New York: Longman's, 1907).

26. For the first Holmes quote, Menand cites Sheldon Novick, *The Collected Works of Justice Holmes*, vol. 1 (Chicago: University of Chicago Press, 1995); for the second, Menand cites Liva Baker, *The Justice from Beacon Hill* (New York: HarperCollins, 1991). For more on pragmatism, see Menand, *Pragmatism: A Reader* (New York: Vintage, 1997).

27. Quotations from *The Art of War* by Sun Tzu (1963). Reprinted by permission of Oxford University Press, Inc.

28. For the history of Tao and Zen, see John Blofeld, *Taoism* (Boston: Shambhala, 1985), and Heinrich Dumoulin, *A History of Zen Buddhism* (New York: Pantheon, 1963). In a preface to the 1963 edition of *The Art of War*, Samuel Griffith notes that the book reached Europe in a French translation in 1772, but we don't know whether Napoleon read it. See also *Sun Tzu and the Art of Business* (New York: Oxford University Press, 1996) by Mark McNeilly, who explains, "My interest in writing this book resulted from the combination of insights I gained working as a business strategist for a major global corporation, the thoughts I'd compiled from my readings as an amateur military historian, and my interest in Sun Tzu's strategic philosophy."

29. Quotations from *A Book of Five Rings*, by Miyamoto Musashi, translation by Victor Harris. © 1974 by Victor Harris. Reprinted with permission of The Overlook Press.

Chapter 3: The Art of Success

1. Quotations from *Hard Drive* © 1992 by James Wallace and Jim Erickson. Reprinted by permission of John Wiley and Sons, Inc.

2. Quotations from "The Creative Response in Economic History," by Joseph Schumpeter, *Journal of Economic History*, vol. 7, No. 2 (November 1947). Reprinted with the permission of Cambridge University Press.

3. Joseph Schumpeter, "Change and the Entrepreneur," in Harvard University Research Center in Entrepreneurial History, *Change and the Entrepreneur: Postulates and the Patterns for Entrepreneurial History* (Cambridge, MA: Harvard University Press, 1949). The article also appears as "Economic Theory and Entrepreneurial History" in a collection of Schumpeter's articles, *Essays on Entrepreneurs, Innovations, Business Cycles, and the Evolution of Capitalism* (New Brunswick, NJ: Transaction, 1989).

4. Joseph Schumpeter, "The Instability of Capitalism," *Economic Journal* September 1928. For a study of how imitation from history works in political decisions, see Richard Neustadt, *Thinking in Time* (New York: Free Press, 1986).

5. For reviews and compilations of the strategy literature to contrast with Bhidé's empirical study, see Henry Mintzberg, Bruce Ahlstrand, and Joseph Lampel, *Strategy Safari* (New York: Free Press, 1998); Richard Koch, *Financial Times Guide to Strategy* (London: Financial Times Prentice-Hall 2000); Financial Times Editors, *Mastering Strategy* (Upper Saddle River, NJ: Prentice-Hall, 2000); Henry Mintzberg and James Quinn, *The Strategy Process* (Upper Saddle River, NJ: Prentice-Hall, 1996); and Henk Volberda and Tom Elfring, *Rethinking Strategy* (London: Sage, 2001).

6. Quotation from *The Origin and Evolution of New Businesses* by Amar Bhidé © 2000 by Oxford University Press, Inc. Reprinted by permission of the publisher.

7. For a critique of *Built to Last*, see Richard Foster and Sarah Kaplan, *Creative Destruction* (New York: Doubleday, 2001), which bears the subtitle, "Why Companies That Are Built to Last Underperform the Market." Foster and Kaplan's study of 1000 companies overturns the whole notion of "built to last." Nothing lasts: You have to keep changing. But as we saw, *Built to Last* mostly agrees with this. Collins and Porras based their title on their method, not on their results: They studied companies that have lasted, and found that they do so by changing. A more fitting title for *Built to Last* might be *Change to Last*. Alas, no company succeeds forever: Foster and Kaplan cite Enron as a shining example of corporate excellence.

8. Quotations from *Strategy and Structure* by Alfred Chandler (1962). Reprinted by permission of MIT Press.

9. Quotations from *The Mind of the Strategist* by Kenichi Ohmae © 1982 The McGraw-Hill Companies. For other studies of the Japanese model, see Richard Pascale and Anthony Athos, *The Art of Japanese Management* (New York: Simon & Schuster, 1981); William Ouchi, *Theory Z: How American Business Can Meet the Japanese Challenge* (Reading, MA: Addison-Wesley, 1981); Masaaki Imai, *Kaizen: The Key to Japan's Competitive Success* (Chicago: Irwin, 1986); and Takeshi Yuzawa, *Japanese Business Success: The Evolution of a Strategy* (New York: Routledge, 1994).

10. Quotation from *The Growth of Firms in Japan* by Ryuei Shimizu (1980). Reprinted by permission of Keio University Press. Partial funding for Shimizu's studies came from the Fukuzawa Memorial Fund of Keio University. Yukichi Fukuzawa was a master of the art of what works in the nineteenth century, using creative imitation of Western achievements to help Japan catch up. Fukuzawa founded Keio University to assist in that task. See especially Fukuzawa's *Autobiography* (Tokyo: Hokuseido, 1948).

11. For Japan's decline in recent decades, see Edward Lincoln, *Arthritic Japan: The Slow Pace of Economic Reform* (Washington, DC: Brookings Institution, 2001).

12. Quotations from *Control Your Destiny or Someone Else Will* by Noel Tichy and Stratford Sherman (1993). Reprinted with permission of Doubleday. There is irony in Tichy and Sherman's title. Jack Welch did not "control" his destiny, but behaved more like Napoleon in this quote cited earlier: "I had few really definite ideas, and the reason for this was that, instead of obstinately seeking to control circumstances, I obeyed them. . . . Thus it happened that most of the time, to tell the truth, I had no definite plans but only projects." See also Welch's autobiography, *Jack: Straight From the Gut* (New York: Warner, 2001).

13. For more on von Moltke, see "The Nineteenth Century," in van Crefeld, *Art of War* (London: Cassell, 2000). Von Moltke's first name was Helmuth, not Johannes.

14. Quotations from *Jack Welch and the GE Way* by Robert Slater © 1998 The McGraw-Hill Companies.

15. For more on Work-Out, see Dave Ulrich, Steven Kerr, and Ron Ashkenas, *The GE Work-Out* (New York: McGraw-Hill, 2002).
16. Confirmation of GE's definition of a good idea or best practice comes from Steve Kerr, personal communication, November 2001.
17. Quotations reprinted by permission of Harvard Business School Press. From *Leading the Revolution* by Gary Hamel. Boston, MA. © 2000 by Gary Hamel, all rights reserved. Imagination also ruled Hamel's earlier book with C. K. Prahalad, *Competing for the Future* (Boston: Harvard Business School, 1994): "We had to conclude that some management teams were simply more 'foresightful' than others. Some were capable of imagining products, services, and entire industries that did not yet exist and then giving them birth." In a later chapter on competitive strategy, we will see that *Competing for the Future* nevertheless provides valuable insight on "creative" versus "adaptive" analysis along the lines of Schumpeter.
18. Theresa Amabile, *Creativity in Context* (Boulder, CO: Westview, 1996); Harvard Business Review, *Breakthrough Thinking* (Boston: Harvard Business School, 1999).
19. Quotations from "The Phone Guy," © 2001 by Michael Specter. First appeared in *The New Yorker*, February 26, 2001. Reprinted by permission of International Creative Management, Inc. For the history of digital phone systems, see the GSM Association Web site, *www.gsmworld.com*.

Chapter 4: Plan-to versus Can-do

1. For Egypt's early bureaucracy, see Toby Wilkinson, "Administration," in *Early Dynastic Egypt* (London: Routledge, 1999); Jaromir Malek, *In the Shadow of the Pyramids: Egypt during the Old Kingdom* (Cairo: American University in Cairo Press, 1986); and James Breasted, "The Pyramid Builders," in *A History of Ancient Egypt* (New York: Scribner's, 1905).
2. Max Weber, *The Theory of Economic and Social Organization* (Glencoe, IL: Free Press, 1947).
3. Peter Drucker, *The Practice of Management* (New York: Harper, 1954).
4. Robert Kaplan and David Norton, *The Strategy-Focused Organization* (Boston: Harvard Business School, 2000); Brian Becker, Mark Huselid, and Dave Ulrich, *The HR Scorecard: Linking People, Strategy and Performance* (Boston: Harvard Business School, 2001); Douglas Smith, *Make Success Measurable!* (New York: Wiley, 1999).
5. W. Edwards Deming, *Out of the Crisis* (Boston: MIT Press, 1982). See "Appendix: Transformation of Japan" for the coup d'oeil and resolution of Japanese engineers in the 1950s and 1960s to adopt and improve the methods that Deming showed them. For Walter Shewhart's original techniques, see his *Economic Control of Quality of Manufactured Product* (New York: Van Nostrand, 1931).

6. Quotations from *Out of the Crisis* by W. Edwards Deming (1982). Reprinted by permission of MIT Press.
7. For the Lucent story, see especially Stephanie Mehta, "Lessons from the Lucent Debacle," *Fortune*, Feb. 5, 2001; and Jonathan Weil, "Lucent's Sales Outlook Is Central to Suit Filed by Former Official," *Wall Street Journal*, Dec. 20, 2000.
8. Quotations from *The Rise and Fall of Strategic Planning* by Henry Mintzberg. © 1994 by Henry Mintzberg. Reprinted with permission of The Free Press, a division of Simon & Schuster Trade Publishing Group. The Simon quote that follows comes from "Making Management Decisions: The Role of Intuition and Emotion," in *Academy of Management Executive*, February 1987.
9. Quotations from *Strategy Safari* by Henry Mintzberg, Bruce Ahlstrand and Joseph Lampel. © 1998 by Henry Mintzberg, Ltd., Bruce Ahlstrand and Joseph Lampel. Reprinted with permission of The Free Press, a division of Simon & Schuster Trade Publishing Group.
10. C. E. Lindblom, "The Science of Muddling Through," *Public Administration Review* 19 (1959).
11. Quotation from *The Financial Times Guide to Strategy* by Richard Koch (Financial Times Prentice-Hall, 2000). Reprinted with permission of Pearson Education Ltd.
12. Sydney Finkelstein and Donald Hambrick, *Strategic Leadership* (Minneapolis/St. Paul: West, 1996).
13. Kathryn Harrigan, *Strategic Flexibility* (Lexington, MA: Lexington, 1985).
14. See Richard Pascale, "Perspectives on Strategy: The Real Story behind Honda's Success," *California Management Review*, Spring 1984.
15. The two articles are Henry Mintzberg, "The Design School: Reconsidering the Basic Premises of Strategic Management," *Strategic Management Review* 11 (1990); and Michael Goold, "Design, Learning and Planning: A Further Observation on the Design School Debate," *Strategic Management Review* 13 (1992). Mintzberg's quote on riding motorcycles around Des Moines comes from yet another article, "Reply to Michael Goold," *California Management Review*, Summer 1996.
16. Wesley Truitt, *Business Planning: A Comprehensive Framework and Process* (Westport, CT: Quorum, 2002). Truitt endorses flexibility too, following an article by Clayton Christensen, "Making Strategy: Learning by Doing," *Harvard Business Review*, November–December 1997.
17. Baldrige National Quality Program, *Criteria for Performance Excellence* (Washington, DC: National Institute of Standards and Technology, 2002).
18. Wilbur Cross and Alice Richey, *Encyclopedia of Model Business Plans* (Englewood Cliffs, NJ: Prentice-Hall, 1994).
19. Quotation from the Web site of Lucent Technologies, Inc., 2002. Reprinted with permission.
20. Rosabeth Kanter, *The Change Masters* (New York: Simon & Schuster, 1983).

21. Gary Hamel and C. K. Prahalad, "Strategic Intent," *Harvard Business Review*, May–June 1989. See also "Strategy as Stretch," in Hamel and Prahalad, *Competing for the Future* (Boston: Harvard Business School, 1994).
22. Quotations from *Reviewing Strategy* © 2002 by Willie Pietersen. Reprinted by permission of John Wiley and Sons, Inc.
23. Quotations reprinted by permission of Harvard Business Review. From "The Core Competence of the Corporation," by C. K. Prahalad and Gary Hamel, May–June 1990. © 1990 by Harvard Business School Publishing Corporation; all rights reserved. See also "Building Gateways to the Future" and "Embedding the Core Competence Perspective," in Hamel and Prahalad, *Competing for the Future*.
24. In *Competing for the Future*, Hamel and Prahalad tell us more about how to build new core competencies: "Given that it may take five, ten, or more years to build world leadership in a core competency area, consistency of effort is key. Consistency depends first of all on a deep consensus about which competencies to build and support, and second, on the stability of the management teams charged with competence development. Such consistency is unlikely unless senior managers agree on what new competencies should be built." So core competencies—old or new—are mostly a matter of senior managers deciding what to be good at. That's fine—as long as they start with what works. Quotation reprinted by permission of Harvard Business School Press. From *Competing for the Future* by Gary Hamel and C. K. Prahalad. Boston, MA. © 2000 by Gary Hamel and C. K. Prahalad, all rights reserved.

Chapter 5: Change versus Charge

1. Quotations from *The Fifth Discipline* by Peter Senge (1990). Reprinted by permission of Doubleday. A rich literature followed *The Fifth Discipline: The Art and Practice of the Learning Organization* (New York: Doubleday, 1990), including Karen Watkins and Victoria Marsick, *Sculpting the Learning Organization* (San Francisco: Jossey-Bass, 1993); Peter Kline and Bernard Saunders, *Ten Steps to a Learning Organization* (Arlington, VA: Great Ocean, 1993); Michael Marquardt, *Building the Learning Organization* (New York: McGraw-Hill, 1996); Senge et al., *Fifth Discipline Fieldbook*, (New York: Doubleday, 1994) and Senge's *The Dance of Change: The Challenges to Sustaining Momentum in Learning Organizations* (New York: Doubleday, 1999).
2. Brian Dumaine, "Mr. Learning Organization," *Fortune*, Oct. 17, 1994.
3. For "Beyond Bureaucracy," see Warren Bennis, editor, *American Bureaucracy* (Chicago: Aldine, 1970).
4. Bennis emphasizes the skills of everyone in the group as much as the skill of the leader. The idea that great strategy starts with great

people is also featured in *Good to Great* (New York: HarperCollins, 2001), by James Collins, one of the coauthors of *Built to Last*.

5. For the Manhattan Project, see Richard Rhodes, *The Making of the Atomic Bomb* (New York: Simon & Schuster, 1986).

6. For the Disney story, see Richard Schickel, *The Disney Version* (New York: Simon & Schuster, 1968); and Bob Thomas, *Walt Disney: An American Original* (New York: Simon & Schuster, 1976). For a view that matches that of Bennis, see Bill Capodagli, *The Disney Way: How to Implement Walt Disney's Vision of "Dream, Believe, Dare, Do" in Your Own Company* (New York: McGraw-Hill, 2001).

7. Peter Block, *Stewardship* (Berrett-Koehler, 1993); John Redding, *The Radical Team Handbook: Harnessing the Power of Team Learning* (New York: Wiley, 2000).

8. Chris Argyris and Don Schon, *Organizational Learning* (Reading, MA: Addison-Wesley, 1978).

9. Rudy Ruggles, "The State of the Notion: Knowledge Management in Practice," *California Management Review*, Spring 1998.

10. Carla O'Dell and C. J. Grayson, "If Only We Knew What We Knew: Identification and Transfer of Internal Best Practice," *California Management Review*, Spring 1998.

11. For the International Benchmarking Clearinghouse study, see Gabriel Szulanski, *Intra-Firm Transfer of Best Practices* (Houston: American Productivity and Quality Center, 1994). For more recent research, see Jeffrey Pfeffer and Robert Sutton, *The Knowing-Doing Gap* (Boston: Harvard Business School, 2000).

12. This account of the Trotter matrix comes from "Learning Culture 2: Stealing Shamelessly," in Robert Slater, *The GE Way Fieldbook* (New York: McGraw-Hill, 1999); George Anderson, personal communication, April 2001; and Steven Kerr, personal communication, November 2001.

13. Quotations from *Jack Welch and the GE Way* by Robert Slater (New York: McGraw-Hill, 1998).

14. John Kotter, "Leading Change: Why Transformation Efforts Fail," *Harvard Business Review*, March–April 1995.

15. John Kotter, *Leading Change* (Boston: Harvard Business School, 2000).

Chapter 6: Forces versus Sources

1. Michael Porter, *Competitive Strategy* (New York: Free Press, 1980).

2. Michael Porter, *Cases in Competitive Strategy* (New York: Free Press, 1983) and *Competitive Advantage* (New York: Free Press, 1985).

3. Quotations from *A Concept of Corporate Planning* by Russell Ackoff. © 1969 by Russell Ackoff. Reprinted by permission of the author. For economists who entered the field after Porter, see especially P. Milgrom and J. Roberts, *Economics, Organization and Management* (Englewood Cliffs, NJ: Prentice-Hall, 1992); Sharon Oster, *Modern Competitive Analysis* (New York: Oxford University Press, 1999); and

D. Besanko, D. Dranove, and M. Shanley, *Economics of Strategy* (New York: Wiley, 2000).

4. Porter first introduced the five forces in "How Competitive Forces Shape Strategy," *Harvard Business Review,* March–April 1979.

5. Pankaj Ghemawat, "Competition and Business Strategy in Historical Perspective," Harvard Business School Note no. N9–797–136, 1997, cited in Amar Bhidé, *The Origin and Evolution of New Businesses* (New York: Oxford University Press, 2000). Ghemawat credits especially a survey by Richard Shmalensee.

6. Quotations from "What Have We Learned about Generic Competitive Strategy?" by Colin Campbell-Hunt, *Strategic Management Journal,* 21 (John Wiley and Sons Limited: February 2000). Reproduced with permission. Campbell-Hunt uses all 17 studies to find out whether there is enough real-world evidence for Porter's three generic strategies to measure their performance. There is. He then assesses performance using only the 10 studies that measure it. That cuts the sample size by about half, to three thousand.

7. From "From Competitive Advantage to Corporate Strategy," by Michael Porter, *Harvard Business Review,* May–June 1987. Reprinted by permission of Harvard Business Review.

8. The Boston Consulting Group model appears in Bruce Henderson, *Henderson on Corporate Strategy* (Cambridge, MA: Abt, 1979).

9. Quotation reprinted by permission of Harvard Business School Press. From *Competing for the Future* by Gary Hamel and C. K. Prahalad. (Boston: MA). © 2000 Gary Hamel and C. K. Prahalad, all rights reserved.

10. Clayton Christensen, *The Innovator's Dilemma* (New York: HarperBusiness, 1997); Richard Foster and Sarah Kaplan, *Creative Destruction* (New York: Doubleday, 2001).

11. "The Process of Creative Destruction" appeared in Joseph Schumpeter, *Capitalism, Socialism and Democracy* (New York: Harper & Brothers, 1942).

12. Sydney Finkelstein and Donald Hambrick, *Strategic Leadership* (Minneapolis/St. Paul: West, 1996). Hambrick is also the author of the first empirical study of competitive strategy that Campbell-Hunt cites in his meta-analysis. See Donald Hambrick, "High Profit Strategies in Mature Capital Goods Industries: A Contingency Approach," *Journal of Management* 10 (1983). Campbell-Hunt also adopts the term *contingency.* His meta-analysis "suggests that contingency theories of performance may now offer more powerful insights into the origins of effective competitive strategy." In *Strategic Leadership,* Finkelstein and Hambrick adapted their categories of executive behavior from D. Keirsey and M. Bates, *Please Understand Me* (Del Mar, CA: Prometheus, 1978); W. Taggart and D. Robey, "Minds and Managers: On the Dual Nature of Human Information Processing and Management," *Academy of Management Review* 6

(1981); and D. K. Hurst, J. C. Rush, and R. E. White, "Top
   Management Teams and Organizational Renewal," *Strategic
   Management Journal* 10 (1989).

13. Barney Glaser and Anselm Strauss, *The Discovery of Grounded Theory*
   (Chicago: Aldine, 1967).

14. For more on grounded theory, see Anselm Strauss and Juliet Corbin,
   *Basics of Qualitative Research: Grounded Theory Procedures and
   Techniques* (Thousand Oaks, CA: Sage, 1998); Karen Locke, *Grounded
   Theory in Management Research* (Thousand Oaks, CA: Sage, 2001); and
   Howard Becker, *Tricks of the Trade* (Chicago: University of Chicago
   Press, 1999).

15. On "insight," Glaser and Strauss cite Eliot Hutchinson, "The Period
   of Frustration in Creative Endeavor," *Psychiatry* 3 (1940) and "The
   Period of Elaboration in Creative Endeavor," *Psychiatry* 5 (1942); and
   Morris Stein and Shirley Heinze, *Creativity and the Individual* (New
   York: Free Press, 1960).

16. For Southwest Airlines versus the automobile, see Subrata
   Chakravarty, "Hit 'Em Hardest with the Mostest," *Forbes*, Sept. 16,
   1991. For the benchmark study, see Icon Group International,
   *Southwest Airlines Co.: International Competitive Benchmarks and
   Financial Gap Analysis* (2000).

17. Seth Schiesel, "Trying to Catch WorldCom's Mirage," *New York
   Times*, June 30, 2002.

18. From "What Is Strategy?" by Michael Porter. *Harvard Business Review*,
   November–December 1996. Reprinted with permission. © 1996 by
   Harvard Business School Publishing Corporation, all rights reserved.
   Here Porter cites Japan as a case of organizational effectiveness
   replacing strategy, with dire results. In their heyday, Japanese firms
   "rarely developed distinct strategic position," thanks to their great
   organizational effectiveness. But in the 1990s, now that other countries have caught up on that score, "Japanese companies will have to
   learn strategy." This will be hard for them to do, because strategy
   "requires hard choices." The Japanese face a huge obstacle: their
   "deeply ingrained service tradition that predisposes them to go to
   great lengths to satisfy any need a customer expresses," so that they
   become "all things to all customers." This is an unusual twist on the
   Japan story. In contrast, we saw earlier that Japanese companies were
   great strategists, even without much formal planning, much like
   Bhidé's successful entrepreneurs. And Porter accuses them of being
   too nimble—being "all things to all customers"—in recent times,
   whereas most other observers claim the opposite: The Japanese have
   become rigid and bureaucratic, both within companies and in government policy that overprotects them.

19. In this article, Porter does not abandon his three generic strategies.
   The article just helps you understand them "to a greater level of
   specificity." And yet, even if they are necessary, they are hardly sufficient. There are countless possibilities for what your generic strat-

egy should look like in practice. For success versus failure, those details make all the difference.

Chapter 7: Arrows in the Quiver

1. Alex Osborn, *Applied Imagination* (New York: Scribner's, 1953). For the date and definition of *brainstorming*, see *Webster's Collegiate Dictionary* (on-line).
2. Osborn published an earlier version of his book as *Your Creative Power* (New York: Scribner's, 1948). All citations here come from the 1963 edition of *Applied Imagination* (New York: Scribner's, 1963). A lively literature followed Osborn, for example, Charles Clark, *Brainstorming: The Dynamic New Way to Create Successful Ideas* (New York: Doubleday, 1958).
3. For the brainstorming study, see Arnold Meadows and Sidney Parnes, "Evaluation of Training in Creative Problem Solving," *Journal of Applied Psychology* 43 (1959).
4. Quotations from *Applied Imagination* by Alex F. Osborn (1963). Reprinted with permission from the copyright holder, Creative Education Foundation, 289 Bay Rd., Hadley, MA 01035.
5. A second study of brainstorming supports deferment of judgment. See Arnold Meadows, Sidney Parnes, and Hayne Reese, "Influence of Brainstorming Instructions and Problem Sequence on a Creative Problem Solving Test," *Journal of Applied Psychology* 43 (1959).
6. Amabile reports on her research in *The Social Psychology of Creativity* (New York: Springer-Verlag, 1983) and *Creativity in Context* (Boulder, CO: Westview, 1996). Amabile directs us to a study on successful creativity, but the measure turns out to be whether a firm innovated, not whether the innovation succeeded. See R. D. Russell and C. J. Russell, "An Examination of the Effects of Organizational Norms, Organizational Structure, and Environmental Uncertainty," *Journal of Management* 18 (1992).
7. Edward de Bono, *Lateral Thinking* (New York: Harper & Row, 1970); *Serious Creativity* (New York: HarperBusiness, 1992); *Six Thinking Hats* (Boston: Little, Brown, 1985).
8. This version of the six thinking hats comes from de Bono, *Serious Creativity*.
9. Arthur VanGundy, *Creative Problem-Solving* (New York: Quorum, 1987).
10. Paul Schoemaker and J. Edward Russo, "A Pyramid of Decision Approaches," *California Management Review* 36 (1993).
11. Schoemaker and Russo put bootstrapping in the larger category of "Importance Weighting." Here we use *bootstrapping* to mean the whole category. They draw especially from an article by Colin Camerer, "General Conditions for the Success of Bootstrapping Models," *Organizational Behavior and Human Performance* 27 (1981). Most recently, Daniel Kahneman won the 2002 Nobel Prize in economics for work on intuition as a major force in decision making.

You can't trust it completely, but you can improve it by knowing what biases are at play, especially in expert systems. See especially Daniel Kahneman, Paul Slovic, and Amos Tversky, *Judgment under Uncertainty* (Cambridge: Cambridge University Press, 1982).

12. James Surowiecki, "The Buffett of Baseball," *New Yorker* (Sept. 23, 2002).
13. Earnshaw Cook, *Percentage Baseball* (Baltimore: Waverly Press, 1964).
14. Xerox Corporation, *Leadership through Quality* (1989). In the same year as this guide, 1989, Xerox won the Baldrige Quality Award.
15. Thomas Kuhn, *The Structure of Scientific Revolutions* (Chicago: University of Chicago Press, 1969).
16. Kathryn Brown, "Biotech Speeds Its Evolution," *Technology Review,* November–December 2000. See the diagram "Evolution: Maxygen Style," by Betsy Hayes.
17. Although we lack an overall method for reporting business results for particular strategies, business research is chipping away at the problem. In a 2002 working paper, "The Road to Drug Discovery: Experience and Exploration along Different Dimensions" (New York: Columbia Business School, 2002), Atul Nerkar gives empirical evidence that business success in developing new drugs comes from scanning other laboratories' results rather than from working harder in your own. His results recall Roger Bacon's advice on the scientific method: to look first to "those who have made experiments" before your own experience. Nerkar humbly limits the relevance of his research to the pharmaceutical industry. But now that he has shown the way, perhaps others will try a similar analysis for other industries.
18. Michael Porter, *Competitive Strategy* (New York: Free Press, 1980).
19. Sydney Finkelstein and Donald Hambrick, *Strategic Leadership* (Minneapolis/St. Paul: West, 1996). Finkelstein and Hambrick cite especially an article by W. Starbuck and W. Milliken, "Executives' Perceptual Filters: What They Notice and How They Make Sense," in Donald Hambrick, *The Executive Effect* (Greenwich, CT: JAI, 1988). See also Donald Hambrick, "Environmental Scanning and Organizational Strategy," *Strategic Management Journal* 3 (1982).
20. The Mitchell quotes come from Lao Tzu, *Tao Te Ching* (translated by Stephen Mitchell, New York: Harper Perennial, 1992).
21. Stanley Herman, *The Tao at Work* (San Francisco: Jossey-Bass, 1994); Les Kaye, *Zen at Work* (New York: Crown, 1997).
22. J. M. Juran, *Quality Control Handbook* (New York: McGraw-Hill, 1998).
23. Mikel Harry and Richard Schroeder, *Six Sigma* (New York: Currency, 2000); George Eckes, *The Six Sigma Revolution* (New York: Wiley, 2001); Peter Pande, Robert Neuman, and Roland Cavanagh, *The Six Sigma Way* (New York: McGraw-Hill, 2000); Greg Brue, *Six Sigma for Managers* (New York: McGraw-Hill, 2002).
24. Peter Senge, *The Fifth Discipline Fieldbook* (New York: Doubleday, 1994).
25. Michael Hammer and James Champy, *Reengineering the Corporation* (New York: HarperCollins, 1993).

26. From *Co-opetition* by Adam Brandenburger and Barry Nalebuff. (New York: Doubleday, 1996). Reprinted with permission. See also John von Neumann and Oskar Morgenstern, *Theory of Games and Economic Behavior* (Princeton, N.J.: Princeton University Press, 1944); Nalebuff also wrote an earlier book on game theory in business with Avinash Dixit, *Thinking Strategically* (New York: Norton, 1993). See also Avinash Dixit and Susan Skeath, *Games of Strategy* (New York: Norton, 1999).
27. Figure adapted from "Quality Matrix," from *Jack Welch and the GE Way Fieldbook* by Robert Slater © 1999 The McGraw-Hill Companies.
28. Gabriel Tarde, *The Laws of Imitation* (New York: Henry Holt, 1903).
29. U.S. Army, "A Leader's Guide to After-Action Reviews," Training Circular 25–20, 1993. The after-action review replaced the after-action report, which only the commanding officer wrote. As the commander cannot be everywhere during the event, a review by everyone provides more insights than a report by one person.
30. See Thom Shanker and Eric Schmitt, "Service Chiefs Say Afghan Battle Will Help Military Get Smarter, Stronger and Faster," *New York Times*, Sept. 10, 2002.
31. The Patton quote comes from the U.S. Marine Corps, *Warfighting* (New York: Doubleday, 1994).
32. Excerpt from *The Patton Papers 1940–1945*, edited by Martin Blumenson © 1974 by Martin Blumenson. Reprinted by permission of Houghton Mifflin Company. All rights reserved.
33. George Patton, *War as I Knew It* (Boston: Houghton Mifflin, 1947).

Chapter 8: The Art of Synthesis

1. For a history of management consulting and the different roles consultants have played, see Clive Rassam and David Oates, *Management Consultancy* (London: Mercury, 1991).
2. For a review of strategy methods used by the consulting field in general, see Sugata Biswas and Daryl Twitchell, "Appendix I: Fifteen Essential Frameworks," in *Management Consulting: A Complete Guide to the Industry* (New York: Wiley, 2002).
3. For a brief profile of Bower, see Curt Schleler, "Consulting Innovator Marvin Bower," *Investor's Business Daily*, Nov. 9, 2000. McKinsey revenue comes from *Ward's Business Directory* (2001), which ranks McKinsey fifth among U.S. management consulting firms in total sales.
4. Larry Bossidy and Ram Charan, *Execution: The Discipline of Getting Things Done* (New York: Crown, 2002).
5. Ethan Rasiel, *The McKinsey Way: Using the Techniques of the World's Top Strategic Consultants to Help You and Your Business* (New York: McGraw-Hill, 1999); Ethan Rasiel and Paul Friga, *The McKinsey Mind: Understanding and Implementing the Problem-Solving Tools and Management Techniques of the World's Top Strategic Consulting Firm* (New York: McGraw-Hill, 2001).

6. Quotations from *The McKinsey Way* by Ethan Rasiel © 1999 The McGraw-Hill Companies.
7. Rachel Silverman, "Growth at McKinsey Hindered Use of Data," *Wall Street Journal*, May 20, 2002.
8. Diagram, "McKinsey Problem Solving Process" from *The McKinsey Mind* by Ethan Rasiel and Paul Friga © 2001 The McGraw-Hill Companies.
9. For Interaction Associates, see interactionassociates.com. For Objexis, see objexis.com.
10. The *Oxford English Dictionary* gives various technical definitions for *synthesis* from philosophy, chemistry, grammar, and physics. The definition used here is the general one.
11. There really is a Keri S. This picture of how she works is based on personal observation and communication (2001).

Chapter 9: The Way of What Works

1. J. C. Herold, *The Age of Napoleon* (New York: American Heritage, 1963).
2. Definitions come from the *Oxford English Dictionary* (on-line).
3. Conference Board, *Special Consumer Survey Report*, "Job Satisfaction on the Decline," July 2002. The report shows a decline in job satisfaction from 59 percent in 1995 to just under half in 2002.
4. Carol Sansone and Judith Harackiewicz, *Intrinsic and Extrinsic Motivation* (New York: Academic, 2000); Daniel O'Keefe, *Persuasion: Theory and Research* (Newbury Park, CA: Sage, 1990); Robert Beck, *Motivation: Theories and Principles* (Englewood Cliffs, NJ: Prentice-Hall, 1978); Douglas Moock, *Motivation: The Organization of Action* (New York: Norton, 1987); Tory Higgins and Arie Kruglanski, *Motivational Science* (Philadelphia: Psychology Press, 2000); John Atkinson, *An Introduction to Motivation* (Princeton, NJ: Van Nostrand, 1964). Most of Moock's chapter "Images, Goals, and Plans" explains "how actions are implemented." At the end of the chapter, Moock asks, "How do we decide what action to take?" His answer is "subjective probabilities," which are your "idea of the likelihood of various events." Yet where does that idea come from? Moock doesn't tell us. In the art of what works, it comes from expertise. Sansone and Harackiewicz also cover goals in a chapter, "Achievement Goals and Optimal Motivation." They give two kinds of achievement goals: "When pursuing mastery goals, an individual's reason for engaging in an achievement activity is to *develop* his or her competence in the activity. In contrast, when pursuing performance goals, an individual's reason for engagement is to *demonstrate* his or her competence relative to others." In the art of what works, you undertake an "achievement activity" not to master or prove a skill, but to succeed in what you want to achieve.
5. For Feather's work, see "The Relationship of Persistence at a Task to Expectation of Success and Achievement-Related Motives," *Journal of Abnormal and Social Psychology* 63 (1961); and "The Study of Persistence," *Psychological Bulletin* 59 (1962).

6. Chérie Carter-Scott, *If Life Is a Game, These Are the Rules* (New York: Broadway, 1998); *If Love Is a Game, These Are the Rules* (New York: Broadway, 1999); *If Success Is a Game, These Are the Rules* (New York: Bantam, 2000).

7. Quotation from *If Success Is a Game, These Are the Rules* by Chérie Carter-Scott (2000). Reprinted by permission of Broadway Books.

8. Quotation from *Think and Grow Rich* by Napoleon Hill (1937). Reprinted with permission of the Napoleon Hill Foundation. The quotes cited here come from pages 213 and 206 of the original edition. More recent editions omit reference to the "ether." Hill's most important predecessor was Samuel Smiles, author of *Self-Help* (New York: Harper & Brothers, 1859). Smiles preached the Victorian values of hard work, thrift, and perseverance through portraits of successful people of his own and earlier times.

9. The Carnegie quote comes from an 1896 lecture at Cornell University, cited in Joseph Wall, *Andrew Carnegie* (New York: Oxford University Press, 1970).

10. Thomas Peters and Robert Waterman, *In Search of Excellence* (New York: HarperCollins, 1982).

11. For the Sanford Bernstein study, see Tom Petrano, "Why Investing Is Still a Toss of the Dice," *Los Angeles Times*, Oct. 2, 1995. For the market average, the study used the S&P 500's annualized return of 14.5 percent from 1980 to 1994.

12. Quotation reprinted with permission of Simon & Schuster Adult Publishing Group from *Unlimited Power: The New Science of Personal Achievement* by Anthony Robbins. © 1986 by Robbins Research Institute.

13. Stephen Covey, *The Seven Habits of Highly Effective People* (New York: Simon & Schuster, 1989).

14. Wayne Dyer, *A Spiritual Solution to Every Problem* (New York: HarperCollins, 2001).

15. Quotations from *The Seven Spiritual Laws of Success* © 1995, Deepak Chopra. Reprinted by permission of Amber-Allen Pub., Inc. P. O. Box 6657, San Rafael, CA 94903. All rights reserved.

16. Laura Day, *Practical Intuition* (New York: Random House, 1996); and *Practical Intuition for Success* (New York: Harper Collins, 1997).

17. Quotations from *Life Strategies* © 1999 by Philip McGraw, Ph.D. Reprinted by permission of Hyperion Books.

18. For Carnegie's steel business, see "Steel Is King, 1873–1881," in Wall, *Andrew Carnegie*.

19. Quotations from *The Arc of Ambition* by James Champy and Nitin Nohria (1999). Reprinted by permission of Perseus Book Group.

20. Joseph Campbell, *The Hero with a Thousand Faces* (Princeton, NJ: Princeton University Press, 1949); Robert McKee, *Story* (New York: ReganBooks, 1997); Aristotle, *Poetics* (translated by S. H. Butcher, New York: Hill & Wang, 1961).

Appendix: Right versus Might

1. For a direct application of business methods to the social sector, see Mary Hatten, "Strategic Management in Not-for-Profit Organizations," *Strategic Management Journal* 3 (1982).
2. Carol Weiss, *Evaluation Research* (Englewood Cliffs, NJ: Prentice-Hall, 1972).
3. Harry Hatry, *Performance Measurement* (Washington, DC: Urban Institute, 1999); Bryan Barry, *Strategic Planning Workbook* (Saint Paul, MN: Wilder Foundation, 1997); John Bryson, "Strategic Planning and Action Planning for Non-Profit Organizations," in Robert Herman, *Handbook of Non-Profit Leadership and Management* (San Francisco: Jossey-Bass, 1994); Paul Joyce, *Strategy in the Public Sector* (New York: Wiley, 2000).
4. For the learning organization in government, see Janice Cook, Derek Staniforth, and Jack Stewart, *The Learning Organization in the Public Services* (Brookfield, VT: Gower, 1997).
5. Peter Senge, *Schools that Learn* (New York: Doubleday, 2000).
6. Sharon Osler, *Strategic Management for Non-Profit Organizations* (New York: Oxford University Press, 1995).
7. Michael Porter, "Competitive Solutions to Societal Problems," in *On Competition* (Boston: Harvard Business School, 1998); Michael Porter and Mark Kramer, "Philanthropy's New Agenda," *Harvard Business Review*, November 1999. For Porter and Kramer's organizations, see effectivephilanthropy.org and foundationstrategy.com.
8. Kevin Kearns, *Private Sector Strategy for Social Sector Success* (San Francisco: Jossey-Bass, 2000).
9. Quotations from *Common Purpose* by Lisbeth Schor (1997). Reprinted by permission of Doubleday.
10. K. A. Opuni, "Project GRAD—Houston Program Evaluation Reports," 1997–2002, cited in K. A. Opuni and Lynn Ellsworth, "Project GRAD: A Comprehensive School Reform Model That Works" (forthcoming).
11. Quotations from *Scaling Up Successful Work* (video) by Junko Chano © 2002 by The Ford Foundation. Chano's videos, at grantcraft.org, offer a rare glimpse of successful strategy in action.
12. Quotations from *The Elusive Quest for Growth* by William Easterly (2001). Reprinted by permission of MIT Press. Easterly uses 88 countries to test the aid-to-investment link, and 138 for the investment-to-growth link.
13. Quotations from *Globalization and Its Discontents* by Joseph E. Stiglitz. © 2002 by Joseph E. Stiglitz. Used by permission of W. W. Norton & Co., Inc. Although Stiglitz concentrates on the IMF, he covers the World Bank and the World Trade Organization as well. Much the same critiques and recommendations apply.
14. To contrast strategic synthesis with the way strategy typically unfolds in development assistance, see Derick Brinkerhoff, *Improving Development Program Performance* (Boulder, CO: Lynne Reinner, 1991).

Index

A

A priori assumptions, 141

AARs (*see* After-action reviews)

ABB, 173

Abbottston Elementary (Baltimore),
  237

Accounting, false, 145

Achievement motivation, 214

Achievement networks, 125

Ackoff, Russell, 131

Acquisitions, 136

Adaptive response, creative vs.,
  45–47

Administrative problems, 59, 60

Administrators, 140

Advertising, 60

Afghanistan, 188, 189

After-action reviews (AARs),
  187–191

The Age of Napoleon (J. C. Herold),
  211

Agreement-based analysis, 206

Ahlstrand, Bruce, 91

Aikido, 171

Airline catering, 54, 58, 104

Airline industry, 144

Akerlof, George, 3

Alcoa, 60

Alexander, 5, 19

Alice in Cartoonland (short films),
  117

Alice in Wonderland (film), 117

Aligning systems to vision, 126

Allen, Paul, 43–46

Allied Signal, 173

Allies, 204

Altair (microcomputer), 44–46

Amabile, Teresa, 78, 158, 159

Ambition, 225–226

American Airlines, 182–183

American Express (AmEx), 54–55,
  57

American quality movement, 88–90

America's War on Poverty, 234

AmEx (*see* American Express)

Analytical approach, 236

Anderson, Eric, 79–80

Animated feature films, 116–118

Annie E. Casey Foundation, 235
Apple Computer, 14, 45, 111, 115
Applied Imagination (Alex Osborn),
 152
The Arc of Ambition (James Champy
 and Nitin Nohria), 225–227
Argyris, Chris, 119
Aristotle, 227, 228
Armour, 60
The Art of War (Sun Tzu), 4, 38–39
Astronomy, 34
Asymmetries of information, 3
Atkinson, John, 213–214
Atomic bomb, 115–116
AT&T, 144–145
Attainable vision, 115
Automobile industry, 68
Autonomous operating divisions,
 63
Averages, 89

B
B. F. Goodrich, 152
Babcock, Chip, 222–223
Baby powder, 53
Bacon, Roger, 33
Baldrige National Quality Award,
 97, 100, 173
Baltimore, 237
Bandages, 53
Bangladesh, 244–245
Barry, Bryan, 235
Baseball, 164
BBDO, 152
BCG (*see* Boston Consulting Group)
Beane, Billy, 164
Beck, Robert, 213
Becker, Brian, 88
Behavior, changing, 120
Bell Atlantic, 180
Bell Labs, 88
Benchmarking, 168
Bennis, Warren, 8, 113–116

Bergson, Henri, 31
Berry, Marcellus, 54–56
Bessemer, Henry, 226
Best Practices, 76, 122
Best practices, 120–121, 124
"Beyond Bureaucracy"
 (Warren Bennis), 113
Bhidé, Amar, 6, 48–51, 88, 98
Bidding, 143
Biotechnology, 166
Black belts, 174–175
Block, Peter, 118
Blumenson, Martin, 190
The Book of Five Rings (Miyamoto
 Musashi), 5, 39–40, 99, 189
Bootstrapping, 9, 161–165
Bossidy, Larry, 195–196
Boston Consulting Group (BCG),
 94, 95, 137, 195
Bower, Marvin, 194
Brainstorming, 152–155, 177–178,
 202
Brandenburger, Adam, 181
Breakthrough Thinking, 78
Brue, Greg, 173
Bryson, John, 235
Buddhism, 4, 39, 220
"The Buffet of Baseball" (James
 Surowiecki), 164
Buick, 61
Building on what works, 51–58
Built to Last (James Collins and
 Jerry Porras), 6, 51–52, 56, 58,
 137, 218
Bunge, Mario, 31
Bureaucracies, 86, 114
Business Planning (Wesley Truitt), 97
Business plans, 97–101
Buyers, 132, 144

C
Caesar, 5, 19
California Management Review, 119

Campbell, Joseph, xi, xii, 227, 228
Campbell-Hunt, Colin, 134–135
Campbell's (company), 143
Canon, 105
Career strategy, 212
Carnegie, Andrew, 215, 217, 225–226
Carriage makers, 61
Carter-Scott, Chérie, 215–216
Cartoon strips, 117–118
Case method, 195
Cases in Competitive Strategy (Michael Porter), 130, 142
Cavanaugh, Roland, 173
Center for Effective Philanthropy, 235–236
Central organizations, 63
Champy, James, 179, 180, 225–227
"Chan" Buddhism, 39
Chandler, Alfred, 6, 59–68
"Change and the Entrepreneur" (Joseph Schumpeter), 47
The Change Masters (Rosabeth Kanter), 101
Changing behavior, 120
Chano, Junko, 241
Charan, Ram, 195–196
Chess, 26, 161
Chevron, 168
Chevron Refining, 120–121
Chief executives, 63
Chief Learning Officers, 122
China, 4, 37, 39, 93, 247–248
Chopra, Deepak, 220–221
Christensen, Clayton, 139
CIS (*see* Communities in Schools)
Civil War (U.S.), 18
Classic strategic planning, 8, 16–17, 20, 219, 236
Clausewitz, Carl von, 3–6, 8, 13
    on coup d'oeil and resolution, 22–23
    difficult text of, 21

on imagination, 30
Antoine Jomini vs., 16–18, 20
on past experience, 23–24, 81
on suspending action, 171
Clients, engaging, 202–204
"Climate for Creativity" questionnaire, 158, 159
CMCD (*see* Consistency Management and Cooperative Discipline)
Co-opetition (Adam Brandenburger and Barry Nalebuff), 181–183
Coaches, 140
Coastline Pool Consortium, 98–101
Cognitive school, 91
Coke, 181
Colgate, 60
Collective mindfulness, 177
Collins, James, 6, 51–52, 54–58, 218
Committees, decision making by, 64
Common Purpose (Lisbeth Schor), 236
Communication, 124, 176
Communities in Schools (CIS), 239, 240
Community colleges, 241
Compaq, 181
Competing for the Future (Gary Hamel and C. K. Prahalad), 139
"Competition and Business Strategy in Historical Perspective" (Pankaj Ghemawat), 134
Competitive Advantage (Michael Porter), 130, 142
Competitive analysis, 143
Competitive insight, 145–147
Competitive intuition, 138–140
"Competitive Solutions to Societal Problems" (Michael Porter), 235
Competitive strategy, 8, 129–148, 236

Competitive strategy *(continued)*
  expert analysis in, 147–148
  five sources for, 144–145
  and grounded theory, 140–143
  and insight, 145–147
  and intuition, 138–140
  and social sector, 233, 235–236
  studies of, 134–138
  tools from, 9
Competitive Strategy (Michael
  Porter), 129–133, 143, 168
Competitors, 181
Complementors, 181
Computer models of expert
  decision making, 26
A Concept of Corporate Planning
  (Russell Ackoff), 131
Conference Board, 212
Consensus, 206
Consistency Management and
  Cooperative Discipline
  (CMCD), 239, 240
Consulting (*see* Strategy consulting)
Cook, Earnshaw, 164
Copernicus, Nicolaus, 33, 34
Coping, 132
"The Core Competence of the
  Corporation" (C. K. Prahalad
  and Gary Hamel), 104–105
Core competencies, 104–106
Core ideology, 57, 58
Core of uniqueness, 147
Corrective interventions, 237
Costs, switching, 132
Coup d'oeil, 3, 8, 25–26
  von Clausewitz on, 22–25
  at Honda, 96
  as insight, 6
  of Steve Jobs, 15
  of Ray Kroc, 14
  as motivator, 225
  of Napoleon, 19
  at Nokia, 79–80

in science, 30–35
in social sector, 242
Tao on, 38
vision following, 104
Covey, Stephen, 219–220
Creative Destruction (Richard Foster
  and Sarah Kaplan), 139
Creative imagination, 29, 215
Creative imitation, 48–51
Creative planning, 106–107
Creative Problem Solving (Arthur
  VanGundy), 160
Creative response, adaptive vs.,
  45–47
"The Creative Response in
  Economic History"
  (Joseph Schumpeter), 6, 45
Creative stimulation, 157–161
Creative strategy, 229–231
Creative structure, 58–68
Creative success, 80–81
Creativity, 14–15, 28–29, 77
Creativity in Context (Teresa
  Amabile), 78
Credit-card business, 182
Cross, Wilbur, 97–98
Crotonville Institute, 72, 75, 76,
  122–124, 183–185
Crown Cork and Seal, 142
Culture, 120
Cumulative learning, 109
Current competitors, 132, 144
Curtis Publishing, 60
Customers, 173, 181
Czech Republic, 248

D
Daewoo Corporation, 244
Daimler-Benz, 200
Darwin, Charles, 56, 154
Databases, 200–201
Davis High School (Houston), 239
Day, Laura, 221–222

De Bono, Edward, 159–160

Decentralized structure, 67

Decision making:

  in action, 27

  bootstrapping tool for, 161–165

  by committees, 64

  computer models of expert, 26

  gut-instinct based, 205

  Napoleon on, 161

  recognition-based, 4

Deming, W. Edwards, 88–90,
    172–174

Desh Garments, 244

Dialogue, 175–178

Differentiation, 133

Digital wireless technology, 78–80

The Discovery of Grounded Theory
    (Barney Glaser and Anselm
    Strauss), 140–141

Diseconomies, 138

Disney, 116–118

Distinctive emphasis, 135

District organization, 67

Diversification, 68, 135–136, 137

Divine guidance, 220

Do, 39

Dobbs, Gary, 222

Dodd, Alvin, 67

Dot.com boom, 76–78

Dr. Phil (television show), 224

Drucker, Peter, 86, 87

DuPont, 6, 60–61, 63–64, 168, 170

DuPont, Irénée, 63

DuPont, Pierre, 63

Durant, William, 61–64

Dyer, Wayne, 220

E

E-commerce, 77

East Harlem, 236

Easterly, William, 243–245, 249

Eastern Air Transport, 54

Eastman Kodak, 117

Eckes, George, 173

Economic analysis, 8, 138–139

Economic research, 131, 140, 143

Economics, 45

Economics of information, 3

Economies of scale, 138

Educating Intuition (Robin Hogarth),
    28

Egypt, 85–86

Einstein, Albert, 115, 225

Electric wiring, 218

Electricity, 32

The Elusive Quest for Growth
    (William Easterly), 243

Emergency room nurses, 27

Emergent strategy, 8, 94, 236

Empowerment, 126

Encyclopedia of Model Business Plans
    (Wilbur Cross and Alice
    Richey), 97–98

Engaging the client, 202

Entrepreneurial edge, 146

Entrepreneurs, 6, 46–51, 56, 98

Environmental scan, 236

Erickson, Jim, 44

Ericsson, 79

Error measurement, 173–175

Eugene of Savoy, 5, 19

Evaluation, social sector, 234

Evaluation expectation, 158

Evaluation Research (Carol Weiss),
    234

Evolution, 56–58

Ex ante, 45

Ex post, 45

Excellence, search for, 217–219

Execution (Larry Bossidy and
    Ram Charan), 195

Executives, 140

Expecting the unexpected, 3, 25

  at Honda, 96

  in social sector, 242

  in software applications, 44–45

Experience (of Japanese executives), 71–72
Expert analysis, 147–148
Expert intuition:
  counterintuitiveness of, 21
  definition of, 4
  elements of, 26
  elusive nature of, 13–16
  examples of, 4
  failure from, 80–81
  imagination vs., 78
  and Steve Jobs, 14–15
  and Ray Kroc, 13–14
  and modern coup d'oeil, 26–30
  in social sector, 233–249
  in strategy, 13–41
  strategy determined with, 9
  tools of, 9
  in Western and Eastern philosophy, 35–40
  (*See also* specific headings)
Expertise, 214
Explosives, 60
Export Trade Department, 64, 65

F
Fact-based analysis, 197, 198, 200, 204, 205
False accounting, 145
Father Noah's Ark (short film), 118
Feather, Norman, 214
Fermi, Enrico, 115–116
Field interviews, 168, 169
The Fifth Discipline Fieldbook (Peter Senge, William Isaacs, and Bryan Smith), 176
The Fifth Discipline (Peter Senge), 8, 110, 112–113, 175–176, 235
Financial services companies, 55
Financial Times Guide to Strategy (Richard Koch), 92
Finkelstein, Sydney, 93, 126, 139–140, 170, 196
Finland, 78

Firefighters, 27
"Five forces," 9
Five forces model, 235
Flexibility, 8, 90–94, 102, 215, 221
Flexible evolutionary strategy, 58
Flowers and Trees (short film), 117
"Fluid" theory of electricity, 32, 36
Focus, 133
Food service, 54, 58, 104
Ford, Henry, 61, 80
Ford Foundation, 241
Ford Motor Company, 76, 111
Forgery, 54
Formal planning, 50–51
Foster, Richard, 139
Foundation Strategy Group, 236
Fox, Robert, 218
Fragmented industries, 138
Franklin, Benjamin, 32, 36
Frazer, George, 67
Frederick the Great (Prussia), 5, 19, 23
Frequent-flyer programs, 182–183
Friends, 204
Friga, Paul, 196
"From Competitive Advantage to Corporate Strategy" (Michael Porter), 135

G
Galileo, 33
Game theory, 181–183
Garda, Bob, 204
Gates, Bill, 43–46
GE Capital, 174
GE Financial Services, 73
GE Plastics, 73, 218
"The GE Way," 6, 72–76
General Electric (GE), x, 6, 9, 201
  Best Practices at, 76
  expert intuition at, 72–76
  as learning organization, 121–125
  plagiarizing at, 74–75
  "planful opportunism" at, 74

Six Sigma used by, 90, 173
Trotter matrix used by, 168,
     183–185
Work-Out method at, 75
General Motors-du Pont Antitrust
     Suit, 64
General Motors (GM), 6, 60–64, 80,
     182
General offices, 61–63
Genuine openness, 113
Ghemawat, Pankaj, 134
Glaser, Barney, 140–142
Global social sector, 242–249
Global System for Mobile
     Communication (GSM), 78
Globalization and its Discontents
     (Joseph Stiglitz), 246
GM (*see* General Motors)
GM Card, 182
Goals:
   audacious, 52
   Antoine Jomini on, 17–18
   Gary Klein on reachable, 28
   scientific achievement preceding,
     31
   setting, 8, 88–90, 215, 221
   setting higher, 214
   SMART, 155–156
   and social sector, 234
   switching, 20
   writing down your, 88
Goethals, George W., 66
Goold, Michael, 95
Gould, 143
Government, 234
GRAD (*see* Project GRAD)
GRAD-USA, 240
Grant, Ulysses S., 18
Graphical user interface, 15
Grayson, C. J., 120
Green belts, 174, 175
Grievances, 176
Grinding it Out (Ray Kroc), 13
Grounded theory, 9, 140–143

Group action, 125
Group consensus, 206
The Growth of Firms in Japan
     (Ryuei Shimizu), 6, 70
GS Technologies, 176
GSM (Global System for Mobile
     Communication), 78
Guiding coalition, 126
Gunpowder, 60
Gustavus Adolphus, 5, 19
Gut instinct, 197, 205

H
HAI, 142–143
Hallmark, 180
Hambrick, Donald, 93, 126,
     139 140, 170, 196
Hamel, Gary, 77–78, 102, 104–106,
     139
Hamilton, William, 154
Hammer, Michael, 179, 180
*Handbook of Non-Profit Leadership
     and Management*
     (Robert Herman), 235
Handbook on Creativity (Robert
     Sternberg), 29–30
Hannibal, 5, 19
Hanson Trust, 137
Happiness, 10–11, 212
Harackiewicz, Judith, 213
Hard Drive (James Wallace and
     Jim Erickson), 44, 46
Harden, Orville, 65
Harrigan, Kathryn, 93
Harris Investment Management,
     163
Harry, Mikel, 173
Harsanyi, John C., 181
Harvard Business Review, 78
Hatry, Harry, 235
Herman, Robert, 235
Herman, Stanley, 171
The Hero with a Thousand Faces
     (Joseph Campbell), xi, 227, 228

Herold, J. C., 211
Hero's journey, xi–xii, 211–231
  and creative strategy, 229–231
  and letting go, 220–224
  and motivation, 213–214, 224–229
  to success, 215–220
Hewlett-Packard, 76
Higgins, Tory, 213
High-cost products, 133
Hill, Napoleon, 215–216
History, combinations from, 4,
  23–25 (*See also* Past
  achievements/experience)
Hittle, J. D., 18
Hogarth, Robin, 28
Holmes, Oliver Wendell, 36–37
Honda, 94–96
Horse-drawn carriages, 61
Hospitals, 142–143
Hotels, 54
Household Bank, 182
Houston, 238–242
Houston Endowment, 239
The HR Scorecard (Brian Becker,
  Mark Huselid, and Dave
  Ulrich), 88
Humphries, Stella, 113
Huselid, Mark, 88
Hyatt Roller Bearing, 62

I
IBM, 111, 161, 173
IBM Credit, 179–180
Icon Group, 144
If Life Is a Game, These Are the Rules
  (Chérie Carter-Scott), 215
If Love Is a Game, These Are the Rules
  (Chérie Carter-Scott), 215
"If Only We Knew What We Knew"
  (Carla O'Dell and C. J.
  Grayson), 120
*If Success Is a Game, These Are the
  Rules* (Chérie Carter-Scott), 215
Imagination, 115

creative, 29, 215
  expert intuition vs., 78
  intuition vs., 30
  strategy driven by, 76–78
IMF (*see* International
  Monetary Fund)
Imhotep, 85–86
Imitation:
  creative, 48–51
  innovation leading to, 47, 48
  and S-curve, 185–187
Imperfect information, 3
Implementation, strategy, 202–203
Implementation plan, 203
Improvisation, 102
In Search of Excellence (Thomas
  Peters and Robert Waterman),
  217–218
Inc. magazine, 48
"*Inc.*-500" list, 48, 50
Incremental approach, 236
Industrial organizations (IOs), 134
Industrial Revolution, 211
Industry demand, 142
Information, imperfect, 3
Initial hypothesis, 198–200
Innovation:
  imitation from, 47, 48
  and S-curve, 185
  as source of business success,
  146
The Innovator's Dilemma
  (Clayton Christensen), 139
Insight, 3–4, 6
Intel, 181
Intent, strategic, 101–104
Interaction Associates, 206
Internally consistent, 133
International Benchmarking
  Clearinghouse, 120
International Harvester, 60
International Monetary Fund (IMF),
  242, 245–248
Internet, 183

Interviews, 168, 169
Intrinsic and Extrinsic Motivation
(Carol Sansone and Judith
Harackiewicz), 213
An Introduction to Motivation
(John Atkinson), 213
Intuition:
and data, 205
imagination vs., 30
Napoleon on, 19
science and study of, 30–31
Herbert Simon on, 91
skill of, 28
study of, 26
teaching of, 5
Intuition and Science (Mario Bunge),
31
Intuitive sensitivity, 70
Invenire, 211
Inventors, 211
IO (industrial organization), 134
Isaacs, William, 176, 177
Issue trees, 198–199, 207
ITE, 143

J
J. C. Penney, 66, 67
James, William, 4, 35, 36
Japan, 4–5, 6, 39, 68–72, 88–89, 173,
174
Jobs, Steven, 14–15, 33, 49, 115
Johns Hopkins University, 237
Johns-Manville, 60
Johnson & Johnson, 53, 57
Jomini, Antoine, 16–18, 20
Jones, James, 188–189
Joyce, Paul, 235
Juran, J. M., 173

K
Kaizen, 75
Kan (sixth sense), 70
Kanter, Rosabeth, 101–102
Kaplan, Robert, 88

Kaplan, Sarah, 139
Kasparov, Garry, 161
Kaye, Les, 171
Kearns, Kevin, 236
Keith, Michael G., 144–145
Kepler, Johannes, 33
Kerr, Steven, 122–125
Ketelsen, James, 239–242
Ketelsen, Kathryn, 239
Keynes, John Maynard, 246
Kilmer, Fred, 53, 56
Klein, Gary, 4, 27–28
Knowledge management, 119–121
Knowledge of tactics, 189
Koch, Richard, 92–93
Kodak, 173
Kosovo, 188
Kotter, John, 125–127
Kramer, Mark, 235
Kroc, Ray, 13–14, 31, 33, 141,
169–170
Kruglanski, Arie, 213
Kuhn, Thomas, 4, 31–35, 58, 166,
234

L
Lampel, Joseph, 91, 109–110
Lao Tzu ("Old Master"), 4, 37, 171
The Last Supper (painting), ix
Lateral thinking, 159
*Lateral Thinking, Six Thinking Hats,
and Serious Creativity*
(Edward de Bono), 159
Law, 36–37
Laws of Imitation (Gabriel Tarde),
186
"A Leader's Guide to After-Action
Reviews" (U.S. Army), 188
Leadership, 102, 126, 170, 190–191
"Leading Change" (John Kotter),
125–126
Leading from the front, 102
Leading the Revolution (Gary
Hamel), 77

Learning organizations, 8, 109–127
  and the Fifth Discipline, 109–113
  GE example of, 121–125
  and hero's journey, 219–220
  knowledge management in,
    119–121
  and organizational change,
    125–127
  and social sector, 233, 235, 236
  teams in, 113–119
  tools from, 9
  vision in, 111
Learning school, 91–92
Leonardo da Vinci, ix, 217
Letting go, 220–224
Lexan, 218
Life and death decisions, 27
Life Strategies (Phillip McGraw),
  221
LIN Broadcasting, 182
Lindblom, Charles, 92
Logical incrementalism, 8
Los Alamos (New Mexico), 115
Low-cost products, 133
Lucent Technologies, 90, 100

M
Macintosh computer, 15, 115
Madden, Nancy, 237
Mail-order business, 66
Make Success Measurable! (Douglas
  Smith), 88
Management by objectives (MBO),
  86, 89–90
Management consulting, 194
Management engineering, 194
Manhattan Project, 115–116
Mao Tse-tung, 93
Market models, 246–247
Market segmentation, 80, 133,
  135
Marketing, 60
Marriott, J. W., 53–54, 56, 58, 101,
  104, 106, 143, 170

Marriott Corporation, 53–54, 57,
  101–102, 137
Martial arts, 39, 171, 174–175
Master black belts, 175
MasterCard, 182
Mathematics, 33
Maxygen, 166
Mayer, Richard, 29–30
MBO (*see* Management by
  objectives)
McDonald's, 13–14, 31, 33, 141, 170
McGraw, Phillip, 221–224
McKee, Robert, 227
McKinsey, 193–205
McKinsey, James O., 194
The McKinsey Mind (Ethan Rasiel
  and Paul Friga), 196, 203–206
The "McKinsey way," 193
The McKinsey Way (Ethan Rasiel),
  196–204
MECE (mutually exclusive,
  collectively exhaustive), 198
Medawar, Peter, 33
Meetings, 176
Menand, Louis, 4, 36–37
Mental models, 110
Mercer Management, 194–195
Merit-based ranking, 86
Merseles, Theodore, 66–67
Meta-analysis, 134
The Metaphysical Club
  (Louis Menand), 4, 36
Microsoft, 44–46
Middle-level managers, 203
MIM (*see* Move it Math)
The Mind of the Strategist (Kenichi
  Ohmae), 6, 68–69
Mintzberg, Henry, 8, 90–92, 94–96,
  109, 130, 215, 234
Mission statements, 180
Mitchell, Stephen, 171, 172
MITS, 44, 45
Mobile war, 18
Model business plans, 97–98

Model T (Ford), 61
Modeling, 219
Moltke, Johannes von, 74
Mona Lisa (painting), ix
Money orders, 54–55
Montgomery Ward, 66, 67
Moock, Douglas, 213
Moral commitment, 233
Morgan, J. P., 63
Morgenstern, Oskar, 181
Motivation, 213–216, 219–221,
    224–229
Motivation (Douglas Moock), 213
Motivation Management Service
    Institute, 215
Motivation (Robert Beck), 213
Motivational effect, 214
Motivational Science (Tory Higgins
    and Arie Kruglanski), 213
Motorcycles, 94–96
Motorola, 78, 79, 90, 173
Move it Math (MIM), 239–240
Musashi, Miyamoto, 5, 39–40, 99,
    189
Mutually exclusive, collectively
    exhaustive (MECE), 198

N
Nalebuff, Barry, 181
Napoleon Bonaparte, 3–6, 8–9, 16
    on circumstances, 22
    and creative strategy, 230
    on decision making, 161
    flexibility of, 20
    merit-based rise of, 86
    past battles studied by, 18–19
    pyramid structure used by, 88
    tactical knowledge of, 189
    on unity of command, 208
    at Waterloo, 80
Nash, John F., 181
Natural evolution, 56–57
Natural scientists, 35
NBC, 88

NEC, 106
Networks, achievement, 125
Neuman, Robert, 173
Neumann, John von, 181
New Ideas about New Ideas (Shira
    White), 15
New York Times, 144–145, 188–189
New Yorker, 79
Newton, Isaac, 14, 33
No-distinctive emphasis, 135
Nohria, Nitin, 225–227
Nokia, 78–80, 141
Normal science, 9, 32, 34, 165–167,
    227
Norton, David, 88
Nuovo, Frank, 79
Nurses, 27

O
Oakland A's (baseball team), 164
Objectives, 86
Objexis, 206
O'Dell, Carla, 120
Ohmae, Kenichi, 6, 69, 71–72
O'Keefe, Daniel, 213
The Old Mill (cartoon), 118
Olds, 61–62
On-line retail sales, 183–185
On War (Carl von Clausewitz), 3,
    13, 16, 21, 22, 24, 171
Openness, 113
Operating divisions, 63
Operating systems, 44
Oppenheimer, Robert, 115–116
Opportunism, planful, 74
Opportunistic experimentation,
    52
Opportunities, seizing, 57
Opuni, K. A., 240
Organizational change, 125–127
Organizational charts, 86
Organizational Learning (Chris
    Argyris and Donald Schon),
    119

Organizing Genius (Warren Bennis), 8, 113, 114, 118

The Origin and Evolution of New Businesses (Amar Bhidé), 6, 48

Origin of Species (Charles Darwin), 56

Osborn, Alex, 152–154, 177

Oster, Sharon, 235

Out of the Crisis (W. Edwards Deming), 89, 174

Outsourcing, 144, 194

Overall cost leadership, 133

Ownership of strategy, 194–196, 204

P

Panama Canal, 66

Pande, Peter, 173

Papyrus, 86

Participatory strategic planning, 112, 206–209

Partnership initiatives, 235

Pascale, Richard, 94

Past achievements/experience, 9, 14
  von Clausewitz on, 23–24
  of countries, 243
  as GE model, 73
  and IMF, 246
  Thomas Kuhn on, 32, 34
  and McKinsey databases, 201
  Napoleon's study of, 18–19
  and pragmatism, 36
  scanning of, 167–170
  scientific continuity of, 34
  with strategic planning, 85–90
  Tao on, 38

Patton, George, 189–190

The Patton Papers (Martin Blumenson), 190

PCs (*see* Personal computers)

PDNET, 200–201

Pepsi, 181

Percentage Baseball (Earnshaw Cook), 164

Performance Measurement (Harry Hatry), 235

Personal computers (PCs), 15, 44–46

Personal happiness, 10–11, 212

Personal mastery, 110

Personal strategy, 212

Persuasion (Daniel O'Keefe), 213

Peters, Thomas, 217–218

Pharaoh, 85–86

"Philanthropy's New Agenda" (Michael Porter and Mark Kramer), 235

Philosophy, expert intuition in, 35–40

Picasso, Pablo, 29

Pietersen, Willie, 103–104, 141

Place-based neighborhood transformation initiatives, 238

Plagiarizing, 74–75

Plan (definitions), 50

"Planful opportunism," 74

Planning:
  classic strategic (*see* Classic strategic planning)
  creative, 106–107
  Kenichi Ohmae on, 71

Poetics (Aristotle), 228

Poincaré, Henri, 30–31

Poland, 248

Polaroid, 111

Policy, 243–244

Popular Electronics, 44

Porras, Jerry, 6, 51–52, 54–58, 218

Porter, Michael, 8, 129–133, 135–139, 141–143, 145–148, 168–169, 235

Potential entrants, 132, 144

Practical Intuition for Success (Laura Day), 221

Practical Intuition (Laura Day), 221

The Practice of Management (Peter Drucker), 86

Pragmatism, 4, 35–37, 70, 71, 103
Pragmatism (William James), 35
Prahalad, C. K., 102, 104–106, 139
Prelude Corporation, 133
Presence of mind, 3
   von Clausewitz on, 24–25
   of Ray Kroc, 14
   and letting go, 220
   Miyamoto Musashi on, 39–40
   and responsibility, 220–221
   in social sector, 242
   Tao on, 38
Price premium, 139
Private Sector Strategies for Social
   Sector Success (Kevin Kearns),
   236
Problem-solving models, 165–167,
   197–202
"The Process of Creative
   Destruction" (Joseph
   Schumpeter), 139
Procter & Gamble, 60
Products, 133
   cost of, 135
   quality of, 135
Project, 20
Project GRAD (Graduation Really
   Achieves Dreams), 238–242
Proofs, 33
Published reports, 168, 169
Purposeful evolution, 58
"A Pyramid of Decision
   Approaches" (Paul
   Schoemaker and J. Edward
   Russo), 161
Pyramidal structures, 114
Pyramids, 86, 230

Q
Quader, Mr., 244, 245
Quality, 135, 172–175
Quality Control Handbook (J. M.
   Juran), 173
Quinn, James, 8, 92

R
Radial tires, 142
The Radical Team Handbook
   (John Redding), 118
Rasiel, Ethan, 196–201, 203, 205
Rational model, 218
R&D (research and development)
   department, 142
Recognition-based decision
   making, 4
Recognition of problems, 70
Recognition-primed
   decision-making model (RPD),
   27–28
Redding, John, 118
Reengineering, 178–181
Reengineering the Corporation
   (Michael Hammer and James
   Champy), 179
"Reflections and Suggestions"
   (George Patton), 190
Reinventing Strategy (Willie
   Pietersen), 103
Reports, published, 168, 169
Research and development (R&D)
   department, 142
Resolution, 3–4, 25
   von Clausewitz on, 22, 24
   and evolution, 57
   of Honda, 96
   as insight, 6
   of Ray Kroc, 14
   and strategy consulting, 196
Responsibility, 220–221
Retail business, 66–67, 183
Retention, 136
Revolution, 76
Richey, Alice, 97–98
The Rise and Fall of Strategic
   Planning (Henry Mintzberg), 8,
   90, 91, 94–96, 215, 234
Robbins, Anthony, 219
Rockefeller, John D., 64
Roosevelt, Franklin, 115

RPD (*see* Recognition–primed decision–making model)
Ruggles, Rudy, 120
Russia, 247–248
Russo, J. Edward, 161–164

S
S-curve, 185–187
Sakaguchi, Jeff, 204
Sanford Bernstein (investment firm), 218
Sansone, Carol, 213
Saqqara pyramid, 86, 230
Scaling Up Successful Work (Junko Chano), 241
Scans, what-works, 9, 167–170
Scheme of action, 50
Schoemaker, Paul, 161–164
Schon, Donald, 119
Schools, 235, 237–242
Schools that Learn (Peter Senge), 235
Schooten, Frans van, 33
Schor, Lisbeth, 236–238, 241
Schroeder, Richard, 173
Schumpeter, Joseph, 6, 45–47, 58–59, 69, 138–139, 230, 244
Science, 30–35
"The Science of Muddling Through" (Charles Lindblom), 92
"Science of science," 4, 30
Scientific method, 9, 32, 96
Scoville, 60
Sears, 6, 66–68, 95, 183
Self-help, 228
Self-improvement, 212
Self-renewal, 109
Selten, Reinhard, 181
Senge, Peter, 8, 110–113, 119, 126, 175–176, 235
Serendipity, 49
The Seven Habits of Highly Effective People (Stephen Covey), 219
The Seven Spiritual Laws of Success (Deepak Chopra), 220

SFA (*see* Success for All)
Shakespeare, William, 225
Shared vision, 110–112, 126
Sheean, Vincent, 190
Shewhart, Walter, 88, 173
Shimizu, Ryuei, 6, 70–71
Siemens, 79
Sigma, 173
Simon, Herbert, 4, 26–27, 91, 161
"Six Forces" model, 235
Six Sigma Academy, 173
Six Sigma for Managers (Greg Brue), 173
Six Sigma (Mikel Harry and Richard Schroeder), 173
Six Sigma Research Institute, 173
The Six Sigma Revolution (George Eckes), 173
Six Sigma system, 90, 173–175
The Six Sigma Way (Peter Pande, Robert Neuman, and Roland Cavanaugh), 173, 174
Sixth sense, 70
Slater, Robert, 72, 74–76, 124
Slavin, Robert, 237
Sloan, Alfred, 61–64
SMART goals, 155–156
Smith, Bryan, 176
Smith, Douglas, 88
Smith, Webb, 117, 118
Snow White and the Seven Dwarfs (film), 116–118
Social scientists, 35, 234
Social sector, 233–249
    global, 242–249
    GRAD example of, 238–242
    schools of strategy for, 234–236
    studies of, 236–238
Society for Organizational Learning, 113
Software industry, 44–46
Soldiers, 27
Solution trees, 207
"Solve everything at once," 238

Sony, 142
South Korea, 244, 245
Southwest Airlines, 144
Specter, Michael, 79
Spence, Michael, 3
A Spiritual Solution to Every Problem
    (Wayne Dyer), 220
Standard Oil, 6, 64–65
Standard products, 133
Standards, wireless, 78
Start-ups, 136
"The State of the Notion" (Rudy
    Ruggles), 120
Steelmaking, 226
Step organizations, 86–87
Sternberg, Robert, 29–30
Stewardship (Peter Block), 118
Stiglitz, Joseph, 3, 245–248
Stoneman, Dorothy, 236–237
Story (Robert McKee), 227
Storyboards, 117–118
Strategic Flexibility (Kathryn
    Harrigan), 93
"Strategic Intent" (Gary Hamel and
    C. K. Prahalad), 102
Strategic Leadership (Sydney
    Finkelstein and Donald
    Hambrick), 93, 139, 170,
    196–197
*Strategic Management for Non-Profit
    Organizations* (Sharon Oster),
    235
Strategic Management Review
    (Michael Goold), 95
Strategic planning, 84–107, 220
    in business, 97–101
    classic (*see* Classic strategic
        planning)
    Coastline Pool Consortium
        example of, 98–101
    and core competence, 104–106
    creative, 106–107
    flexible, 90–94
    in hero's journey, 215–216

Honda example of, 94–96
    and intent, 101–104
    participatory, 112, 206–209
    past experience with, 85–90
    in social sector, 234–235
"Strategic Planning and Action
    Planning for Non-profit
    Organizations" (John Bryson),
    235
Strategic Planning Workbook
    (Bryan Barry), 235
Strategic synthesis, 206–209
Strategies for Change (James Quinn),
    92
Strategists, 140
Strategy:
    von Clausewitz on, 3–6
    competitive, 8
    elements of, 3–4
    emergent, 8
    imagination driving, 76–78
    problem of, 3–11
    schools of, 8, 91–92
    studies of, 6
    successful Japanese business, 69
Strategy and Structure
    (Alfred Chandler), 6, 59
Strategy consulting, 193–209
    McKinsey way of, 196–205
    and ownership of strategy,
        194–196
    participatory, 206–209
    steps of, 196
The Strategy-Focused Organization
    (Robert Kaplan and
    David Norton), 88
Strategy in the Public Sector
    (Paul Joyce), 235
Strategy Safari (Henry Mintzberg,
    Bruce Ahlstrand, and Joseph
    Lampel), 91, 94, 109
Strauss, Anselm, 140–142
Structure:
    choice of, 59

Structure *(continued)*
  decentralized, 67
  strategy follows, 59
The Structure of Scientific Revolutions
  (Thomas Kuhn), 31, 58, 166, 234
Subforces, 132
Substitutes, 132, 142, 144
Success:
  building on, 40
  search for, 215–220
Success for All (SFA), 237, 239, 240
"Successive integration of problem
  elements," 160
Summary of the Art of War
  (Antoine Jomini), 16–18
Sun Tzu, 4, 38–39
Suppliers, 132, 144, 181
Surowiecki, James, 164
Switching costs, 132
SWOT analysis, 156–157
Synthesis, strategic, 206–209
Systems thinking, 111, 112, 126

T
Tact, 37
Tactics, 189
T'ai chi, 171
Talc, 53
The Tao at Work (Stanley Herman),
  171
Tao Te Ching (Lao Tzu), 4, 11, 37–38,
  171
Taoism, 4, 37–38, 171, 220, 221, 227
Tarde, Gabriel, 186–187
Tarde's S-curve, 186–187
Teagle, Walter, 64–65
Team leaders, 208
Team learning, 110
Teams, 8, 113–119
Technicolor, 117
Techniques
  (*see* Tool(s)/technique(s))
Technology, 245

Technology Review, 166
Tenneco, 238–239
Textile industry, 244–245
Theories, 20
  history-based, 24
  William James on, 36
  and McKinsey model, 200
  scientific achievement preceding,
    31
  for self-instruction vs. battle, 25
*Theory of Games and Economic
  Behavior* (John von Neumann
  and Oskar Morgenstern), 181
Thinking about business problems,
  196–197
Three Little Pigs (cartoon), 116
Tichy, Noel, 72–74, 76
Timex, 133
Tool(s)/technique(s), 9, 151–191
  after-action reviews as, 187–191
  bootstrapping, 161–165
  brainstorming, 152–155
  creative stimulation as, 157–161
  dialogue as, 175–178
  game theory as, 181–183
  normal science as, 165–167
  quality as, 172–175
  reengineering as, 178–181
  S-curve as, 185–187
  SMART goals as, 155–156
  SWOT analysis as, 156–157
  Trotter matrix as, 183–185
  wei wu wei as, 171–172
  what-works scans as, 167–170
Tradition, 77
Traveler's checks, 55
Trotter, Lloyd, 122
Trotter matrix, 9, 122–124, 168,
  183–185, 201, 206
Truitt, Wesley, 97
Tulane University, 142–143
Tunisia, 243
Turenne, 5, 19

U
Ulrich, Dave, 88
Unique products, 133
Uniqueness, 153
United Motors, 62
United States, 234
Unity of command, 208
University of Buffalo, 152
Unlimited Power (Anthony
 Robbins), 219
Urgency, sense of, 126
U.S. Army, 187, 188
U.S. Tire Company, 60

V
Value, 153
VanGundy, Arthur, 160
Viète, 33
Vicksburg, battle of, 18
Vision, 9
 aligning systems to, 126
 attainable, 115
 coup d'oeil before, 104
 in learning organizations, 111
 and strategy, 126
Vision statements, 97
Visionaries, 140
Visionary firms, 52
Visioning approach, 236
Vlasic, 143

W
Walk-through, 179–180
Walkman, 142
Wall Street Journal, 201
Wallace, James, 44
Wallis, John, 33
War as I Knew It (George Patton), 190
Waterloo, battle of, 80

Waterman, Robert, 217–218
Waterway Accessories, 99
Weber, Max, 86
Wei wu wei (doing-not-doing),
 171–172, 174, 177, 221
Weisberg, Robert, 29
Weiss, Carol, 234
Welch, Jack, x, 72–76, 81, 88, 124, 218
"What Have We Learned about
 Generic Competitive
 Strategy?"
 (Colin Campbell-Hunt), 134
"What Is Strategy?"
 (Michael Porter), 145
What-works scans, 9, 167–170
White, Shira, 15
White belts, 175
Whitecap Pools, 99
Who Framed Roger Rabbit (film), 117
Winfrey, Oprah, 221–224
Wood, Robert, 66–67
Work-Out method, 75, 122–124
World Bank, 242–245
WorldCom, 144–145
Wozniak, Steven, 15
Writing things down, 86–88
Written strategic plan, 100

X
Xerox, 15, 33, 45, 165

Y
Yin-yang, 227, 228
Youth-Build program, 236–237

Z
Zen, 4–5, 39, 171, 220
Zen at Work (Les Kaye), 171
Zwerling, Steven, 241–242